Childhood, Generational Order and the Welfare State: Exploring Children's Social and Economic Welfare

Volume 1 of COST A19: *Children's Welfare*

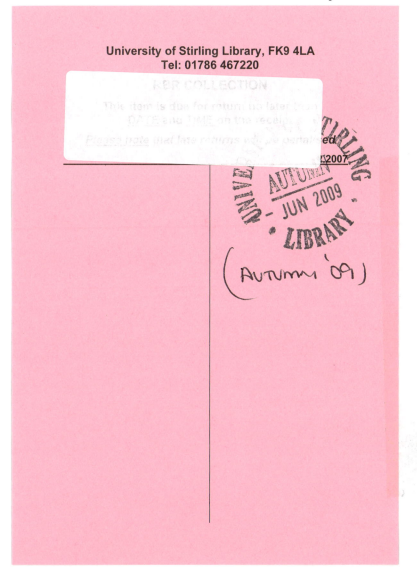

*Helmut Wintersberger, Leena Alanen, Thomas Olk
and Jens Qvortrup (eds)*

Childhood, Generational Order and the Welfare State: Exploring Children's Social and Economic Welfare

Volume 1 of COST A19: *Children's Welfare*

2007

Childhood, Generational Order and the Welfare State:
Exploring Children's Social and Economic Welfare
Volume 1 of COST A19: *Children's Welfare*

Price: 62.25 Euro per set of two volumes.

This book has been financially supported by
COST, European Cooperation in the field of Scientific and Technical Research
The Research Council of Norway

COST is an intergovernmental European framework for international cooperation
between nationally funded reserch activities. COST creates scientific networks and enables
scientists to collaborate in a wide spectrum af activities in research and technology.
COST activities are administered by the COST Office.
Website: www.cost.esf.org

Neither the COST Office nor any person acting on its behalf is responsible for the use of which
might be made of the information contained in the present publication.

Published by
University Press of Southern Denmark
Campusvej 55
5230 Odense M
Denmark

University of Southern Denmark Studies in History and Social Sciences vol. 337

Set and printed by Narayana Press

ISBN13 97-887-7674-201-0 (vol. 1)
ISBN13 97-887-7674-208-9 (vol. 1 and vol. 2)

TABLE OF CONTENTS

HELMUT WINTERSBERGER, LEENA ALANEN,
THOMAS OLK AND JENS QVORTRUP
Introduction   9

THEORIZING CHILDHOOD AND CHILDREN'S WELFARE

LEENA ALANEN
Theorizing Children's Welfare   27

ILONA OSTNER
Whose Children? Families and Children in »Activating« Welfare States   45

THOMAS OLK AND HELMUT WINTERSBERGER
Welfare States and Generational Order   59

MEASURING CHILDREN'S WELFARE

JONATHAN BRADSHAW
Some Problems in the International Comparison of Child Income Poverty   93

DONALD J.HERNANDEZ, NANCY A. DENTON AND SUZANNE E. MACARTNEY
Child Poverty in the U.S.: A New Family Budget Approach
with Comparison to European Countries   109

JONATHAN BRADSHAW
Child Benefit Packages in 22 Countries   141

Negotiating Childhood and Children's Welfare

Tess Ridge
Negotiating Child Poverty: Children's Subjective Experiences
of Life on a Low Income   161

Mona Sandbæk
Children's Rights to a Decent Standard of Living   181

Máire Nic Ghiolla Phadraig
Working Children and the 'Descholarization' of Childhood   201

Anna-Liisa Närvänen and Elisabet Näsman
Age Order and Children's Agency   225

European Childhood in Perspective

Jens Qvortrup
European Childhood – Diverging or Converging?   253

Contributors to this volume   275

FOREWORD

The two volumes *Childhood, Generational Order and the Welfare State* (volume 1) and *Flexible Childhood?* (volume 2) are the last publications from COST A19 – Children's Welfare. The background of the Action, which began in 2001, was the all-European experience of population ageing which currently is causing concern in practically all countries of Europe and the insufficient attention – both scientific and political – paid to one highly significant part of the population, namely children. They are logically becoming much fewer in this process of ageing, but in a number of other ways children and childhood have been impacted by processes taking place simultaneously and intertwined with population ageing and its consequences.

These processes are identified, described and analysed in the Country Reports – Children's Welfare in Ageing Societies – and in the two volumes that are now published. It is important however to underline that the Action has hosted also a huge number of meetings with a lot of interventions from both external lecturers and members from the Action itself. While creating space and time for creative de-liberations among participants from more than 20 countries, the Action has in the truest sense of the word constituted a network for both more and less experienced researchers. This is, in fact, one of the rationales of the COST framework. It has been a network that has conveyed and been conveyed with blood and flesh in terms of conceptual, substantial and methodological contents, which – so it is hoped – will be of value and inspiration also to practitioners and politicians in their effort to improve the welfare of children as well as of adults and the elderly.

The Action has been made possible first of all by the COST framework. A number of its officers have been very helpful in guiding us through this system. We are grate-ful for all the help and compliance we have received. The Action has also been met with generosity from The Norwegian Research Council which has been helpful with financial assistance.

We wish to express our gratefulness also to Karin Ekberg, senior executive officer at the Norwegian Centre for Child Research. She has used her efforts and long standing experience to smooth the process and keep the wheel running.

In the very last moment we were lucky enough to have Petra Essebier, University of Halle, with us in Trondheim. She kindly offered her expertise for the proof reading and provided assistance in an efficient and professional manner, for which we thank her very much.

Last but not least, we wish to convey warm thanks and gratitude to all our colleagues who have ventured to embark on this long journey and who have shown confidence in and been supportive of this endeavour.

We do hope that the Action will leave quite a few positive imprints in its wake – not least in terms of carrying forth the plenty of unanswered not to say unaddressed problems that have come up during the Action.

An-Magritt Jensen, Chair of Action
Jens Qvortrup, Co-ordinating Editor

INTRODUCTION

Helmut Wintersberger, Leena Alanen, Thomas Olk and Jens Qvortrup

The Rationale

When COST-Action A19 on Children's Welfare was initiated in 2000, two developments had – among others – influenced the public perception of childhood in modern society throughout the last decade of the 20th century:

- the UN Convention on the Rights of the Child (CRC) and its almost universal acknowledgement by the international community as a set of normative regulations guiding child welfare practice and childhood policies both nationally and internationally;
- innovations in childhood research, above all in social research, finding its expression in the discovery if a new sociological arena, the sociology of childhood and/or children as well as the establishment of new related research networks and committees.

New childhood studies

It is obvious that the first development did get much wider attention than the second one. However, for the departure of a new research oriented action dealing with children's welfare as COST A19, developments concerning the state of the art in childhood research were of at least the same relevance as the CRC. Let us, therefore, start the discussion with innovations concerning childhood research. In this respect two innovations have to be considered which turned out to be at the basis of two new research paradigms, structure oriented childhood and actor oriented child research, both distinct from the dominant developmental psychological paradigm.

In the frame of the structure oriented approach childhood is considered as a social category or permanent structure in society, and children as a population group of their own. With a view to the developmental paradigm the main factors of distinction are the level of analysis (society instead of the individual) and the permanent nature of childhood as social category (contrary to the transient perception of a child developing towards adulthood). Along with the structural approach we might consider children as a minority group, which is – according to Wirth's definition – a group singled out from the rest of the society, in this case the dominant group of adults, for special treatment, in particular protective as well as repressive discrimination. In the present volume this conceptual orientation is being followed up and further developed towards a generational view of childhood, which means comparing for instance the distribution of material and other resources among different generations or age groups, and in particular towards an analysis of children's position with a view to the welfare state and its generational order.

In actor oriented child studies the categorical assumption of children's immaturity and incompetence is questioned (for any age) by drawing the attention rather on children's competences and contributions. This change of perspective is not at all completely new and restricted to the sociological discipline; it may build upon previous findings in both psychological and pedagogical research.

On the one hand the new research orientations are different and distinct theoretically and practically, on the other hand – as the present volume demonstrates – they are interdependent and mutually indispensable for further developing discourses on children's welfare. Also the usefulness of the developmental child research paradigm is not questioned in principle, however, its instrumentality has to be judged depending on purpose and level of the exercise. If the objective is, for instance, to define or monitor the implementation of childhood policies at the macro-political level, the structure oriented childhood paradigm is definitely a more adequate theoretical tool than any other one, and therefore indispensable.

The Convention on the Rights of the Child

As to the Convention on the Rights of the Child (CRC), this piece of international law was adopted by the General Assembly of U.N. in 1989, and meanwhile ratified by the entire international community (except for the U.S.A. and Somalia). It had a major impact on public attitudes with a view to children and childhood. In European countries at least, it has led to the emergence of new institutions such as children's ombudspersons, child commissioners etc., and it has to some degree also influenced the work of traditional child (welfare) workers in both the statutory and voluntary sectors. For obvious reasons, the CRC is being discussed predominantly in the frame of a legal, especially a human rights discourse, rather than of a welfare discourse providing more or less the conceptual framework for this volume.

However, also in this context it would be wrong to disregard the CRC, not only for its impact on child welfare and childhood policies caused by the afore mentioned shifts with a view to public attitudes and professional identities, but the CRC is also a valuable source of normative premises for the generation of new models for conceptualising childhood and the generational order of welfare. Due to its general acceptability there cannot be any question whether norms enshrined in it may be used at all, but we might argue only with a view to interpreting the given norms.

Some fundamental principles contained in the CRC, such as non-discrimination, the best interest of the child, the freedom of thought and speech, are good examples of norms, which are being acknowledged as legal standard without any further questioning, their translation and interpretation for a social welfare discourse is, however, to be implemented with great care, and must be open to criticism. On the other hand, the welfare state analysis contained in this volume may be instrumental for a children's rights discourse by providing a conceptual and empirical framework for better understanding, for instance, the notion of the child citizen with particular regard to the welfare state.

Children's welfare

On the whole, childhood and welfare discourses involve different research constituencies, and therefore we are faced with a mutual neglect: welfare analysis tends to neglect childhood and children as population group, while childhood studies tend to neglect welfare theory and policies at large. With a view to the 3 Ps, the principles of protection, provision and participation, under which the majority of specific norms contained in the CRC are often structured, provision oriented rights are particularly neglected. While protective rights were immediately taken up and redefined by the traditional fraction of »child savers«, and while participation rights got the immediate attention by the new fraction of »kiddie libbers«, rights of provision have remained somehow in the shade. This is not to say that there were no theoretical or political debates on providing for children in cash or care at all. However, usually these debates did not take place in the frame of childhood discourses, but in other arenas, such as general social, labour market, family and women's policies.

Only in recent years we have witnessed a fundamental change in the »welfare architecture,« which has caused a shift in the position of children, women and families with a view to welfare. By adapting modern welfare states to a changing economic and social environment, not to mention overcoming the functional deficits of the old welfare regime, new ideas and concepts are being propagated. The new priorities and measures for restructuring welfare regimes derive either from the visions and concepts of an »activating social policy« or the social investment state (Giddens 1998). The idea underlying this concept is that the state should not – as up till now – merely protect the social positions of particular »at risk« groups in a reactive manner (such as by granting social security benefits), but should rather build »human capital« or »social capital« by investing in individuals. In this way target groups of social policy should be enabled to deal with their personal matters themselves, and thus overcome risks or inferior social status by means of their own power.

Mediated by the discourse on child poverty and the demographical developments, a stronger integration of child-oriented questions into social policy and welfare state research as well as the corresponding policy in terms of «new welfare architecture« is argued for. The most prominent example is Gøsta Esping-Andersen's (et al.) (2002) book »Why We Need a New Welfare State«. Beginning with the heading »Investing in Children, Families and Women« this book proposes a differentiated and broad strategy of investment by the welfare state in a »good« childhood (not in family as such!) as an effective instrument against poverty, social exclusion, and the inheritance of marginalized life chances by the next generation.

The concept of the social investment state promotes the expansion of a public system of early childcare and education, and thus a shift in the responsibility from the private sphere of the family household to the public sphere of social services and institutions. By realizing the ideas of an activating social policy and the social investment state, the »responsibility mix« concerning the welfare of children changes. Women will be discharged from their family obligations, and will be de-familialized in order to improve their chances for participation in the labour market. To enable this activation of mothers, children must also be de-familialized. The increased participation in the labour market by both parents reduces the time they can spend with their children. Increasingly, the contribution of fathers and mothers to the welfare of their children focuses on the securing of the material living conditions made possible by gainful employment. The children, on the other hand, become more and more clients of childcare institutions provided by state and market. Thereby they will be liberated from their family, and attain a public status.

At first glance the strategy of investing in children seems to improve their position with a view to the generational order of welfare. By providing an extended provision of childcare institutions the welfare state takes on more responsibility for the welfare of children. Nevertheless, this strategy has a different kind of citizenship in mind than that connected to a really child-oriented perspective. The status of children moves away from »the private property« of the parents to a concept of the child as a »citizen-worker of the future«. This means that the quality of childhood in the here and now risks being overshadowed by a pre-occupation with the development of children as future citizen-workers. The investment in children is not aimed at improving the quality of childhood in the present, but at gaining economic returns in the future. The right to receive benefits is linked to benefits in return given by the children in the future.

In conclusion, within the social investment regime the citizenship rights of children are limited in two respects: First, the child is not »being a citizen», but rather a »citizen-in-becoming«. And second, the citizen-status is reduced to the economic dimension of the productive citizen-worker-of-the-future, and weakens the political and social dimensions of full citizenship. Therefore, the integration of childhood and welfare discourses in the frame of a new welfare architecture including also the generational dimension is still an open task on the agenda, and the emphasis placed in this volume on issues like child poverty, child oriented financial transfer systems, services, particularly child care services under a childhood policies perspective, is a first step on this way.

Class, gender and generation

Generational analysis in the sense of confronting the condition of children at large with the condition of adults is one of the most recent developments in structure oriented childhood research, adding a third structural level to the existing ones of class and gender in particular.

While social class in the Marxist understanding has been a dangerous concept for the ruling classes (therefore having been strongly opposed by any economic and political leadership in the capitalist world), the story of gender is different. The feminist movement and women's research were originally attacked not only by the cultural bourgeoisie but also – ironically – by the Marxist camp, and by the latter in terms of an accusation for contributing to splitting up the working class. It was argued that women's belonging to social classes was more significant than their sharing common condition under patriarchal regimes. Women's research rejected the charge – not because it denied the diverse lives that women lead, but because it insisted – and rightly so – that women first and foremost had something in common which cut through classes.

The assumption of a generational research is, as we see it, that different generational segments, such as for instance childhood, adulthood and old age, relate and interact with each other in particular ways under various historical and societal circumstances. This assumption presupposes a certain degree of commonness among members of each of the generational segments – in terms of for instance rights, power, law, discourses, access to welfare, to space etc.

To some extent the process of introducing the generational perspective has similarities with the difficult journey of the feminist movement towards establishing gender (besides social class) as a recognised structural level in welfare analysis. Interestingly, however, it seems as if not least gender researchers and the feminist movement are annoyed about the introduction of generational research. They keep insisting that gender – i.e. the division of childhood into a girl- and a boy-childhood – becomes a vital part of childhood studies. In other words they insist on a singular notion of womanhood while at the same time they advocate the plural notion of childhoods.

History repeats itself: capitalists oppose the unity of workers, workers oppose the unity of women, and women oppose the unity of children. However, the interaction between feminist and childhood research and policies can and should be interpreted also in a more constructive way, as this was done by Therborn (1993) in the following paragraph:

> »The rise of women made two central contributions to the emergence of child politics. One was of visibility, the other of conceptualisation. Women's fights for entry into participation in public life, in the labour market, in public debate, in places of power made children more visible to public discourse … The 'family' was individualised, comprising individual members, who had but who should not have unequal rights and powers. This individualist egalitarianism (or egalitarian individualism) first and most explicitly asserted the individuality of the woman. But in so doing, it undermined also the the patriarchal collectivism of the family, and opened up a space for discussing the individuality and the rights of the child as well.«

Recently, the diversity approach has been supported also by child researchers who insist on what is called multiple identities at the cost of what unites children categorically. There are plenty of good reasons to conduct small-scale childhood studies, but only if they are subsumed under insight about childhood in general. There may also be fundamental differences between gender and generation at structural levels (as there are between class and gender), but this cannot be used as a principal argument against the introduction of the generational level. A sustainable childhood research can, in our view, be pursued only if childhood is ascertained as unit in a generational structure. Such were lessons learned about the position of workers and women. Why should a childhood research ignore these lessons?

Overview of Chapters

Theorizing childhood and children's welfare

In the first Chapter Leena Alanen focuses on promoting a conceptual integration of welfare research and childhood studies. The aim is to clear some ground for developing understandings of children's welfare that are compatible with sociological approaches to children and childhood. The chapter first surveys the many different notions of welfare used in the welfare research literature and discusses their relations with each other. It then asks how children and childhood are dealt with in this research, and further, can we just »add« children to existing welfare studies' frameworks? The conclusion is: in order to make the tools and knowledge of social science significant with a view to children and childhood, while simultaneously avoiding the »adultist« distortions of welfare research, more is required than an addition alone. In the chapter it is suggested that some of the analytical tools that have been developed in child-hood studies – a sociology of children, a deconstructive sociology of childhood, and structural approaches to children and childhood – are useful in the needed critique and deconstruction of existing welfare frameworks, and in developing »missing parts« for a more adequate and comprehensive framework. In this chapter the author begins to sketch such a framework based on a systemic, multilevel and processual view of welfare production.

In the next Chapter Ilona Ostner discusses how families and children are affected by the shift towards »activating« welfare states. »Positive activation« is a key-principle in the frame of a »social investment« welfare state, which is to be seen in contrast to the traditional philosophy of merely »distributive« or »consumptive« welfare. While for adults this development directly and explicitly aims at increasing labour market participation in particular with a view to women, for children the consequences are more complex: as receivers of maternal care they might be negatively affected if this care resource is being eroded; more positively, as future workers they are increasingly seen as an asset, and adequate child benefits and services as investments in human capital (Esping-Andersen 2002). Ostner begins with recalling the emergence and institutionalisation of »childhood« as a social category separate from and independent from adulthood. She describes children's changing status, the growing individualisa-tion as driven by law and the barriers to children's legal individualisation by drawing upon Therborn (1993). Then she outlines »legal individualisation« as part and parcel of a process of societal individualisation that in turn implies new and more direct forms of state intervention into individual lives. Women and men of employable age are expected above all to be employed, and parents thereby meet their obligations towards their children by supporting them. On the other side, children have to enter educational institutions earlier than ever, and consequently family childhood will fur-ther erode. In turn, societies offer services to worker-citizen-mothers and –fathers as well as to future worker-citizen-children. However, this utilitarian »activating« welfare state invests first of all in areas which and in people who promise returns. In the end the family seems to be left for those who do not promise returns.

The difficult relationship between childhood and the welfare state is also at the centre of the following chapter on »Welfare states and generational order« by Thomas Olk and Helmut Wintersberger. The authors start with registering a two-fold neglect: On the one hand, childhood research has neglected welfare state theory and welfare policies for children and families. In most cases, childhood research focuses on different aspects of the life worlds of children or special dimensions of their living conditions like child poverty, sexual abuse, child discrimination. On the other hand, welfare state theory and research have also treated children and children's welfare as a marginal issue. Dominant welfare state theories – Esping-Andersen's influential typology of welfare state regimes as well as feminist theories – bear adultist characteristics. Therefore, discussing political options and strategies for an adequate integration of childhood and children into welfare theory poses major problems. Esping-Andersen's welfare state typology is restricted to a conventional understanding of work and income in industrial societies, while suppressing gender oriented and generational aspects of the system of inequality in post-modern societies. In this respect feminist attempts to extend welfare state theory make sense. Along the lines of feminist welfare state theory we can also ask about the relationships between children as a social category, on the one side, and a given welfare state arrangement, on the other. However, in feminist theory there are also fundamental objections against using age (or generation) as a structural dimension for defining a generational mode of production and a generational order of welfare. For this reason, existing theories and typologies cannot contribute essentially to a child-oriented theory of welfare state. A child-oriented welfare state theory has to create independent criteria and indicators which make it possible to differentiate given welfare states according to their »child-orientation«. The authors elaborate on some of the shortcomings of existing welfare state theories. Then they argue that selecting generation as structural dimension is not only feasible in a theoretical, but also desirable in a normative perspective: it coincides with political and legal developments concerning the position of children in society at large. The main part of the chapter is dedicated, however, to explicating more in detail how to extend welfare state theory and practice to childhood, age and the generational dimension with particular emphasis on two relevant areas: monetary child benefit packages as well as childcare services.

Measuring children's welfare

The previous three theoretical chapters are followed up by a sequence of empirical chapters addressing issues of child poverty, generational income distribution and child-related public benefit packages. Child poverty is probably the most important indicator of child well-being and this has been recognised by the European Union in that child poverty rates are the only child-based indicator published as one of the nine primary indicators of Social Inclusion. The availability of comparative data on child poverty has been much improved in recent years. The Luxembourg Income Study (LIS) has enabled a comparison of child poverty rates on a consistent basis for now 31 countries and UNICEF have used this data for their League Tables of child poverty in rich nations. Independently of LIS, the OECD has gathered child poverty rates from member states' national sources on a consistent basis. Then there is the data for the EU countries that has emerged from the European Community Household Panel Survey, which is now being replaced by the Survey of Income and Living Conditions covering the EU25.

Despite this rich variety of sources there are a number of serious problems with this data, which Jonathan Bradshaw addresses in his first Chapter on »Some problems in the international comparison of child income poverty«. First of all, the data available is all very out of date, and for national governments comparative data that is five or six years old is only of historical interest. Secondly, while child poverty rates are based on income, income is only an indirect indicator of living standards, less reliable than multiple deprivation. Thirdly, the child income poverty measure being employed mostly is a relative one, a problem which has become more salient with the expansion of the EU to include a larger number of countries with very much lower living standards. Fourthly, most child income poverty is analysed using rates – the proportion of children below a threshold, but rarely how far below the threshold children are. There is an argument to be had about whether it is better for a country to have a large number of children a little or a smaller number of children a long way below the threshold. Fifthly there is a debate to be had about whether those countries with high but dynamic/short term child poverty are better or worse than those countries with lower but more persistent child poverty. And finally there are also methodological problems with arbitrary income thresholds and equivalence scales.

Based on this demonstration Bradshaw concludes that income poverty measures have become the dominant way in which child poverty is represented and compared, and that this is likely to continue in the EU. However in his view one should be developing a wider repertoire of measures. There is potential for the use of deprivation indicators and subjective measures and indeed using overlapping measures. There is potential for exploring other indicators of child well-being and indeed UNICEF in its Innocenti Report Card series has already made a distinguished start. One should move away from income poverty measures in comparative research and operationalise indicators of child well-being – some of which could be income measures.

There is the widespread opinion that – with a view to social welfare in general and children's welfare and child poverty in particular – the United States is different from Europe. In their Chapter on »Child poverty in the U.S.: a new family budget approach with comparison to European countries«, Donald Hernandez, Nancy Denton and Suzanne Macartney present a new poverty measure for the U.S. using Census 2000 data, and interpret results vis-a-vis extant internationally comparable estimates, before they lead us through a long and controversial history of poverty measurement in the U.S. As the most important conceptual advance in the evolution of poverty measurement the authors see the paradigm shift from »pauperism« to the modern social science concept of »poverty« based on a subsistence budget reflecting the amount that a family must spend in order to live at a minimally adequate level. When an official poverty measure was adopted in 1965, the threshold was set at a level essentially identical to one-half median family income, though not as a matter of principle. But over time the U.S. measure has lagged further and further behind the one-half median family income standard, because it has been adjusted only for inflation, not for increases in the real standard of living. Consequently, the official measure has come under increasing criticism. Drawing upon previous work by both the National Academy of Sciences and the Economic Policy Institute, the authors have developed new Basic Budget Poverty rates for the U.S. using Census 2000 data and other sources.

The results indicate that their Baseline Basic Budget Poverty rate for children in 1999 is slightly lower than the rate estimated by UNICEF based on median family income. However, insofar as children in Europe and other rich countries generally have access to government funded national health insurance, and formal child care or early education arrangements, and, if they are infants or toddlers, to parents who can care for them at home because of government-guaranteed, job-protected, paid maternal or parental leave arrangements, and insofar as federal support for these services in the U.S. lags far behind, a more comprehensive approach to comparing the circumstances of children in the U.S. and other rich countries requires an adjustment for child care/early education and health coverage. Their most fulsome measure incorporating these factors yields a Basic Budget Poverty rate of 38.3% for U.S. children, compared to 2-10% in a variety of European countries. These high poverty levels, in combination with large race-ethnic differentials, merit increasing public policy attention because it is projected that race-ethnic minority children will constitute a majority of U.S. children by 2030. The current circumstances and future prospects of U.S. children do not compare favorably to their European peers, the authors conclude.

Every industrial country has a 'package' of tax allowances, cash benefits, exemptions from charges, subsidies and services in kind, which assist parents with the costs of raising children. This package plays a part, along with labour market income, in tackling market driven child poverty. Parts of the package assist parents in employment: by subsidising low earnings, subsidising childcare costs, creating or structuring financial incentives or disincentives to be in employment or to work part-time or full-time or, in couples, have one parent or two parents working. Other parts of the package assist parents to stay out of the labour market, enabling them to stay at home to care. The package may influence the number of children a women will have and the birth spacing. It may also have an impact on family form making it more or less easy for a parent to separate or bring up a child alone.

In his other Chapter Jonathan Bradshaw investigates the variations in the structure and level of these child benefit packages in 22 OECD-countries as at July 2001. To compare social policies on a systematic basis a model family method was applied. The procedure is to identify a specific range of model families (couples with 1-3 and lone parents with 1-2 children, children's ages ranging from under 3 to 17), as well as to specify a variety of income cases for each family type. The policies that are taken into account in the package are tax benefits, income related cash benefits, non income related cash benefits, social insurance contributions, rent/housing benefits, local taxes/benefits, child care costs/benefits, social assistance, guaranteed child support and other support. Housing costs and any charges for schooling as well as a standard package of health care are taken into account, too. A ranking of the 22 countries according to the generosity of their child benefit packages may be seen as the most condensed way of presenting the results of the study. This ranking shows that the countries with the most generous overall child benefit package are not those which employ a substantial element of targeting, either through tax credits, or income related benefits. They are the countries that deliver most if not all their value as a non-income related child benefit.

As to factors explaining variations, it appears that it is not the level of the wealth of a nation, nor the character of its labour market, nor the level of earnings but rather its social expenditure and especially the share of its social expenditure going to families, as against the elderly, that determines the child benefit package. As to impact, the level of the child benefit package achieved is also associated with success in reducing market-generated levels of child poverty and it is possibly also associated with higher fertility rates. Those countries that make most effort to transfer resources horizontally have the most generous child benefit packages. Nations make choices. The policies that they choose have an impact on the financial burdens born by parents raising children. The advantages of the model family method is that it can produce up-to-date comparisons, fairly easily, which give insights into how different family types are treated within and between countries by their tax and benefit systems.

Negotiating childhood and children's welfare

While the previous three empirical chapters are clearly quantitative, the following chapter by Tess Ridge on »Negotiating child poverty: Children's subjective experiences of life on a low income« is a qualitative piece of research. The chapter takes a subjective approach to understanding the lives and experiences of low-income children, and draws on children's accounts and discourses to explore how they negotiate their lives and manage their relationships in the context of restricted social, material and structural environments. In general, children living in poverty have been seen as passive victims of poverty and disadvantage, rather than as reflexive social agents whose lives are organised by the constraints of a poor childhood. Based on her as well as other studies, Ridge develops quite a different view: Although poverty is an intense and for many children an enduring backdrop to their lives, one should not overlook that these are 'ordinary' children, busy in the everyday social world of childhood, determined to stay connected to the social milieu, and striving to be accepted and included in the cultural exchanges of their peers. Children are thoughtful, responsive and sensitive actors within their homes and families, where making ends meet and sustaining family life on a restricted income are a daily challenge. Access to work is a key strategy employed by children to generate some measure of autonomy.

It is apparent from children's accounts that they are not passive victims of poverty but equally it is important to recognise the manifold constraints on their lives and the challenges these present to their capacity for self realisation. Low-income children are reflexive social agents, who engage with their lives and their circumstances, constructing and reconstructing their lives in dynamic and imaginative ways. They are also thoughtful and competent social agents who are fully aware of social and economic realities of their lives. However, their childhoods are organised around the constraints of poverty, therefore any understanding of childhood poverty, while encompassing the discourse, agency and identity of the child, must also recognise the social, material and cultural boundaries, constructions and institutions that shape the life worlds of children who are poor.

While based on the previous chapter, one could claim that letting children's perceptions of their needs inform definitions of child poverty may facilitate children's social inclusion, in the following a main argument is that child-specific policies can open up chances for children in poor families by not letting the family's economy restrict their access to school and leisure activities. In the next Chapter on »Children's rights to a decent standard of living« Mona Sandbaek starts with asking: What kind of claims do poor children have on society when it comes to their material living conditions? In modern welfare states, there is an interplay between state and parents to ensure children's welfare. However, this policy does not go so far as to guarantee all children a basic living standard. In her article she presents existing knowledge about poor children's exposure to risk, but also factors that can play a protective role. In order to explore their situation in greater depth, she draws upon a recent Norwegian study. Finally, she discusses how a policy can be developed which is directed towards children themselves, based on their own rights as citizens. However, a rights-based approach puts the role of the state on the agenda: the measures discussed in the chapter, seem to presuppose an active state, which may appear contradictory to the trend prevailing in many European countries.

Although Sandbaek advocates a rights-based approach to fight child poverty, she also finds it necessary to draw attention to some pitfalls such approach may entail: one of them is to overestimate children and put too much responsibility on their shoulders; another is to underestimate children and approach them with an idealized perception of what childhood should be like; and thirdly, a rights-based approach in order to secure children's needs should also not be practised in a way that creates contradictions between parents and children, on the contrary, there is reason to build on parents' efforts and willingness to take care of and give priority to children. Many pay a high price for protecting their children, in terms of worries and health problems. It is likely to be perceived as a positive contribution if the state shares the responsibility for safeguarding the rights to a decent standard of living of the youngest generation, while at the same time recognising the efforts made by most parents to bring up their children.

The 'modern concept of childhood' defines children's place as in family, care and school settings. The extension of universal schooling was identified as one of the major elements in the social construction of modern childhood. This view is questioned by Máire Nic Ghiolla Phadraig in her Chapter on »Working children and the 'descholarisation' of childhood«. She sets out to review the studies of the combination of full-time schooling with part-time economic activity by children and young people in the affluent industrialised countries. Far from being a thing of the past, levels of participation have increased in recent years. This observation has prompted responses regarding the developmental implications both positive and negative. Explanations have ranged from the structural – such as continued hidden poverty, and the demands of the labour market – to the pressures of consumerism. Indeed, working children and young people are reduced to victims by such explanations. It is argued that the increase can only be understood as part of a complex interplay of schooling, continued poverty, labour market, cultural and family factors which give rise to a new 'generational division of labour'. Furthermore, the phenomenon may also be viewed as a way in which children and young people exercise agency to negotiate the boundaries between childhood and adulthood.

It is also important, Nic Ghiolla Phadraig argues, to note that part-time work promotes early school-leaving in some cases and dilutes grades in others, but it is difficult to unravel the extent to which lower school achievement precedes or follows involvement in part-time work. Part-time work is a hugely important part of a positive self-concept for many children and young people. It affords them recognition that they are growing up and ready to take on more adult-like roles, without taking on the full responsibility of adulthood. For some, at least, the status and recognition of competence at work, helps to compensate for a poor school experience. Parents also mainly support the view that part-time work can be a positive, developmental experience. It may be argued that part-time work has replaced progress through school as a marker of transition to adulthood. The labour market demands for a more educated workforce, which supported a lengthening of years of schooling, have become more nuanced. There are limits to the need for an 'educated' work-force, many unskilled/semiskilled tasks remain to be carried out. The combination of an independent cash flow and their treatment, when at work, as of adult status, is a big attraction to young people, whose growing social competence is largely ignored in the school system. For this group, at least, the secular trend of scholarisation of childhood has ceased and we are now witnessing a process of descholarisation, in which the progressive lengthening of schooling and childhood has gone into reverse, Nic Ghiolla Phadraig concludes.

In the next Chapter on »Age order and children's agency« Anna-Liisa Närvänen and Elisabet Näsman lead us back to the theoretical section when introducing it as a contribution to the discussion on the complex interplay between structure, culture and agency, focusing on children's agency as a part of childhood welfare. Presumably, this focus on agency has two implications: on one hand, they use different concepts in their chapter such as age order and life-course structure; on the other hand, they refer to the dualism of age order (limiting agency) and children's agency (doing age). It is the latter aspect which indicates the position of the chapter in this section. The authors argue, that the age order of the life course institution structures opportunities and constraints, such that the child position shapes and limits agency in any particular context. But children interpret and reflect upon their opportunities and constraints, through past experiences, by anticipating their future and interpreting their present situation when choosing a line of action. They may have and make use of power resources and negotiate, contest, oppose and overcome the constraints of the age order in the specific situation.

European childhood in perspective

In the very last chapter of the book Jens Qvortrup continues discussions about generational aspects. Based upon a special study – initiated by the Norwegian COST-team – he reports about differences between generational segments as to their enjoyment of transfers from the public, whether in cash or in kind. It is not possible to draw conclusions in general terms from this study, but it demonstrates from a methodical point of view that it is possible to deal much more detailed with such comparisons than it has been done so far – and hopefully the results may encourage other countries to carry through similar comparisons.

Generational studies are so far not well developed – in particular not as far as empirical substantiation is concerned. How are resources distributed between generational segments, and how are the responsibility and the 'burden' for a just distribution divided? At a historical juncture, as pension schemes are a hot issue in practically all modern societies, these are questions that are bound to be much more seriously addressed than hitherto.

It is – in these post-modern times – said again and again that our societies and our lives are becoming more and more complex. The first part of Qvortrup's chapter acknowledges these complexities, while at the same time it is paying attention to the fact that in an international context our European countries exhibit clear and remarkable similarities. There is a need in modern analysis to focus on the details and the nuances without, though, overlooking the striking similarities which make Europe and the rich world in general surprisingly alike vis-à-vis the poor part of the world. This is something that should not be forgotten in the midst of what appears complex and fluid.

References

Esping-Andersen, G., G. Duncan, A. Hemerijck and J. Myles (2002): *Why We Need a New Welfare State*. Oxford/New York: Oxford UP.

Folbre, N. (1994): *Who Pays for the Kids? Gender and the Structure of Constrains*. New York/ London: Routledge.

Giddens, A. (1998): *The Third Way*. Polity Press: Cambridge.

Qvortrup, J., M. Bardy, G. Sgritta and H. Wintersberger (eds) (1994): *Childhood Matters. Social Theory, Practice and Politics*. Aldershot: Avebury.

Therborn, G. (1993): »The Politics of Childhood: The Rights of Children in modern times.« Castles, F.G. (ed): *Families of Nations. Patterns of Public Policy in Western Democracies*. Avebury: Dartmouth Aldershot, 241-291.

Wirth, L. (1945): »The Problem of Minority Groups.« Linton, R.: *The Science of Man in the World Crisis*. Columbia/New York: University Press, 347 – 372.

THEORIZING CHILDHOOD
AND CHILDREN'S WELFARE

Theorizing children's welfare

Leena Alanen

During the most recent decade the state of contemporary childhoods and the welfare of children have become a permanent concern in public discourse and in political debates throughout Europe. One reason for this is the worry felt over the rapid ageing of Western societies: people now live longer than earlier generations while children are being born in declining numbers. This raises acute concern about the adequacy of future workers and citizens, in terms of both their quantity and quality. Coinciding with this are diagnoses on the »crisis« of existing welfare states and the need to remake them. It is furthermore argued that the existing models for producing societal welfare also need serious rethinking. What states now need to do is to develop new models that support »investments« in people (that is: in »human capital«) instead of redistributing cash and benefits. Children, in particular, are a strategic subpopulation to invest in, and »child-centred social investment strategies« should take central place in the new programs proposed for moving »beyond the welfare state«. (E.g. Pierson 1998; Bonoli et al. 2000; Esping-Andersen et al. 2002.)

These discussions are taking place in policy-developing arenas, with social scientific research on welfare seeming to lag far behind. Children, especially, have never been centrally present in welfare research (see more below). Child advocacy agencies worldwide (such as UNICEF) and children's rights initiatives (e.g. children's poverty groups) have been the leaders in producing and distributing information on children's status in the world and in individual countries. Over the years several other initiatives have also been taken to establish both national and cross-national systems of indicators for measuring children's well-being, mostly for the purpose of informing and guiding policy-making, testing the performance of policies and (more recently) providing reliable data for extensive social reporting on children's status and living conditions.

In each of these cases, the question of *what children's welfare actually means* is given an answer in one way or another, although it often remains implicit and in many cases relies on publicly accepted »truths« on the subject. In the world of policy-making this is perhaps to be expected, as the rationalities of policy-making and of science tend not to coincide (cf. Hudson and Lowe 2004). So far it seems that the theoretical grounding of efforts to promote children's welfare has taken second place to the more immediate aim of developing common protocols and consistent, shared measures, and summary indices of children's well-being (cf. Hauser et al. 1997; Gasper 2004; Manderson 2005). However, now that children and childhood are becoming a more prominent issue in rethinking and reorganizing societal welfare, the social sciences are being asked for their contribution. In responding to this call, the (»new«) Childhood Studies provide important new resources.

This chapter aims to clear some ground in order to develop a response from the perspective of Childhood Studies. First, the starting points, experience and results of the COST A19 Children's Welfare project are reviewed and discussed. How should we think of welfare, in the case of children? How should we go on to develop a sociological understanding of children's welfare? The chapter surveys the bewildering multitude of different notions of welfare that are on display in the research literature as this obviously is one of the bedrocks in relation to which any sociology of children's welfare is to develop. It is then asked how children and childhood are dealt with in this research: are they present in welfare research, and if they are, in what way?

Based on this reading, the suggestion is that to progress in understanding children's welfare an encounter needs to take place between Childhood Studies and welfare studies. Are contemporary forms of thinking of welfare straightforwardly applicable in the case of groups and categories whose welfare has not been considered so far? Can we just »add« children to welfare studies' frameworks? The experiences gained in developing the social study of children and childhood during the last two decades will raise some doubts of the success of an additional strategy. It tells us rather that theories and concepts, methodologies and measures of both classical and modern social science have mainly been constructed from a normative *adult* viewpoint.[1] The exclusion of children from its concerns has been the rule. Therefore, to bring the tools and knowledge of social science to be of significance in the case of children and childhood, while simultaneously struggling to avoid their »adultist« distortion, will require more than an addition alone: first, a critique of existing welfare research and deconstruction of its ways of thinking will be needed, both constructed from an explicit children's standpoint. In the chapter it is suggested that some of the analytical tools that have been developed in Childhood Studies can be profitably used in the inspection of the utility for a sociology of children's welfare of existing welfare frameworks.

Unravelling 'welfare': Useful distinctions

To support its arguments this chapter makes use of a distinction that Ruth Lister (2004) develops in her reading of poverty research. The focus of her critical consideration is the state of this research and especially the diversity in ways that researchers have handled the term 'poverty'. Across the literature many different uses of the same term can be found, which then also carry over to policy-making. Lister underlines that to understand the phenomenon of poverty it is important to differentiate between *concepts, definitions and measures* (Lister 2004: 3-8). Concepts operate at a fairly general level and they provide the framework within which definitions (of concepts) and measurements (operationalisations of definitions) are developed. Definitions (and therefore also measures) mediate concepts in the sense that implicit in definitions of poverty are in fact explanations of poverty and its distribution. For this reason it is important, first, that definitions are not divorced from their wider conceptualisations, and second, that their relationships to wider conceptual frameworks (and we may envision these frameworks as networks of interrelated concepts) are clarified. Only then, she contends, can definitions function as an adequate basis for developing measures.

The problem in much poverty research, Lister notes (2004: 6-7), is that researchers typically begin their work with definitions of poverty, and then go on to develop measures of poverty, but in this they tend to *mistake* their definition for a concept, or simply *conflate* definitions and concepts. The result is that the frameworks on which different understandings of poverty are actually grounded are lost from sight (and analysis), and the historical and political constructedness of the adopted notion of poverty is left without full consideration. This, of course, has crucial implications for the politics of poverty as concepts never stand outside history and culture, they are contested, and they have practical effects. Equally, the fuzzy notion of (children's) welfare needs to be taken as seriously as 'poverty' in poverty research: theorizing children's welfare requires that welfare is properly conceptualized and the frameworks in which our concepts of children's welfare are to function are explicated.

A further guideline for thinking how to theorize children's welfare is provided by O'Brien and Penna (1998) who in their general discussion on welfare theorizing distinguish between two interconnected components of welfare theory: (1) a theory of *social welfare,* and (2) a *social theory* of welfare.

In theorizing social welfare the focus is on »how distributions of resources and opportunities and social patterns of access, participation, inclusion and exclusion support, or contribute to or undermine individual and collective welfare. In short, it is a theory of the organization of social relations and of the impacts of this organization on individual and collective well-being.« (O'Brien and Penna 1998: 4.)

This form of theorizing is essentially a theory *for* welfare policy as it aims to (theoretically) open up the particular views of social and political life that are implicit in the policy and welfare frameworks that are intended to generate more 'effective', more 'rational', more 'just', more 'humanitarian' or otherwise more 'appropriate' policy operation and outcome. The premises and basic assumptions of such frameworks are typically about people's behaviour, learning or interacting, the formation and change of their attitudes, or how people generate resources and share them. They are the premises of welfare frameworks in that they guide the making of social policies and welfare programmes as well as their implementation; and they will tell us how welfare will be provided and life will be experienced when the policy or programme is implemented (ibid: 4-5).

O'Brien and Penna (1998) point out that this sort of theorizing is essentially *normative:* it tells us how we think people should act and what beliefs they should have, how political or economic institutions should operate and how organizations should relate to the populations they serve if we are to make our policies and programmes work »better«, that is: to produce the intended efficiency or outcomes.

It is important to note that in no way does one need to take a theory with such a normative logic in a negative sense, as if it would necessarily refer to manipulation and the direction of people's beliefs and behaviours. In fact many historical as well as more recent strands of critical social and political theorizing – such as liberal, Marxist or ecological theories – show great concern for changing people's behaviours or social institutions in order to create more just, more egalitarian, or more democratic structures and relations, and thereby, welfare – in whatever way it is defined in each case.

The point about the normativity in theorizing social welfare alerts us to the importance of recognizing the concept of welfare that we are in fact using when specifying what we mean by children's welfare. In policy-making they mostly remain implicit whereas a sociology of (children's) welfare would need to be clear on the normative criteria of welfare used in each case.

The second component of a theory of welfare is one that focuses on »how existing social policies and welfare programmes emerged in the first place and how they came to take the form they do, and what the relationships are between the policies and programmes and the societies in which they are situated.« (O'Brien and Penna 1998: 6.)

The premise for developing this sort of *social* theory of welfare is the (sociological) insight that welfare policies, programmes and institutions – and the welfare state as an apparatus of such policies, programmes and institutions – do not just distribute and redistribute income and other benefits to people, even where this is the benign intention of policies. They also impact on the social relations between people and sometimes in very powerful ways, by including or excluding, bringing some people into the centre of recognition and marginalising others, acting towards the liberation of some and perhaps the oppression of others. John Clarke, for instance, writes of Western welfare state development in the 1960s and 1970s that it was »not simply the enlargement of a pre-given field of benefits and services; it was also marked by a series of intersecting and overlapping struggles to make differences, divisions and forms of inequality recognized as a basis for social claims on welfare states (Clarke 2004: 9).

Welfare theory in this sense of the term involves theorizing the political and cultural struggles over welfare, the agents active in these struggles and the creation of social relations and divisions as their outcome. These two components of welfare theorizing are not alternative or competing ways to understand welfare; rather, together they delineate a comprehensive research programme with several levels and dimensions. The task of any one research project is more modest than such a full research programme.

'Children's welfare' and the COST project

The aims of the COST project were given in its work plan (Memorandum of Understanding, or MoU, 2000) in a fairly vague manner: it did not specify what exactly the project would need to look at, and how, in order to be able to account for children's welfare across several European countries. The project aimed at

1) improving the understanding of children's welfare under the impact of globalisation, internationalisation, and the market, as growing factors in children's lives;
2) ameliorating understandings of differences in welfare, space and time use between children and between generational groupings (e.g. children vs. adults);
3) improving the understanding of children's provision from public (state) budgets;
4) making children's welfare transparent as far as the intergenerational distribution of resources and children's use of space and time are concerned.

The basic motivation for launching the project was the recognition that children and childhood have not been fully considered in European welfare research and the discussion on welfare policy. The project therefore made its purpose to bring children and childhood more prominently into welfare discourse, and to begin to produce knowledge that is relevant also (although not limited) to European child policy concerns. This would be achieved by basing the work of the project on the tenets and developments of the (»new«) social studies on children and childhood (Childhood Studies). Accordingly, the approach adopted in the collecting, handling and interpreting of secondary (national) data was a *generational* one (see Introduction in Jensen et al. 2004).

Two »pillars« of welfare were initially specified in the MoU to guide the project towards the direction from which an improved understanding of children's welfare would be sought. First, children's *economic and social welfare* would be studied, and second, their *access to space and use of time*. These two »pillars« also served as the general guidelines for the researchers when they began to compile the country studies to report on children's welfare in each of the participating countries.[2] Two working groups were established to specifically delve into each of the »welfare pillars«, thereby defining the two-fold focus in the project's subsequent work towards understanding children's welfare.

Much more conceptual guidance beyond this was not initially provided for the work of the national research teams. Also, although the project plan did discuss several »welfare issues«, or »dimensions« (particularly children's poverty), it did not commit project members to any particular tradition or approach in the area of welfare research. This also seems a very reasonable starting point, considering the method of work in the project (interpretive secondary analysis) and the immense variation in both quantity and the kind of childhood-related data available in the participating countries. Also the varying disciplinary backgrounds of the researchers involved in the project (although broadly social scientists) do matter; this would also be reflected in the country's reports and the project's further products. Finally also the understandings of 'welfare' adopted by individual researchers can hardly be separated from the political and cultural contexts of their work in their own national contexts, and therefore the national reporting on children's welfare would be expected to also reflect local meanings and understandings.

Meanings of welfare

The idea and the concept of welfare is of course far older than welfare research as a domain of scientific work, or welfare policy as a domain of social praxis. Since its origin in political philosophy (Barry 1999), diverse old and new meanings have been added to and removed from the notion. Universal conceptions of human welfare have a long history and are now part of international discourse, as exemplified by the UN Development Programme's Human Development Reports (Clark & Gough 2005). Today political philosophy and modern economics – two very different discourses – are the dominant producers in the welfare studies field (Gasper 2004). With the evolution and growth, particularly in the latter half of the 20th century, of the social, political and administrational apparatus that we presently know as the welfare state, the uses of the term have multiplied and new subfields have been opened within welfare research. Social policy analysis is presently a (third) strong voice in the study of welfare. The political concern around the »crisis« of the welfare state, especially during the 1990s, and the search for a new »welfare architecture«, have also added to the proliferation of meanings of welfare.

The present multitude of notions of welfare and the trouble in grasping how they differ from and relate to each other becomes evident when surveying even a small part of the now huge welfare research literature. The following (non-exhaustive) sample, picked from the massive, and ever-growing, social scientific literature, is sufficient to demonstrate this.[3]

'Welfare', we are told, can be taken to mean
- the wealth, health, happiness (*eudaimonia*), or fortunes of a person or a group,
- a utility (i.e. individual preferences, as in welfare economics),
- the quality of everyday life (of individuals or groups), or
- human development.

These definitions of welfare point to qualitative assessments of the material, physical or social situation of individuals, or groups of them, and therefore, basically refer to the state of individuals *being* well, *doing* well or *faring* well. In much welfare research and policy literature, well-being is typically treated interchangeably with welfare in this specific understanding of the term (Gasper 2004: 2-3). Particularly in traditions of quantitative measuring of individual welfare, well-being appears to be the term mostly used (cf. Rapley 2003: 26-62).[4]

What the meaning of being, doing or faring well actually is in each case, is a normative issue that is decided separately from its measuring (Corbett 1997). Social indicators, particularly, are developed as instruments for the testing, management and governance of social policies; with the help of indicators a new policy may be tested to see what it does for the targeted social group (see e.g. Ben-Arieh and Wintersberger 1997; Corbett 1997). The main focus is on the performance of the policy, and not the processes by which the final output of the policy is generated (Corbett 1997: xix), so social indicators are meant to be tools for measuring the output of policy, such as the status of children/childhood. Accordingly, one principal meaning of children's welfare is the status of individual children in relation to some defined condition of the children's being, e.g. health, education, economic security, or problem behaviour.

Indicators of children's well-being along these lines have been developed already for more than two decades by UNICEF, in order to regularly monitor the State of the World's Children. A newer development in several European countries is the inclusion of similar measurement systems on children's welfare (well-being) within the social reporting tradition.[5]

A second, partly different and more comprehensive set of understandings of 'welfare' includes
- financial, and other forms of assistance given to poor people,
- organized provision of educational, cultural, medical, and financial assistance to the needy,
- systems of service provision whose ostensible aim is to promote social well-being and alleviate social distress, or
- statutory procedures designed to promote the basic physical and material well-being of people.

These more 'systemic' uses of the term have been increasing since the evolution and growth of welfare states. 'Welfare' now names the diverse (so far national) systems of benefits and services provided by the (welfare) state. Particularly the UK literature uses the term 'child welfare' (and not 'children's welfare') to point at particular *policy areas* that are understood to provide for the nation's children or various categories of them (e.g. »children in care«) in one of the above meanings. Alternatively in this literature, 'child welfare' functions as a short-hand for the social, political and administrative *apparatus* that is institutionalized for such provision (cf. Frost & Stein 1989; Stevenson 1999; Hendrick 2003; 2005).

In the United States literature, the systemic usage is not nearly as clear and, instead, 'welfare' is used in a much narrower sense than in Europe. The term now appears mostly in the context of particular programmes of public assistance (as in »welfare reform«) or the stigmatizing/stigmatized condition of being dependent on such programmes, as in »being on welfare«; »welfare dependency«; »welfare mothers« (Currie 1995; Barry 1999, 126; Bloch et al. 2003; Clarke 2004: 21-22). The semantically more limited use may be understood to derive from the more limited scope of the American welfare system compared to European welfare state structures.[6]

In a sociological treatment the systemic use of 'welfare' described above will expand to cover the totality of the welfare state system (and even beyond it): welfare can be usefully made to refer to all the welfare state institutions, policies and practices, and we may well speak of different welfare cultures (cf. Chamberlayne et al. 1999). This comprehensive sense of welfare also covers the actors making and upholding the system of institutions, policies and practices, and the relations between them: managers, administrators, service providers and »clients« or »welfare subjects.[7]

Within the more complex, systemic understanding of welfare, the individualized notions of welfare (or well-being) introduced earlier may now be taken to refer to the outcomes of the organized welfare activities, practices and relationships making the welfare system, on the level of its »end users« that are individual citizens and groups of them. The idea of 'welfare' production implies furthermore that not just the state agents, but also all other agents that participate in the production of welfare are included within 'welfare'.[8] The interplay between different agents, the relations that are formed between actors, the individual-level outcomes and the social divisions that are (re-)created in the interplay are important elements in the whole of welfare. To account for such a multi-level, multi-agent dynamic welfare system, either quantitatively or qualitatively or both, is a demanding task for research and can be approached from many different viewpoints.

These two meanings seem to be the main usages of 'welfare'; both of them can also be related to the welfare/well-being of children (as well as other subpopulations). Beyond them, a third and different usage is also cropping up in welfare discourse, now linked particularly to macro-economic and environmental concerns. Among these more recent notions are the sustainability, »livability« or social cohesion of a society (e.g. Berger-Schmitt 2000); their attention as directed to the social and economic quality of entire societies and populations as a whole.

Children in welfare research: some observations

The basic motivation for launching the COST project was, as mentioned above, the recognition that children and childhood have not yet been considered in European welfare research and welfare policy work. Scanning through welfare research literature the general observation confirms this: children's welfare issues are either totally *absent* or they are taken account of only *indirectly*, by being related to some other (main) issue such as parents' working time problems and needs for child care while at work.

In the cases where children are expressly included, the treatment tends to be on a *single issue* at a time: poverty, health, mortality, neglect, crime, abuse, exclusion from education, and even life satisfaction (e.g. Micklewright and Stewart 2000); under the theme of children's welfare what is discussed is their poverty, or health or other welfare issues. Rarely is children's welfare as such in focus. In these (rarer) cases children's welfare is typically discussed by *instrumentalizing* children. The recent policy discourse promoting »child-centred social investment strategies« (Esping-Andersen 2002, critically e.g. Beauvais & Jenson 2001, Lister 2002) is one example: children are looked upon and valued as the workers and the citizens of the future; they do not come forward as what they are and their welfare is today. Attention is drawn to children mainly because their societal value is expected to materialize in the future (in adulthood), and therefore they are presented as reasonable objects of economic, social or cultural (educational) »investments« today – children are instrumentalized for the best of the future society. Investments are proposed in the form of alleviation of childhood poverty, provision of benefits to families with children or good quality day-care services. These are »investments« in the sense that societal returns can be expected to be reaped from them some time in the future. And children count because they are the society's resources – instruments – for better welfare futures.[9]

The sociologist will easily recognize here one or another conventional idea of 'socialization' at work: the basis of understanding children's social nature is the unquestioned assumption that they are people still in the process of becoming (James, Jenks and Prout 1998; Alanen 1992). They therefore come to count mainly as future adults (workers, taxpayers, citizens), not as the children of today.

The (»new«) social studies of childhood has for some time developed the alternative viewpoint of children as also existing as social beings living their daily lives and relationships in the present societies. Children, too are social actors and participants in the network of relations that comprise their society; through their participation children today also contribute to their societies, and not only in their adulthood.

Such »new« perspectives on children and childhood, or results from childhood studies, seem not to have impacted child welfare discourses thus far. Janet Fink makes this observation (Fink et al. 2001: 113, 164) and notes herself that

> »… childhood and children are largely invisible within comparative work [on European welfare policy], with its dual emphases on the origin and development of welfare states and the measurement of social insurance performance and provision. Extensive surveys have been conducted of provisions for young children in Europe (…) but more analytical approaches of the relationships between the child, its family and the state tend either not to be integrated into mainstream social policy and comparative social policy (…) or to be marginalized as 'childhood studies' …« (Fink 2001:172).

In 'Children, welfare and the state' Barry Goldson and his colleagues (Goldson et al. 2002) make a commendable attempt in this direction. The first chapters introduce the »new sociology of childhood« and the importance of »listening to children's voices« (ibid: 42-58); however, the rest of the chapters follow the tradition of discussing one welfare issue at a time (poverty, education, work, crime, abuse, …) without relating to the ideas on the »new« perspectives on childhood presented in the opening chapters.

This points the relative fruitlessness of the »add children to science« strategy that is a repetition of the first effort (in the 1970s) to bring women and their lives and experiences into social science (see Harding 1986; for parallels in childhood research see Alanen 1992). It was found not to be adequate for women's (and feminist) concerns; it is an inadequate way also for including children in welfare research: more integrative approaches are needed.

Janet Fink (2001, 173-174) goes some way in this direction in her treatment of family policy analysis. She believes that the issue of children is truly significant for policy analysis, and in three ways: first, children's invisibility helps to leave unacknowledged the ways in which shifting ideas about childhood impact upon and shape the family-oriented policies, second, the positioning of children as dependents has effects on the construction of parenthood with its attendant rights and responsibilities, and third, the 'familialization' of children makes them disappear within the family, which in turn helps to maintain the belief that children's needs are met by serving the family's needs. She concludes: »attention to the nature of such discourses [of childhood] would […] foreground the child, as subject, within welfare policy and practice so that the 'closed box' of the family within comparative social policy is opened…« (Fink 2001: 174). This proposal of an approach is respectful of children's agency and thereby in line with one of the basic tenets in Childhood Studies (see below).

Moving to another area of welfare research: although childhood is a creation of modernity and the institution is strongly maintained by the welfare state, welfare state research has strangely »forgotten« children and childhood. In the introduction to a book on children and the welfare state, Renate Kränzl-Nagl, Johanna Mierendorff and Thomas Olk (2003) explain why this is so: the welfare state is an »adultist« construction, created in struggles about and around adult concerns, and the policies of the welfare state are policies for adults. Childhood policies (Kinderpolitik) seem to be appearing (in discourse) first with the observation that social and economic policies (i.e. policies for adults) impact also on children. In fact, an absence of a well-developed childhood policy is in this way, indirectly, creating in public discourse the recognition that the welfare state needs an explicit childhood policy.

Childhood Studies and Welfare Studies: towards a productive encounter

The ambitions of the COST project were grounded on a view of children and childhood that has been developing since the 1980s across several social sciences. While Childhood Studies is not a coherent school of scientific thought, and does not provide a homogeneous paradigm, a number of assumptions on children and childhood are widely shared.

One of these strongly underlined assumptions is that children (too) are 'social actors' and active participants with contributions to the everyday life of societies. Children's long-lived invisibility in most social science research is seen to be linked to various forms of developmental and socialization thinking which presents children as being in several concomitant processes of 'becoming'. The contrasting starting point given in the assumption of children's (social) agency implies for research that they are addressed as the (sociological) equals to adults or any other social category of people.

The second significant basic assumption in Childhood Studies concerns the institution of childhood: this is a historically, socially and politically »constructed« formation that has been institutionalized for the younger members of societies to 'inhabit'. Social childhoods (and not just individual childhoods) therefore are many; they vary in both time and space, and to assume that there is a universal and »normal« childhood is to fall for a modernist fiction. What these basic tenets imply for disciplines (sociology, anthropology, economics, social policy, history etc.) varies; for sociologists in childhood research the development can be described in terms of three different working approaches.[10]

A sociology of children has been growing out of the early critique of children's invisibility in social science knowledge and the subsequent correction of existing research approach to include children. In the new studies, children were placed in the centre of sociological attention and studied 'in their own right', and not as appendices or attachments to the rest of the social world. The ending of the sociological discrimination of children also required that researchers include in their research material the views, experiences, activities, relationships and knowledges of children, directly and first-hand. Children now were taken as units of research, and seen as social actors and participants in the everyday social world, contributing to its events and thereby also reproducing and transforming their social world. Qualitative research methods, particularly ethnography, have been preferred within this strand of new childhood research.[11]

A second, *deconstructive sociology of children and childhoods* emerged from discussions in social sciences around post-positivist and broadly constructionist methodologies, and their implications for how the social world should be understood and researched. Now the notions 'child', 'children' and 'childhood', and their many derivations, were seen as historically formed cultural constructs. Such notions are significant for children's everyday reality as they are incorporated in social models of action, cultural practices and social policies, and they provide cultural scripts and rationales for people to act in relation to, and on, children and childhood. Discourses of childhood derive their political significance centrally from this. Accordingly, the task of the deconstructive researcher is to »unpack« such constructions by exposing their creators and the social circumstances of their formation, as well as the political processes of their production, interpretation, communication and practical implementation. This sociology aims to disclose the (discursive) power of cultural constructs in social life.

A third, *structural approach to childhood* has also been developing. Here childhood is taken as the unit of analysis and understood as a social structure. 'Structure', however, is a multi-meaning concept, and there are varieties of structural analysis. They share a focus on macro-analysis. Structural-*categorical* approaches involve thinking in terms of children as an aggregate. It »enables us to describe the population of children according to a number of variables: it is important to know what is common for all children« (Qvortrup 1993: 19). The actual living children, each with their different and individually experienced childhoods – which is the central concern of the sociology of children described above – now receive little or no attention and are assembled under the socially established *category* of children. The task is to link empirical observations at the level of children's lived everyday lives (e.g. experience of poverty, use of time, social exclusion) with their macro-level contexts. The aim is to identify the specific social structures and large-scale processes which in interplay with other structures and linked processes impact children's daily lives and living conditions, and »produce« the observed poverty, patterns of time use or exclusion. Quantitative (statistical) methods of research are particularly useful in accounting for the social features that children share, and their structural contexts.

Another structural approach employs *relational* thinking: childhood is conceptualized as a socially generated position within a generational structure, and defined as the figuration of specifically generational relations with which children, on a daily basis, engage themselves in practical relations (i.e. in practices) with other generational groups (Alanen 2001a). The aim is to identify the generational *practices* within which children co-construct themselves as 'children', i.e. as occupiers of a particular generational position, in relation to a number of other agents (Alanen 2001a, 2001b). The advantage in studying children's issues relationally is that it helps to produce a more *dynamic* analysis than the categorical approach. A second advantage is that not only can the *outcomes* of the enacted 'generationing' processes be studied for features that children display, but also the actual processes and relations within which those outcomes are produced. Therefore also the *agency* aspect in children's activity comes more prominently into view, as children are studied as the co-constructors of their own objective and subjective, structured and structuring conditions.

In encountering welfare studies with Childhood Studies, basic questions in developing children's welfare studies are:
• to what extent are the frameworks, conceptualizations and approaches in today's welfare studies able to take in the »new« perspectives introduced by Childhood Studies?
• to what extent are they in fact »adultist« constructions that resist including children within their frameworks, or do so only on condition of a reduced understanding of children?
• can they be adjusted or reoriented in order to contain the more developed childhood perspectives?

These questions imply a stage of *critique* of welfare research frameworks and *deconstruction* of their ways of thinking for developing children's welfare studies. The approach suggests a critical stance towards the notions used in the approaches currently applied in the welfare research field: the context and standpoint of their emergence and basic assumptions they hold on children and childhood, family, citizenship, justice, etc.

In the COST project, material, social and cultural resources, such as income and wealth, space and time, have been viewed from the point of view of their being constraints, opportunities and limitations for children to practice their agency. And agency, as presented above, is the main concern in the sociology of children. The subjective experience of constraints, opportunities and limitations as well as the use (or non-use) of available resources can be taken to importantly constitute the lived and experienced childhoods, and they therefore can be seen to indicate children's welfare/well-being. Clearly the *sociology of children* approach works well as a framework in studying children's welfare. The work of Tess Ridge (2002, and the chapter in this book) on children's experience of poverty demonstrates the use of the approach to reach the subjective, active, experiential dimension of children's welfare. This approach also opens up towards frameworks of welfare that specifically conceptualize the cultural and experiential (subjective) dimensions of welfare (e.g. Chamberlayne et al. 1999; Williams et al. 1999).

The methodology proposed in the COST project's MoU makes the *structural-categorical* assumption that children form an institutionally and culturally established category of people. Based on this, children's access to and use of a number of valued and welfare-relevant resources can be described, analyzed and compared cross-nationally. At its barest, this approach conflates with that of social indicator studies, quality of life studies and statistical studies on diverse »dimensions of welfare«. To provide for a sociology of children's welfare, the structural-categorical approach needs to enrich such analytical descriptions by enveloping them within arguments on the structural contexts that appear to produce the observed phenomena. Structural-categorical theorizing in turn can be enriched and developed into more dynamic, *relational* theorizing of children's welfare. This will require the observing and measuring – and not just abstract theorizing – of systemic and dynamic realities, such as generational structures and generationing processes, and the processes whereby meanings of welfare are produced and enacted.

In summary, the proposal for advancing in the theorizing of children's welfare is that we begin to integrate welfare research and the sociological study of childhood
- by submitting existing welfare research frameworks, paradigms and approaches and their normative definitions of welfare to critical deconstruction from the standpoint of childhood;
- by employing a systemic, multilevel and processual view of welfare (see above) we bring generational divisions, relations and positions to bear on this conceptualization; and
- by using the analytical tools, suggested by a structurally and relationally informed perspective on childhood we rethink and reorient the conceptual resources provided by welfare research towards incorporating children and childhood.

This view of theorizing implies a »mobile« sort of analytic thinking. Thinking children's welfare will therefore also always be unfinished as it will orient us »towards the problems of trying to understand the present as a conjuncture of the complex and multiple routes that brought to this point« (Clarke 2004: 4-5). The vision, and ambition, therefore cannot be to deliver *a theory* on children's welfare.

References

Alanen, L. (1992): *Modern childhood? Exploring the 'child question' in sociology.* Jyväskylä: University of Jyväskylä, Institute for Educational research. Publication Series A: Research reports 50.

Alanen, L. (2001a): »Explorations in generational analysis.« Alanen, L. and B. Mayall (eds): *Conceptualizing Child-Adult Relations.* London: Routledge: 11-22.

Alanen, L. (2001b): »Childhood as a generational condition: children's daily lives in a central Finland town« Alanen, L. and B. Mayall (eds): *Conceptualizing Child-Adult Relations.* London: Routledge: 129-143.

Barry, N. (1999): *Welfare.* Buckingham: Open University Press.

Beauvais, C. and J. Jenson (2001): Two policy paradigms: Family responsibility and investing in children. CPRN Discussion Paper No. F/12, Ottawa. http://www.cpm.org

Ben-Arieh, A, and H. Wintersberger (eds) (1997): *Monitoring and Measuring the State of Children: Beyond Survival.* Eurosocial Reports 62, Vienna: European Centre.

Berger-Schmitt, R. (2000): *Social Cohesion as an Aspect of the Quality of Societies: Concept and Measurement,* Eureporting Working Paper No. 14. Mannheim: Centre for Survey Research and Methodology (ZUMA).

Berger-Schmitt, R. and H.-H. Noll (2000): *Conceptual Framework and Structure of a European System of Social Indicators.* Eureporting Working Paper No. 9. Mannheim: Centre for Survey Research and Methodology (ZUMA).

Bilton, K. (1999): »Child welfare: Whose responsibility?« Stevenson, O. (ed.): *Child Welfare in the UK.* Oxford: Blackwell: 22-41.

Bloch, M., K. Holmlund, I. Moqvist and Th. Popkewitz (2003): »Global and local patterns of governing the child, family, their care, and education.« Bloch, M., K. Holmlund, I. Moqvist and Th. Popkewitz (eds): Governing Children, Families and Education. New York: Palgrave Macmillan: 3-31.

Bonoli, G., V. George and P. Taylor-Gooby (2000): *European Futures.* Cambridge: Polity Press.

Carrington, K. (1993): »The Welfare/Justice Nexus.« Mason, J. (ed.): *Child Welfare Policy. Critical Australian Perspectives.* Sydney: Iremonger: 69-88.

Chamberlayne, P., A. Cooper, R. Freeman and M. Rustin (eds) (1999): *Welfare and Culture in Europe. Towards a New Paradigm in Social Policy.* London: Jessica Kingsley.

Clarke, J. (2004): *Changing Welfare, Changing States. New Directions in Social Policy.* London: SAGE.

Clarke, D.A. and I. Gough (2005): »Capabilities, needs and wellbeing: Relating the universal and the local.« Manderson. L. (ed.) (2005): *Rethinking Well-being.* Perth: Australian Research Institute: 69-90.

Corbett, Th. J. (1997): »Foreword« Hauser, R.M., B.V. Brown and W.R. Prosser (eds) (1997) *Indicators of Children's Well-Being.* New York: Russell Sage Foundation: xix-xxi.

Currie, J.M. (1995): *Welfare and the Well-Being of Children.* Chur: Harwood Academic Publishers.

Esping-Andersen, G. (1990): *The Three Worlds of Welfare Capitalism.* Cambridge: Polity Press.

Esping-Andersen, G. (2002): »A child-centred social investment strategy.« Esping-Andersen, G. with D. Gallie, A. Hemerijck and J. Myles: *Why We Need a New Welfare State.* New York: Oxford University Press: 26-67.

Evers, A. and Th.Olk (Hrsg.) (1996): *Wohlfahrtspluralismus. Vom Wohlfahrtsstaat zur Wohlfahrtsgesellschaft.* Opladen: Westdeutscher Verlag.

Falkingham, J. (2001): »The impact of economic change on child welfare in Central Asia.«Vleminckx, K. and T.M. Smeeding (eds) (2001): *Child Well-Being, Child Poverty and Child Policy in Modern Nations. What Do We Know?* Bristol: The Policy Press.

Fink, J. (2001): »Silence, absence and elision in analyses of 'the family' in European social policy.« Fink, J., G. Lewis and J. Clarke (eds) (2001): *Rethinking European Welfare.* London: SAGE/The Open University: 163-180.

Fink, J., G. Lewis and J. Clarke (eds) (2001): *Rethinking European Welfare.* London: SAGE/The Open University.

Frost, N. and M. Stein (1989): *The Politics of Child Welfare.* Hemel Hempstead: Harvester Wheatsheaf.

Gasper, D. (2004): *Human Well-Being: Concepts and Conceptualizations.* Discussion Paper No. 2004/06. Helsinki: United Nations University WIDER.

Giullari, S. (2003): *Welfare Quadrangles and the Moral Character of Increasingly Elective Social Ties of Support.* Paper presented at the conference 'Welfare and the Social Bond'. Tilburg University. Tilburg, March 26-27, 2003. http://spitswww.uvt.nl/fsw/espanet/documents/doc/giul.doc

Goldson, B., M. Lavalette and J. Mckechnie (2002): *Children, Welfare and the State.* London: SAGE.

Gough, I. (2003): *Lists and Thresholds: Comparing the Doyal-Gough Theory of Human Need with Nussbaum's Capabilities Approach.* ESRC Research Group on Wellbeing in Developing Countries: WeD Working Paper 01.

Harding, S. (1986): *The Science Question in Feminism.* Ithaca: University Press.

Hauser, R.M., B.V. Brown and W.R. Prosser (eds) (1997): *Indicators of Children's Well-Being.* New York: Russell Sage Foundation.

Hendrick, H. (2003): *Child Welfare. Historical Dimensions, Contemporary Debate.* Bristol: The Policy Press.

Hendrick, H. (ed.) (2005): *Child Welfare and Social Policy.* Bristol: The Policy Press.

Hengst, H. (2003): »Kinder und Ökonomie. Aspekte gegenwärtigen Wandels.« Kränzl-Nagl, R., J. Mierendorff and Th. Olk (eds): *Kindheit im Wohlfahrtsstaat. Gesellschaftliche und politische Herausforderungen.* Frankfurt/New York: Europäisches Zentrum/Campus: 235-266.

Hudson, J. and S. Lowe (2004): *Understanding the Policy Process.* Bristol: The Policy Press.

James, A., C. Jenks and A. Prout (1998): *Theorizing Childhood.* Cambridge: Polity Press.

Jensen, A.-M. et al (eds) (2004): *Children's Welfare in Ageing Europe.* Trondheim: Norwegian Centre for Child Research, Norwegian University of Science and Technology, Vols 1-2.

Jenson, J. (2004): Changing the paradigm: Family responsibility or investing in children. Canadian Journal of Sociology 29(2): 169-192.

Joos, M. (2001): *Die Soziale Lage der Kinder. Sozialberichterstattung über die Lebensverhältnisse von Kindern in Deutschland.* Weinheim & München: Juventa.

Kränzl-Nagl, R., J. Mierendorff and Th. Olk (eds) (2003): *Kindheit im Wohlfahrtsstaat. Gesellschaftliche und politische Herausforderungen.* Frankfurt/New York: Europäisches Zentrum/Campus.

Laderchi, C.R, R. Saith and F. Stewart (2003): *Does It Matter that We Don't Agree on the Definitions of*

Poverty? A Comparison of Four Approaches. University of Oxford, QEH Working Paper Series, Number 107. http://www2.qeh.ox.ac.uk/pdf/qehwp/qehwps107.pdf

Lister, R. (2002): *Investing in the Citizen of the Future: New Labour's 'Third Way' in Welfare Reform.* Paper presented at Annual Meeting of American Political Association. http://www.fas.umontreal.ca/pol/ cohesionsociale/publications/lister.pdf

Lister, R. (2004): *Poverty.* Cambridge: Polity Press.

Manderson, L. (ed.) (2005): *Rethinking Wellbeing.* Perth: Curtin University of Technology, Australia Research Institute.

Memorandum of Understanding. COST A19 Children's Welfare (2000). http://www.svt.ntnu.no/noseb/costa19/

Micklewright, J. and K. Stewart (2000): *The Welfare of Europe's Children.* Bristol: UNICEF/The Policy Press.

O'Brien, M. and S. Penna (1998): *Theorising Welfare. Enlightenment and Modern Society.* London: SAGE.

Pierson, C. (1998): *Beyond the Welfare State.* Cambridge: Cambridge University Press.

Qvortrup, J. (1993): »Children at risk or childhood at risk. A plea for a politics of childhood«. Heiliö, P.-L., E. Lauronen and M. Bardy (eds): *Politics of childhood and children at risk.* Eurosocial Report 45/1993. Vienna: European Centre: 19-30.

Rapley, M. (2003): *Quality of Life Research. A Critical Introduction.* London: SAGE.

Ridge, T. (2002): *Childhood Poverty and Social Exclusion, from a Child's Perspective.* Bristol: The Policy Press.

Stevenson, O. (ed.) (1999): *Child Welfare in the UK.* Oxford: Blackwell Science.

Titmuss, R. (1967): The Relationship between Income Maintenance and Social Service Benefits – an Overview. International Social Security Review, XX, 1: 57-66.

Trifiletti, R. (1999): *Southern European Welfare Regimes and the Worsening Position of Women.* Journal of European Social Policy 9 (1): 49-64.

Vleminckx, K. and T.M. Smeeding (eds) (2001): *Child Well-Being, Child Poverty and Child Policy in Modern Nations. What Do We Know?* Bristol: The Policy Press.

William, F., J. Popay and A. Oakley (1999): *Welfare Research. A Critical Review.* London: UCL Press.

Notes

1 For »adultism« in social science, see e.g. Alanen (1992).

2 See the 13 country studies published in Jensen et al. (2004).

3 The examples are taken from Frost (1989), Carrington (1993), Bilton (1999), Chamberlayne & al. (1999), Berger-Schmitt (2000), Berger-Schmitt & Noll (2000), Falkingham (2001), Vleminckx & al. (2001), Goldson & al. (2002), Hendrick (2003), Laderchi & al. (2003) and Gasper (2004).

4 Regarding this, Gasper (2004: 22) notes that etymologically welfare could arguably be a wider

notion than well-being as »'fare' means to travel, travel through life, rather than only to be at a moment«.

5   See Joos (2001) for the case of Germany where social reporting on children is seen as an instrument for developing and assessing the performance of the country's childhood policy (Politik für Kinder). For the range of domains on which children's well-being is measured, for the UK case see Micklewright and Stewart (2000) and for the US case Hauser, Brown and Prosser (1997).

6   Clarke (2004: 21-22) observes the intensive and systematic cultural work in the US in the 1980s and 1990s to reconstruct the meaning of 'welfare'. Built on a political and institutional separation between social insurance-based 'social security' and means-tested and conditional 'assistance, 'welfare' was made to refer to a specific public assistance programme (AFDC); this was moreover »systematically constructed as the hegemonic meaning of welfare« (ibid: 22).

7   Cf. above O'Brien and Penna's (1998) point of »theorizing social welfare«.

8   The many sites and agents of welfare production are in focus in both political and scientific discussions on models of welfare production: they include 'welfare regimes' (Esping-Andersen 1990), 'welfare mix' or 'welfare pluralism' (Evers and Olk 1996) and 'welfare triangle' or 'welfare quadrangle' (Trifiletti 1999).

9   This idea of investing in children has, in recent years, evoked much sympathy and interest in European policy-making communities (as in EU Commission and OECD) and is increasingly proposed as a model for the remaking of European welfare states (e.g. Bonoli et al 2000, 119-138).

10 The »three sociologies« (Alanen 2001a) are to be understood here as different methods of doing childhood research within a shared (broadly constructionist) frame. Each of them has a specific purpose in terms of the knowledge that is sought as well as a specific way of conceptualizing childhood(s); they also utilize specific research methods.

11 Today, this approach quantitatively dominates in Childhood Studies.

Whose Children? Families and Children in »Activating« Welfare States

Ilona Ostner

The Children's Rights Conundrum

Mary Daly (2004) recently pointed to some inconsistencies in ongoing discourses and policies that stress children's rights respectively assume a move towards such rights. The citizenship of children, Daly writes, appears to indicate an interesting point of departure for our understanding and for related analyses of contemporary social policies. The move towards children's rights suggests to be in line with notions of individualisation – as put forward by Ulrich Beck (1983) who speaks about »institutionalised individualism« –

> »whereby most of the rights and entitlements of welfare states are designed for individuals (rather than families)« (Daly 2004: 146).

Drawing upon Daly and Levy (2004), I argue that children's rights have, in fact, ended up in or – if we do not want to assume too much causality here – coincided with social policies specifically designed for children – policies that by design challenge the very idea of rights-based individualism. Child-centred social policies have been part and parcel of what EU Europe has hitherto coined an »activating welfare state« or – to use a term with similar connotations – a »social investment« welfare state – a concept broadly publicised by Esping-Anderson in his programmatic 2002 volume »Why We Need a New Welfare State«. To introduce the concept I rely again on Mary Daly who herself quotes Giddens' understanding. For Giddens a »social investment state« ...

> »engages in positive welfare by investing where possible in human capital rather than (in) the direct provision of economic maintenance [...]. Hence, in a social invest-

ment state social policy is utilitarian, especially having the function of generating resources. Investment in children, therefore, could be seen to be part of a strategy of asset creation and protection« (Giddens quoted in Daly 2004: 146).

»Positive« welfare pertains to »positive activating« measures and to »activation« in a very broad sense. It can encompass early childhood education, bringing people into education and / or jobs, also by providing positive incentives, like »making work pay« measures and other sorts of in-work or for-work benefits. These measures strongly move away from notorious »passive« ones: giving people money without asking for corresponding obligations. They also deviate from negative or punitive measures of activation: tightening eligibility rules, taking away benefits. Jonah Levy distinguishes »thick« and »thin« forms of activation that are accompanied by soft or tough forms of policing and social control. Summing up these trends and ambiguities Daly rightly asks why the new activating or investing – in contrast to »consumptive« – social policies have been phrased in terms of rights and – as one could add – in terms of »guarantees«, a term, Levy frequently uses: e.g. granting children or their parents social rights like access to child-care.

My essay only implicitly answers to this question. It briefly recalls the emergence and institutionalisation of »childhood« as a social category separate from and independent of adulthood; it also points to the rise of children's rights. I first describe children's changing status – the growing individualisation as driven by law – and the barriers to children's legal individualisation by drawing upon Therborn's famous 1993 article. Then, I outline »legal individualisation« as part and parcel of a process of societal individualisation (Ostner 2003) that in turn implies new and more direct forms of state intervention into individual lives. In the course of the 20th century an increasing number of people began to believe that children – not parents – were experts of children's interests. Children's best interests were designed from what was assumed to be a child's point of view. The idea of children as experts of their own lives also entered the UN Convention on Children's Rights. At the end of the 20th century the norm of the individualised child has eventually been established and partly realised (Key 1978).

As a sociologist wedded to the critical sociological tradition I perceive of »the child« in terms of a society that is characterised by the norm of individualisation. Against this backdrop a child can be defined as someone who lacks choice in comparison to significant adults; a child is subjected to other (adult) people's choices. I do not think of a child in bodily terms – as of someone who is growing up – what children surely do. In a sociological not biological perspective children are vulnerable because of their lack of choice and due to their actual or potential subjection to other people's arbitrary actions, mostly their parents' decisions. Legal progress notwithstanding children cannot chose their parents or prevent their parents' separation, re-partnering etc.

– often they are the main victims of parents' choices. De-familisation does not do away with such asymmetries, it only alters the child's minor status. Although a whole set of children's rights has been stipulated, children have not ended to be means to other people's ends.

Children have been increasingly »freed« from the grip of their parents. Lots of former family obligations have been shifted to the societal level and in turn transformed into citizen's – here: family members' – obligations towards the wider society. These obligations are to be met through market related activities that make it possible to pay taxes and contributions to social security schemes; met also by school enrolment and skill formation. »Individualisation« of children via »de-familisation«, on the one hand, and »Vergesellschaftung« of family rights and obligations, on the other – implying a more direct intervention of society into individual lives – can turn out as two sides of the same coin.

The Changing Status of Children

It is well-known how children's economic status changed during the 19th century. Industrialisation and corresponding social differentiation had separated households and economic activity and thereby redefined the roles of family members including children's role and status. The »male breadwinner« came forth. Mechanic solidarity no longer tied family members quasi naturally together. Frail elderly who could not contribute to their own living had always meant a burden to their children – a burden that was hardly made up for by strict norms of filial obligations. Wage dependency further acerbated the load. The child also emerged as a matter of cost and as a growing burden for wage dependants after restrictions of child labour had increased (Ostner 2004).

Historian Harry Hendrick (1994) chronologically enumerates the various status which British society and in particular public policies have conferred to children since the mid 19th century: from the child who worked first full-time then increasingly part-time and combined paid work, school and help in the family's home, to the »school-child« and – since the 20th century – eventually to the »family child«. The latter status has been slowly transformed since then: to the child endowed with rights, the »citizen-child«, but also the »market-child« (Hengst 1998). The incremental expansion of Children's Acts that banned child and restricted youth labour – early measures of what is called today »de-commodification« (granting a person options to exit from the labour market), also »negative« ones that is measures without any compensation for foregone income – drove the transformation of children's status. Children, however, only successively stopped paid work. Wage work outside home, as Hendrick maintains, had contributed to the social status and value of children within their families. Their status had therefore not fully depended upon their families'. Wage work and school hours structured children's daily life and were perceived by many social welfare experts as a perfect means to fight deviance and destitution of labouring parents' children.

As already mentioned, after the definitive abandonment of child labour the child emerged in most families as »family child«. The state and employers, too, came increasingly in to make up for the loss children henceforth constituted for their families. Compensations could take on many forms and served many ends: Germany introduced child-related tax deductions in the 1890s, then entitlements to health insurance based services derived from those of the wage-working parent and orphans' pensions. Early pro-natalist France stipulated the right of mothers and children to free healthcare also in the 1890s. Some countries provided residential care or foster homes for poorer children and other forms of institutional care. Britain did so following her New Poor Law tradition: Hilary Land (1996) recalls typically British systems of support and shelter established by the state in the late 19th and early 20th century for poorer and more vulnerable children – vulnerable, since their parents were poor and could not provide for and protect them. The policies offered to poor parents and their children were modern variants of the »workhouse« system. They consisted of assisting or procuring the emigration of needy children in the care of local authorities to Australia, for instance; or of channelling unemployed boys into the army. Recruits, Land writes (1996: 192-3), alluding (even) to the 1970s in Britain

> »… were not only likely to have *no* educational training (…), (…) 20 per cent did not meet the required literacy or numerical skills. Half of those went to the Royal Army Education Corps' School of Preliminary Education where they received excellent remedial training. (…) Young men from large families or from children's homes, foster homes or from single parent families were over-represented in the latter group (still in 1973 – IO)«.

Land continues to illustrate positive effects of the soldier status of poorer young men after the military salary had been introduced: that there was »every incentive to marry« for young women, hence not to remain unwedded teenage mothers, because the young soldier – the child's father – had an income and was entitled to marriage-related supplements. During the inter-war years British governments had also recognised the need for accommodation when introducing training and job placement schemes for young unemployed or low wage earning people. Taken together, Hilary Land points to earlier de-familising measures that relieved poor parents from obligations to provide for their children by »institutionalising« the latter. Consequently, she is critical about the erosion of such provisions during the later 20th century in Britain – a process that can be called »re-familisation« and that, especially, hurts families with poor means.

Obviously, even in times when the »family child« prevailed, did not all families live up to the norm. Publicly provided accommodation for young working men and women existed in other countries, too, for instance, in Germany, and served as a bridge into adulthood for young blue collar workers and apprentices (Schelsky 1963). In fact, these institutions hindered or at least slowed down the trend towards the encapsulation of adolescents in a family that was becoming inward-looking and self-centred. As families' and young people's income grew, young men and women freely left publicly provided accommodation, returned to their families (»Hotel Mama«) or lived in their own place.

Children's status changed again in tune with the family's new functions (Honig 1999). Many family sociologists of the 1950s already commented that families had become, above all, units of leisure and consumption; hence their main task was teaching children how to consume and deal with disposable time sensibly (ibid.: 145-6). In Schelsky's view, families turned into »consumer-families«, children into »consumer-children«. Economists argued at roughly the same time that children had become either consumer commodities for parent consumers and a matter of preferences, or public goods and hence constituted a serious collective action problem: Why have children, if the gains of having a child are mostly appropriated by the wider society, the cost, however, left with the parents? If the gains of having children were consumed by others, while the burdens suffered by parents, only altruists should be expected to mother or father a child. Since altruists have been rare, numbers of children have declined as a result of new attitudes towards calculating the costs of having or not-having children.

Political scientists, on the other hand, have pointed to the growing concern for children, a concern that has accompanied family change and eventually led to conventions on children's rights (Fuchs 2001). While the »citizen-child« has been increasingly empowered to bring forward her cause, also her cause against her parents, parents' status and related roles including rights as their children's guardians have eroded. Parents do no longer own their children. Children are no longer asked to which estate or household they belong. They introduce themselves with their first names, and these names have in most cases lost any reference to children's ancestors.

The Role of the Law for Individualising Children

Legislation was and still is the catalyst of children's individualisation above all vis-à-vis their parents. Therborn (1993) reconstructs children's steady inclusion in what he calls an »egalitarian individualism«. There are many reasons why »egalitarian individualism« has proceeded to eventually include children: the main driving force has surely been the western enlightened idea that all men are equal, first, before God than before the law. Ideas and norms of equality have become both a means for orientation and for regulation. They have led to a process of continuous comparison – the less equal comparing themselves with more equal people – and corresponding resentment of those perceiving themselves as unequal which, in turn, has always motivated further efforts to equalise.

Men, as Marshall (1950) had elaborated, were the first to attain civil, political and lately social rights, while women enjoyed hardly any rights for long, but had to bear obligations as daughters and wives. Women's legal individualisation weakened men's legal status and saying within the family – but men had nolens volens to successively acknowledge women's equal civic status within and outside marriage and family.

Therborn identifies four elements of the modern legal status of children:

1) a child-centred marriage with equal rights of both parents towards their children – rights that are at the same time based on the idea of children's best interests, welfare and well-being;
2) equal status of marital and non-marital children;
3) recognition of a child's physical, mental and emotional integrity – a »habeas corpus« norm that forbids corporal punishment and other humiliating measures; such recognition is immediately accompanied by the concession of a »continuum« of autonomy, entailing, for instance, a child's right to a minimum of dignity at one end and the right to divorce her parents at the other;
4) children's participation in all matters of their concern follows logically from the idea of »autonomy«.

Therborn tends to suggest that the evolution of children's rights resulted from women's legal individualisation or emancipation. I partly disagree, at least, with regard to the consequences of legal individualisation of the family: as women's marital and family rights have ever since conflicted with men's rights, so have children's rights conflicted with their parents' rights.

To give some examples: Parents, mothers' and also fathers' rights to be economically active on the labour market reduces time for their children or – phrased in terms of Critical Social Theory – time and space for the experience of non-market logics of action. The conflict comes clearly to the fore when Jensen and Qvortrup (2004: 826) write:

> »Children's everyday lives are to a large degree institutionalised and linked to the upsurge in maternal employment. Parental employment influences children's everyday life from an economic, temporal and spatial perspective. A general feature emerging from the reports (COST reports – IO) are the two conditions necessary for children's material and social welfare – economic provision and children's family

life. In terms of children's material welfare – two employed parents are a must. In terms of social welfare – the emerging single-mother family is a worrying feature of modern childhood. Parental break-up may free children from conflict-ridden homes, but it is often followed by less contact with and economic support from the father. (…) children's economic welfare now depends on mother's employment. (…) At the same time, extensive work among both parents (dual-career families) may conflict with children's need for access to parents …«.

Second example: Children have the right to know and or to enjoy both parents. The conflict is apparent. Such a right restricts parents' choices to join, separate and re-partner, if one takes into account that separation and divorce often induces the alienation between the child and the absent parent (mostly the father). It also demands of the parent who lives with the child to concede visiting rights to the former partner. In many instances, recognising children's rights after a divorce can also result in loss of child support, e.g. fathers paying less or no support, once they care for their children during the week. The non-married German mother, also mothers who have for long cohabited with their child's father, have the last say in all custody issues. So far, mothers and courts have assumed this to be in the best interest of the child.

It does not come as a surprise that not all of Therborn's elements have been institutionalised in our western societies, some only partially. Joint custody after divorce has become a norm, to a much lesser extent so a child's right to know (mostly) her (biological) father (Lansdown 2001; Roche 1996). Legal policies often privilege parents' interests at the expense of children's interests. Fathers, especially, never married ones have often minor rights than mothers towards their children but more obligations. Legislators still merge children's and their mothers' interests. Physical punishment was first banned in the Nordic countries, it is banned in Germany – the UK has still to follow. The UK and even more so the US belong to those modern societies that have (re-)invented rather punitive, often humiliating, measures to tackle children's and youth' crime and deviant behaviour, including boot camps, physical punishment, or incarceration of children (Garland 1999; 2004). Sweden and Norway are pioneers in softly policing fathers into taking part of parental leave, Germany has just decided to follow. The Nordic »Daddy Leave« was explicitly introduced to »individualise the right to parental leave« – which meant that the decision about who was to take the leave was not left with the couple. It was argued that couples' free choice was not viable, since traditional gender norms still shaped the couples' decisions. The policy was also justified with reference to the child's best interest and with contributing to individual father's personal development and growth.

Children's rights have continuously met barriers. Parents – even loving and willing ones – mistreat their children and children's best interests. Mistreatment can merely result from a parent's strive to attain his or her own aspirations. The UN

Convention regularly differentiates and graduates children's rights. Graduation and differentiation indicate barriers to children's legal individualisation. In addition, as we all know, children need advocates who formulate their wants and desires. However, even highly entitled children are subjects to adults' interpretations of their needs; also to their parents' actions and choices, as mentioned above. A child is not responsible for the circumstances she enjoys and endures, although some family advisers teach even small children how to properly respond to their working parents needs (with regard to a redefinition and renaissance of child labour, see Hengst 1998). Are their circumstances poor, then moral intuition has hitherto told us (Westerners) that children should be helped. The child used to deserve help. Parents, in contrast, are seen as capable of helping themselves first and via their self-help their children, too. That kind of moral reasoning explains why the focus of poverty has shifted from women, especially, mothers, to children.

While children have been increasingly recognised as being vulnerable – in fact, the whole idea and process of entitling children vis-à-vis their parents and the wider community can be interpreted as resulting from children's vulnerability – the content and ascribed cause of that vulnerability changed as well as the means of dealing with children's vulnerability.

The Multi-Dysfunctional Family, Children as Assets, Family Solidarity Revised

I have argued so far that policies and legislation reacted to children's asymmetric status and restricted choices – restricted if compared with their parents' agency which is also restricted. At present, parents are said not to invest enough or not invest properly into their children and thereby restricting their children's future options, hence, affecting negatively social sustainability. Above all, they are blamed for not having children at all or not having enough children (see, for instance, BMFSFJ 2002).

As Tony Blair has put it during his first term announcing his fight on children's poverty (in my words): »Children make up 20 per cent of our population, but 100 per cent of our future«. Or Esping-Andersen (2002) paraphrasing Blair: »It is in childhood that citizens acquire most of the capital that they will later activate in the pursuit of the good life«. »Health, income poverty, reading to children, social stimuli and guidance are crucial factors in early childhood«, but »we cannot pass laws that force parents to read to their children«. We also cannot prevent homogamy: that lowly educated women partner or marry lowly educated men respectively highly educated and well-to-do women marry their male counterparts, hence reproducing, if not augmenting, social inequalities, inefficiencies and non-sustainability. In a free democratic society such behaviour cannot be forbidden, but compensated. Therefore, investing in children is both functionally and morally desirable. Accordingly, children are not only valuable economic assets, investing in children also corresponds our moral intuition. Similar arguments about family failures abound at present in political discourse and also in research. They are part and parcel of a utilitarian perspective on children and their families. Apparently, children emerge again as objects of adult people's reasoning and doings. Their present or envisioned future social position is perceived as not resulting from their own choices. Therefore, activating and investing measures are well justified.

Women's employment, as already shown with reference to the quotation from Jensen and Qvortrup, has become a crucial factor in any child-centred social investment strategy. It all boils down to women's employment, Esping-Andersen, too, argues. For him, like for many others, enhancing women's employment opportunities is, first of all, a matter of fairness, since it responds to women's (feminist) demands, but secondly, and most importantly, women's employment is also needed, because it yields, like investing in children, increasing returns. Women have been detected now as providers of untapped resources: as a massive labour resource that can help mitigate the burdens of an increasing number of no longer active (unproductively consuming) old people and hence reduce associated financial pressures and shortages of care services. Women's fertility also constitutes a still not sufficiently »tapped« resource of human capital and labour. Finally, women's employment helps fight poverty. Hence, enhancing women's employment is women-, family- and society-friendly.

»Children« and »social investment« provide a very good argument for de-familising policies – policies that »free« families from »care« – decreasingly though from »cash« – obligations towards their family members, albeit some »cash obligations« have become strengthened, lately (child support; families' obligation to provide for their young needy adults). De-familising policies follow naturally from a standpoint that perceives families as failing to properly educate their children, but expects families to still care for the more or less hopeless or less productive ones (as long as these children do not challenge the social order). If we want our children to be better equipped to meet and survive the challenges of the market, the argument runs, we have to protect children from too much family influence. Families are conservative and inward-looking. They do not or not sufficiently prepare for the future. One could write a long list of family failures: Families divorce, reorganise, divorce again which means that they no longer provide the stability and security children need to learn how to cope with increased expectations (flexibility, life-long learning etc.). In addition: Families no longer properly reproduce and prevent children's poverty. The state with the help of the market has to intervene in the best interest of the child.

There is a lot of truth in such arguments. First, families have always failed. Since families have always been highly esteemed and linked to essential emotional needs, they must disappoint. Social investment policies exhibit a remarkable potential of credit claiming – who will dissent and maintain that social investment is a bad thing – those who shall profit – the children – do so immediately, and, most importantly, they are deserving such positive measures. Social investment excels also in blame avoidance. Only weak interests – those of the invisible chronically sick or handicapped or very old – will be hit hard and negatively by social investment. But such interests are politically too feeble to blame politicians and reformers. Social investment policies are therefore divisive policies. Finally, they provide the legitimacy for hitherto »illegitimate« policy. To give an example: In countries where, due to ideological reasons, explicit family policy has not yet existed, social investment encourages to introduce a whole set of family related measures, e.g. the extension of child benefits, childcare etc., which Levy (2004: 200) calls »progressive universalism«, also measures to encourage both parents' employment (tax credits, wage subsidies, care leaves).

Mary Daly (2004: 150) identifies five trends in relation to the family and to children in European welfare states that fit the sketched utilitarian strategy of social investment and corresponding activation:

1) an increased interest of the state in family solidarity (especially, an increased interest in the »cash« and »care« contributions of men); bringing in fathers (or sons), tapping their parental (filial) obligations will inevitably erode women's protected and sometimes privileged status as mothers and serve as a further catalyst for mothers' employment;
2) a move to treat children independently of their families and to grant them individual rights;
3) a tendency to treat both parents as workers;
4) a move towards a greater welfare mix with regard to forms of income and income mixes as well as care provisions;
5) and a move towards gender neutrality for the purposes of social policies – a move also driven by trends 1) and 3): »bringing fathers in« and treating both parents as workers.

Taken together these trends will »de-institutionalise childhood« and »de-familise families« while »institutionalising children«. As Jensen and Qvortrup (2004: 825) emphasised and Land (1996) illustrated: Institutionalisation is not a new phenomenon in children's lives. Families have always given away children for many reasons – and they still do so. The new quality of institutionalisation today results from its utilitarian drive and its affinity to positive eugenic (social investment) measures.

Individualisation of mothers and children can go hand in hand and simultaneously involve greater intervention into family life and practices. Family members are classified and treated according to their labour market attachment which in turn means that state or society seek to affect more directly the division of labour and the performance of tasks within households as well as, as Daly writes, »the nature of the relationship among family members«. The relationship can be described by a de-familised family with two working parents while state or market take care of the child or the elderly in need of care; they do so differently, though, for children versus the elderly.

Elements of a New European Social Model

European Union member states have agreed to boost employment, increase employability of those of workable age (including mothers and older worker) and fight both non-employment and unemployment. The subsequent increase of the number of two-earner-households is thought to tackle the costs of having children. Part of the employability strategy consists of measures to better balance work and family life. Women and men of workable age meet their obligations towards their children by doing paid work and thereby support each other. At the same time, as Daly argues, family solidarity has become redefined. It pertains to solidarity via labour market inclusion that in turn requires de-familisation. Solidarity then means that families must readily give up some of its core activities and leave these with other institutions. Thereby, the family becomes in »Third Way« speak »the partner to a host of other social providers« – its peculiar quality and logic seems to fade.

According to Daly, and here I also fully agree, the promotion of the briefly sketched new family solidarity implies some »anti-familism« which is also apparent in the many discourses on family failures. On the other hand, some anti-familism is needed, if parents are to give away their children after decades of close, intimate and emotional attitudes towards a child who has increasingly become an individual and treated like one. Children have become very special for parents; institutionalisation, however, means inevitably, if only for reasons of institutional fairness, equal (that is »mean« or »median«) treatment. Family failures may have been exaggerated recently in discourse in order to facilitate such institutionalisation of children.

Concluding, I will just point to some back-feeding effects of socialising (de-familising) the family – effects also for children. As already said, de-familisation will transform and has transformed lots of formerly familial obligations into societal obligations which in turn means that families have also become to a larger extent obliged towards the wider society. These obligations are now to be met through market activities. Women and men of workable age, including parents, are expected, above all, to be employed. Children have to enter educational institutions earlier than ever. Family childhood has eroded and will further erode. Market childhood will arise instead and expand. We just have to look at the increasing number of schoolchildren who do paid work and who have since long been discovered as important consumers. In turn, societies offer services to worker-citizen-mothers, worker-citizen-fathers and worker-citizen-children – services paid by taxes and contributions of employees. Obligations are first towards society, in fact, to market needs, then to the family.

The utilitarian social investment and activating welfare state invests above all in areas which and in people who promise returns – increasing returns as far as possible. Related policies »cream« objects of potential investment according to expected returns, hence, tend to be highly selective. This may explain why the recent evolution of children's rights has gone together with increasingly tough policing or mere neglect of »rough« or »hopelessly deviant« children and youth (Goldson 2002). Or why chronically sick or disabled children as well as adults have been confronted so often with rationing of medical treatment. Ironically enough, in the end the family seems mostly left for those who do not promise increasing returns. However, it remains an open question, whether formerly or increasingly de-familised families will be ready to take on such burden in the future.

References

Beck, U. (1983): »Jenseits von Klasse und Stand? Soziale Ungleichheit, gesellschaftliche Individualisierungsprozesse und die Entstehung neuer sozialer Formationen und Identitäten«. Kreckel, R. (ed): *Soziale Ungleichheiten*. Soziale Welt. Special Issue 2. Göttingen: Schwartz: 35-74.

BMFSFJ (2002): *Elfter Kinder- und Jugendbericht*. Bericht über die Lebenssituation junger Menschen und die Leistungen der Kinder- und Jugendhilfe in Deutschland. Bonn: Bundesministerium für Familie, Senioren, Frauen und Jugend.

Daly, M. (2004): »Changing Conceptions of Family and Gender Relations in European Welfare States and the Third Way«. Lewis, J. and R. Surender (eds): *Welfare State Change. Towards a Third Way?* Oxford: Oxford University Press: 135-156.

Esping-Andersen, G. (2002): »A Child-Centred Social Investment Strategy«. Esping-Andersen, G. (with Duncan Gallie, Anton Hemerijck and John Myles): *Why We Need a New Welfare State*. Oxford: Oxford University Press: 26-67.

Fuchs, A. (2001): »Die Umsetzung der UN-Kinderrechtskonvention in Deutschland«, *Recht der Jugend und des Bildungswesens*, Vol. 49 (3), pp 255-262.

Garland, D. (1999): »Editorial. Punishment and Society Today«, *Punishment & Society*, Vol. 1 (1), pp 5-10.

Garland, D. (2004): »Die Kultur der »High Crime Societies«. Voraussetzungen einer neuen Politik von »Law and Order«. Oberwittler, D. and S. Karstedt (eds): *Soziologie der Kriminalität. Theoretische und Empirische Perspektiven*. Kölner Zeitschrift für Soziologie und Sozialpsychologie. Special Issue 43/2003, pp 36-68.

Goldson, B. (2002): »Children, Crime and the State«. Goldson, B. et al (eds): *Children, Welfare and the State*. London: Sage: 120-135.

Hendrick, H. (1994): *Child Welfare in England 1872-1989*. London: Routledge.

Hengst, H. (1998): »Kinderarbeit revisited«, *Zeitschrift für Soziologie und Sozialisation (ZSE)*, Vol. 18 (1), pp 25-37.

Honig, Michael-Sebastian, 1999: *Entwurf einer Theorie der Kindheit.* Frankfurt a.M.: Suhrkamp.

Jensen, A.-M. and J. Qvortrup (2004): »Summary – A Childhood Mosaic: What Did We Learn?« Jensen, A.M. et al (eds): *Children's Welfare in Ageing Europe.* Volume II. Trondheim: Norwegian Centre for Child Research: 813-832.

Key, E. (1978): *Das Jahrhunderts des Kindes.* Königstein: Athenäum (first 1902).

Land, H. (1996): »The Crumbling Bridges between Childhood and Adulthood«. Brannen, J. and M. O'Brien (eds): *Children in Families. Research and Policy.* London: Falmer Press: 189-201.

Lansdown, G. (2001): »Children's Welfare and Children's Rights«. Foley, P. et al (eds): *Children in Society. Contemporary Theory, Policy and Practice.* Houndmills: Palgrave in association with The Open University: 87-97.

Levy, J. (2004): »Activation through thick and thin: progressive approaches to labour market activation«, *Social Policy Review 16.* Analysis and debate in social policy, 2004. Bristol: The Policy Press, pp 187-208.

Marshall, Th. H. (1992): »Staatsbürgerrechte und soziale Klassen«. *Bürgerrechte und soziale Klassen. Zur Soziologie des Wohlfahrtsstaates.* (Edited, translated and introduced by Elmar Rieger), Frankfurt a.M.: Campus: 33-94 (in English first 1950).

Ostner, I. (2002): »Am Kind vorbei – Ideen und Interessen in der jüngeren Familienpolitik«, *Zeitschrift für Soziologie der Erziehung und Sozialisation*, Vol. 22 (3), pp 247-266.

Ostner, I. (2003): »'Individualisation' – The Origins of the Concept and its Impact on German Social policies«, *Social Policy & Society*, Vol. 3 (1), pp 47-56.

Ostner, I. (2004): »'What are Children for?': Reciprocity and Solidarity between Parents and Children«. Knijn, T. and A. Komter (eds): *Solidarity Between the Sexes and the Generations. Transformations in Europe.* Cheltenham: Edward Elgar: 167-184.

Ostner, I. (2004): »Wem gehört das Kind? Von der elterlichen Gewalt zum Recht des Kindes«. Nolte, G. and H.-L. Schreiber (eds): *Der Mensch und seine Rechte.* Göttingen: Wallstein Verlag: 151-170.

Roche, J. (1996): »The Politics of Children's Rights«. Brannen, J. and M. O'Brien (eds): *Children in Families. Research and Policy*, London: Falmer Press: 26-40.

Schelsky, H. (1963): *Die skeptische Generation. Eine Soziologie der deutschen Jugend.* Düsseldorf-Köln: Eugen Diederichs Verlag (first 1957).

Therborn, G. (1993): »The Politics of Childhood: The Rights of Children in Modern Times«. Castles, F. G. (ed): *Families of Nations. Patterns of Public Policies in Western Democracies.* Aldershot: Dartmouth: 241-291.

WELFARE STATES AND GENERATIONAL ORDER

Thomas Olk and Helmut Wintersberger

Introduction

In this chapter we discuss political options and strategies for an adequate integration of childhood and children into welfare theory. This poses enormous problems because a child-oriented welfare state theory does not exist. This is a result of a two-fold neglect (cf. Kränzl-Nagl et al. 2003): On the one hand, childhood research has neglected welfare state theory and welfare policies for children and families. In most cases, childhood research focuses on different aspects of the life worlds of children or special dimensions of their living conditions like child poverty, sexual abuse, child discrimination, etc. On the other hand, welfare state theory and research have also treated children and children's welfare as a marginal issue. Dominant welfare state theories bear adultist characteristics. For example, T. H. Marshall focused on male workers in developing his concept of civil, political, and social citizenship rights; women are only mentioned marginally, and children were excluded because, at that time, it was beyond dispute that the rights of citizenship were assigned exclusively to adults.

Even Gøsta Esping-Andersen's (cf. 1990) influential typology of welfare state regimes is by no means a child-oriented theory of the welfare state. This theory holds that securing of the political, civil, and social citizenship rights does not depend so much on the amount of social expenditure but more on the institutional welfare arrangement and the specific patterns of welfare state intervention. Three criteria are decisive for differentiating the types of welfare state regimes: (1) The criterion of »de-commodification«: this means the extent of reducing the necessity for workers to sell their labour at the market place, (2) the modification of a given societal structure of inequality by a relative autonomous welfare system of stratification, and (3) the relative importance of market, state, and family households by securing the welfare of the population and the interplay of public and private welfare institutions.

Referring to these criteria Esping-Andersen identifies a »liberal,« a »corporatist-conservative,« and a »social democratic« welfare state regime. A given welfare state regime is relevant to a child's welfare. Empirical research demonstrates that children in countries of the social democratic welfare state regime are better off than in countries of a liberal or conservative welfare state regime. However, this is not primarily the result of an explicit child-orientation of welfare institutions. In fact, it is easier in universalistic welfare state regimes to extend citizenship rights from adult male workers to other population groups than in conservative welfare states where the eligibility for social benefits is dependent upon one's position in the labour market or in the liberal welfare state regime, where only restricted social benefits are offered to population groups at risk or with special needs. Esping-Andersen's welfare state typology is oriented around the goals of the Swedish social democratic workers movement, and therefore is restricted to a conventional understanding of work and income in industrial societies, while suppressing gender oriented and generational aspects of the system of inequality in post-modern societies. For this reason, such a typology can not contribute essentially to a child-oriented theory of welfare state (cf. Pringel 1998). A child-oriented welfare state theory has to create independent criteria and indicators which make it possible to differentiate given welfare states according to their »child-orientation«.

In this respect a critical view of feminist welfare state theory may make sense. Although this strand of research is also stamped by adultist thinking, the feminist theoretical concepts are more sensitive to the specific interests and needs of children as a social category than other concepts. Gender-oriented typologies of welfare states analyze the role of women in the context of welfare state policies (cf. Lewis 1992). The first wave of feminist welfare state theory, therefore, differentiated given welfare states with respect to their guaranteeing women equal access to the labour market. New theories go a step further (cf. Daly 2000: 45ff.). The central assumption is that realizing the full citizenship of women relies on an equal access of women and men to the labour market as well as to informal care work in the domestic sphere. This means that the realization of the model of the »universalized breadwinner« has to be completed by an »universalization of care giving«.

Along the lines of the feminist welfare state theory we can also ask about the relationships between children as a social category, on the one side, and a given welfare state arrangement, on the other (cf. Olk 2004). What consequences does a given welfare state regime have for the generational contract? Is the traditional patriarchal hierarchy between men, women, and children strengthened by a given welfare state arrangement or does it support the autonomy and citizenship of children? Questions like these demonstrate that a child-oriented typology of welfare state regimes introduces »social age« and »generation« as additional dimensions of social inequality and stratification analogue to the introduction of »gender« as a criterion of inequality by the feminist movement. In this respect the feminist welfare state theory can not replace a child-oriented analysis of welfare state regimes, for women do not have the same relationship to welfare state institutions as children. For example, mothers may have an interest in defining the extent of their labour market participation according to individual preferences, which could potentially conflict with the interests and needs of their children. Furthermore, women are, by and large, in the position of »care-givers« which implies different interests than those of children who are in the position of »care-receivers«.

However, there are also fundamental theoretical objections against using age (or generation) as a structural dimension for defining a generational mode of production and welfare regime (Folbre 1994). In the following part we will confront this position with some of the findings of new childhood research and show that Folbre is wrong. Then we will argue that selecting generation as structural dimension is not only feasible in a theoretical, but also desirable in a normative perspective: firstly it coincides with political and legal developments concerning the position of children in society at large, ongoing at both international and national levels, and secondly it is effective in the sense that some of the contradictions having hardly any solution in the frame of restricted adultist models are solvable in the generalised model. A major part of the following section will be dedicated, however, to explicating more in detail how to extend welfare state theory and practice by childhood, age and the generational dimension. For pragmatic reasons we will restrict this exercise to two relevant areas, namely the material economic situation of children as well as childcare services.

Capitalism and patriarchy: dual modes of production – And what about adultism?

Folbre (1994) develops her feminist position from a systematic discussion of the main social and economic theories and orientations: traditional neoclassical theory, neoclassical institutionalism, traditional as well as Neo-Marxian theory. Her approach is of interest to us, both methodologically as well as substantively. Methodologically it is an effective and elegant way of identifying the value and limits of traditional theories as well as the value added by theoretical modifications and extensions; and by following her lines of arguing when introducing the feminist position we might learn something with a view to the generational dimension. As to content, she expresses the view that with including gender into welfare state theory the sequence of structural enlargements (or generalisations) of the model should be complete, which means that – according to her – it would not be sound adding to capitalism and patriarchy also adultism as we envisage doing according to the subtitle of this section. Therefore, before going on we have to invalidate her argument, that in addition to class, gender and only gender, but not age or generation may be considered a structural dimension constituting a mode of production and welfare regime.

Patriarchy is a »mode of production both analogous to and intertwined with capitalism«, Folbre (1994, 37) argues, making reference to socialist feminism. Similarities are supposed between gender and class exploitation. Women's biological and social capacities are conceived as a means of production, and the patriarchal family becomes an analogue to the capitalist firm. An essential criterion for considering gender as structural dimension not equal but similar to class, and capitalism and patriarchy as dual systems of production, is women's involvement in production, although for this purpose the notions of »production« and »work« have to be redefined. In the feminist perspective, production is not only production for exchange, but also production for use, and thus work includes (besides market work) non-market work, emotional labour, caring work, sex/ affective production etc. In this way, class and gender become *the* crucial categories, while other forms of collective identity, which cannot be based in production, as nation, race, age, or sexual preference, are contingent or contextual. »These forms of difference often remain on a lower level of theoretical importance, even where they receive careful historical and political attention. Nationalism, racism, ageism, homophobia – these words all imply attitudes rather than structures. They do not comprise 'systems' comparable to capitalism or patriarchy«, Folbre (1994, 38) concludes.

In the following we will not deal with all forms of differences mentioned by Folbre, but only age. The first question we have to ask in this connection is, whether inequalities based on age are just attitudinal, as Folbre suggests, or structural. Folbre is obviously unaware of major developments in childhood research of the last 20 years. It was the main task (and achievement) of the international project »Childhood as a social phenomenon« (Qvortrup et al. eds. 1994) to give rise to formulating theories about childhood as a structural category and to identifying mechanisms in society structurally discriminating children as compared to the rest of the population, namely adults. Therefore we prefer the term adultism to ageism.

In a historical perspective, since the French revolution citizenship, human, political, economic and social rights have been consecutively extended to population groups previously excluded, beginning with the male bourgeois, continuing with the male workers and then the women. Today children form the last big and compact population group, which is still excluded from full citizenship. First changes taking place just now mean a change of the generational relations between children and adults and of the generational order of society as a whole, which means that age/ generation forms a structural dimension.

However, the fact, that the dominant feature of this form of difference is structural, does not imply that there aren't at the same time aspects of adultist discrimination of children which are based on attitudes and prejudices, as this is the case with a view to class and gender relations, too. We also admit that – although we consider age/ generation/ adultism an analogue with a view to sex/ gender/ patriarchy – there are a number of differences between the two categories or dimensions; in particular, while there is generally speaking no trans-gender mobility, all children will eventually become adults, when they reach the age of majority. This is however not in contradiction with the structural nature of the generational dimension, because even if children are becoming adults individually, childhood remains a permanent structural category in any society.

The other question concerns the position of children in the production process. Folbre (1994) holds the view that for establishing a mode of production and a welfare regime along the borderlines of a population group, it is necessary that the group be part of the division of labour. The question therefore is: are children in economically advanced societies part of the generational division of labour? The majority would spontaneously answer this question with no; on the contrary, it is a basic feature of an economically advanced society, that children are scholarised, and that employers are strictly forbidden to employ children. Therefore it is not surprising that also Folbre concludes that there is no basis in the productive system – stretch its definition as you may – for establishing a generational or adultist mode of production. However, in recent literature (Qvortrup 1995; Hengst 2000; Wintersberger 2005) the position of children in the generational division of labour is approached in a totally different way: children's involvement in production and work is seen as a continuous feature of childhood, and scholarisation and human capital formation are not perceived as abolition of child labour, but as child labour adapted to the conditions of an advanced capitalist society. In the course of economic and social development childhood is passing through several productive and economic stages assigning to children the part of agricultural and early industrial producers, human capital, emotional assets, active consumers, and finally post-industrial producers, and the whole process may be interpreted as (formal and real) subsumption of child labour under capital (for a more detailed discussion of this economic evolution of childhood and its impact on the generational division of labour, see chapter on »Working children« by Nic Ghiolla Phadraig, and Wintersberger 2005).

To conclude, children are a part of the generational division of labour, and the generational dimension is as crucial and structural as class and gender are. Therefore, we have invalidated Folbre's assertion as to the unfeasibility of a generational mode of production and welfare: it makes sense to interpret adultism as a mode of production as well as to extend the dualism of capitalism and patriarchy to the triad of capitalism, patriarchy and adultism.

The UN Convention on the Rights of the Child: normative implications for children's welfare

When the General Assembly of the UN adopted the Convention on the Rights of the Child (CRC) in 1989, a new page in the history of childhood was opened. For the first time children were given the role of legal subjects, and in this way the existing generational order of societies and nations was questioned in a fundamental way.

However, the CRC has also shortcomings. As the result of diplomatic negotiations it contains a number of compromises and it leaves much room for interpretation. Some crucial issues, as generational discrimination, are not approached at all, and it contains even some contradictory norms. As other legal documents, it refers to the individual child predominantly. Its perspective is partly developmental, with a focus rather on children's well-*becoming* than well-*being*. Recurrent references to the maturity and capability of the child undermine and erode some of its intentions, in particular those concerning the extension of civil rights to children. It is more explicit with regard to rights and responsibilities of parents, but remains somehow vague concerning both the rights of children and the responsibilities of states vis-à-vis parents and children. In Art 2 concerning discrimination, the text refers only to discrimination among children (e.g. girls and boys), but not explicitly to the most relevant aspect regarding the discrimination of children, generational discrimination between children and adults. We have however to take into account that the CRC had been elaborated in the 1980's when the understanding of childhood was still overwhelmingly dominated by the traditional child sciences and the developmental paradigm in research, as well as by adultist, paternalistic and familistic attitudes in politics and action.

Meanwhile the CRC and the process of its implementation has led to a number of initiatives at national, European and international levels, such as the national action plans for children (NAPs), recommendations concerning childhood policies by both the European Parliament and the Parliamentary Assembly of the Council of Europe, the explicit inclusion of children and their rights in the European (Draft) Constitution as well as ongoing preparations for a substantive Communication of the Commission concerning childhood and childhood policies. The two last initiatives would be of particular importance for establishing the generational dimension in political discourses in Europe, since both inclusion of childhood in the EU Constitution as well as a Communication of the Commission concerning childhood would create a legal basis for addressing childhood and generational issues at the level of the EU, and consequently strengthen this perspective also at national levels.

As to content the CRC contains many articles and paragraphs dealing with children's economic and social welfare, however we will not go systematically through the entire text, but restrict our analysis to interpreting a few articles only, which are central with a view to defining economic and social standards for children. In this

THOMAS OLK AND HELMUT WINTERSBERGER

context we do not make use of the CRC primarily for arguing in the frame of a children's rights discourse, but rather for elaborating on the normative foundations of research and policies with a view to children's economic and social welfare. We take for granted, that drawing upon the CRC in this way is not arbitrary, but highly legitimate, because all European countries have ratified it.

A decent »standard of living« for children

Safeguarding to children a decent standard of living is the main concern of Art 27 CRC. In paragraph 1 States Parties are asked to recognise »the right of every child to a standard of living adequate for the child's physical, mental, spiritual, moral and social development«. We note the developmental orientation in focusing rather on children's well-*becoming* than well-*being*, but dedicate our primary attention to another aspect: the principal request of a desirable living standard for every child, wherever and in whatever conditions he or she may be. Paragraph 2 states that the »parents or others responsible for the child have the primary responsibility to secure, within their abilities and financial capacities, the conditions of living necessary for the child's development«. The family orientation goes like a red thread through the whole CRC. In this connection it means that the responsibility for the material wellbeing of the child is primarily not with the government but with the parents, and therefore, we have also to accept, that children's standard of living may vary along with that of their parents. However, the CRC sets also limits to such variations: in paragraph 3 States Parties are invited, »in accordance with national conditions and within their means, (to) take all appropriate measures to assist parents (…) to implement this right and (…) in case of need (to) provide material assistance and support programmes, particularly with regard to nutrition, clothing and housing«. Obviously the delegation to parents of the principal responsibility for the child's well-being contained in paragraph 2 is not to be understood as a release of governments from any responsibility in this connection. On the contrary, in a preventive way governments may have indirect responsibilities for promoting and maintaining parents' abilities and capacities, and in a subsidiary way, direct responsibilities for the well-being of the child, if parents may not be expected to come up to their responsibilities. Again we note in the list of needs a focus of this article on rather basic needs as nutrition, clothing and housing. This makes sense for those countries of the world where almost 90 percent of children live, while for most European countries a literal interpretation of this wording would not fully correspond to the spirit of the CRC.

Access to social security

Art 26 CRC regulates children's access to social security. In paragraph 1 there is stated that governments »shall recognize for every child the right to benefit from social security, including social insurance, …«, while paragraph 2 states that »the benefits should, where appropriate, be granted, taking into account the resources and the circumstances of the child and persons having responsibility for the maintenance of the child, …«. Similarly to Art 27, also Art 26 acknowledges in paragraph 1 children's citizenship with a view to the distribution of material resources as well as access to social security respectively. However, while the task of safeguarding a decent standard of living is seen as the main responsibility of parents, safeguarding the access to social security remains a primary obligation of the government, which in doing so should however consider the specific needs of the child on one, and the resources available to the child or his/ her parents on the other hand.

Access to childcare services and education

With a view to services we may complement the analysis by drawing attention to Art 28 and 18 CRC, dealing in particular with access to childcare services and education. Art 28 CRC invites States Parties to recognise »the right of the child to education, and with a view to achieving this right progressively and on the basis of equal opportunity, (…) in particular (to) a) make primary education compulsory and available free to all (…)«. By generalising the main message of Art 28 to (public) services we note that, while the CRC accepts to some extent inequalities originating from the different abilities and capacities of the parents, this does not hold true for school or other basic services.

Childcare issues are addressed in Art 18 CRC. As in the case of Art 27, Art 18 paragraph 1 CRC underlines first the responsibility of both parents and states that thereby »the best interest of the child will be their basic concern«. This parallel continues in paragraph 2, in which member states are asked to »render appropriate assistance to parents … in the performance of their child-rearing responsibilities and … ensure the development of institutions, facilities and services for the care of children«. Finally, according to paragraph 3 member states »shall take all appropriate measures to ensure that all children of working parents have the right to benefit from childcare services and facilities for which they are eligible«. From a child centred perspective we discover immediately that a right to day care defined as a »right for children of working parents«, as in Art 18, is − strictly speaking − not a right for children, but for working parents, and should therefore be rather part of an ILO Convention on reconciliation of work and family life. In addition this is in obvious contradiction with a view to article 2 CRC, which forbids any discrimination of children, in particular discrimination on the basis of their parents' economic social or other status.

Synthesis

A careful reader of the CRC will discover similarities and differences with a view to the distribution of rights and responsibilities in Art 18, 26, 27 and 28. In Art 26, 27 and 28 an adequate standard of living as well as access to education and social security are spelled out as rights of every child, while – in the strict sense – according to Art 18 there is not such a right to childcare for every child. Art 18 and 27 emphasise the primary responsibility of parents for their children's welfare, while Art 26 and 28 introduce education and social security as primary responsibilities of the state. From there it follows that concerning standard of living and childcare the CRC accepts inequalities between children along with inequalities existing between their parents, while with a view to basic education and social security it requests more equity. However, Art 18 and 27 oblige also the state and society to support parents economically, for instance with child benefit schemes, and with a view to childcare, for instance by establishing child day-care centres, thereby reducing inequalities transmitted by families. To some extent it is however open to interpretation by governments, how to define the boundaries of parental responsibility and public intervention more concretely.

Generational income distribution and child benefit packages

On one hand, the generational income distribution is better documented than most other dimensions of generational distributive justice; on the other hand, with a view to children's access to basic resources, there is hardly any other area more dominated by adultist preconceptions than access to money. This is obviously connected with the fact, that modern childhood is a priori separated from economic participation, and therefore, the institution of gainful employment, the major source of income for the overwhelming majority of people in modern society, is reserved for adults only. However, in public economics there are concepts such as GDP per capita, in which the whole population of a nation (also children) is included, which means that in those calculations a certain share of the national income is statistically allocated to children, too. This transformation into individual per-capita incomes is generally achieved by applying equivalence scales (see next chapter on »Child income poverty« by Bradshaw) to household incomes for families comprising different numbers of children and adults.

Generational and related distributive dimensions

For the analysis of the generational income distribution of a nation, incomes statistically allocated to individuals are being aggregated and compared with a view to age groups or generations. For economically developed countries this exercise reveals that children are more or less discriminated as compared to the rest of the population, namely adults. This phenomenon referred to also in terms of (generational) child poverty, should, however, not be confused with other phenomena, in particular absolute child poverty in developing and transition countries (present to greater or lesser degree also in rich countries). Behind generational child poverty is a relative poverty concept (Bradbury and Jäntti 1999), which is rather adequate for studying social inequalities and discrimination than absolute poverty and social exclusion.

This reminds us of analogous calculations with a view to gender: incomes statistically allocated to individuals may be and are aggregated also according to gender, and for all countries this shows, that generally (mean as well as median) incomes are lower for the female than for the male population. Theoretically and methodologically, there is no difference between gendered and generational income analysis. However, while for the child population in modern societies gainful employment is – as stated before – not a significant phenomenon, for the (adult) female population it is. Therefore in addition to the gender comparison of statistically standardised incomes (as above), we are familiar also with the comparison of actual female and male incomes from gainful employment (wages, salaries etc.), which again indicates income discrimination of women as compared to men. Consequently, gender income disparities may either be due to open discrimination of women in the sense that they get lower salaries for the same work or less easily promoted than male workers, or structural discrimination in the sense that women in general tend to be concentrated in lower paid jobs than men. Disparities emerging from this more restricted gender income comparison contribute to general gender income inequalities, however, they represent only a part of the problem. An even greater problem is caused by the fact, that a larger share of women (than men) in employable age work part-time only or do not work at all. Both open and structural discrimination of women is rather due to mother- than womanhood (though all mothers are women, not all women are or become mothers), and there are obviously interrelations and overlaps between discrimination of children and mothers as well as between child and maternal poverty (cf. e.g. Beisenherz 2002).

In larger families in particular, the household income has to be shared among more persons, and therefore standardised per capita incomes are statistically lower than in smaller households. Whenever a child is born in a (couple or single) household, it is obvious that per-capita income from the market will decrease for the household due to the presence of an additional member unable to contribute to the household income. If in addition a parent (due to the present gender distribution of housework and care activities this is usually the mother) reduces or cancels her participation in the labour market, this leads even to a decrease of the absolute household income in a situation when an increase would be needed instead just in order to maintain the previous living standard. Depending on accessibility and cost of childcare facilities, the pressure on the mother to reduce working time or withdraw from employment will rise with the number of children to be taken care of. This dynamics draws our attention on another dimension of the income distribution, namely the horizontal distribution focusing on variations in household expenditures depending on the number (and age) of children.

It is obvious, that the generational, gender and horizontal distributions interact also with the vertical dimension, which is the main traditional social policy concern, the distribution between social classes as well as between the rich and the poor. Changes and reforms in one dimension are likely to affect balances with a view to other dimensions, and for each dimension it might be possible to identify stakeholders and discourses. In this context we will obviously focus on children as stakeholders and argue in the frame of a childhood discourse.

Child-related financial transfers: functions and objectives

So far we have considered only one source of household income, namely the market. Since in all economically advanced countries governments allocate some child-related financial resources for families with children, we have to include also these child benefit packages in order to get a realistic picture concerning the generational income distribution. With a view to these programmes there are mainly four functions/ objectives to be distinguished:

A basic income for children
Safeguarding a basic income to children would be a primary objective in the frame of a childhood and children's rights discourse. Such direct financial transfers to children would fully acknowledge the recognition of children as subjects by the UN-CRC. However, we do not know of any nation providing explicitly a basic income to all children. This is not at all surprising, because the CRC itself hints in Art 27 to the primary responsibility of parents for their children's welfare. But even if we have to admit that, for the time being, a basic income for children, though an interesting radical idea, is not a real political option, we may evaluate existing child benefit programmes with a view to their adaptability and compatibility with regard to a basic income for children. Obviously, a universal and substantial child allowance defined equally for all children – even if legally transferred to the child's parents – is closer to a basic income than a child-related tax allowance, which is depending on a number of other (but child-related) conditions.

Family allowances
Family allowances are intended to compensate parents for expenditures on children. Raising children implies a variety of additional expenditures for parents, usually referred to as the children's (direct and indirect) costs. While direct costs may be clearly allocated to children, as baby food, clothing, toys, childcare expenditures etc., indirect costs are hidden in the total household expenditures which cannot be allocated easily to individual family members, as housing costs for instance. For compensating children's costs governments may grant either direct child subsidies or tax allowances to parents. Explicit beneficiaries are parents with economically dependent children or – in the case of the traditional father-breadwinner/ mother-homemaker family – fathers. However, since an increase of the household income implies also an increase for the standardised income of all family members, also the rest of the family, children in particular, benefit indirectly.

Maternity benefits and parental leave allowances
Maternity benefits and parental leave allowances are intended to compensate parents, predominantly mothers, for opportunity costs. Further to parents' additional expenses on children, there may arise also opportunity costs, particularly for income foregone. If parents (mostly mothers) withdraw from the labour market (partly or fully / temporarily or for good) in order to take care of a small child, the difference between the former and the present household income is referred to in terms of opportunity costs. Quite a number of governments have developed policies aiming at compensating temporarily and partly for income losses of parents (usually mothers) due to care responsibilities with regard to small children. While maternity benefits are obviously granted to mothers only for a short period before and after the birth of a child, parental leave allowances may be granted after expiration of the maternity benefit for a restricted period in early childhood, in principle either to mothers or fathers, in reality however mostly to mothers. Both maternity benefit and parental leave allowance are usually dependent on previous employment of the recipients.

Childcare allowances
Childcare allowances are intended to compensate parents, usually mothers, for childcare. Some governments grant a financial benefit to parents (mostly mothers) for socially useful work, particularly childcare. Childcare allowances, though producing similar results as the previous programme, follow quite a different philosophy: direct benefits to parents, mostly mothers, intended as financial compensation for informal activities of social or collective utility. From there it follows, that, differently from the previous programme, childcare allowances are not dependent on the previous (nor necessarily on the present) employment status.

   All these measures may be found in one or the other country participating in

COST A19. For a more systematic discussion of the whole variety of child benefit packages the reader is referred to Bradshaw's chapter on »Child benefit packages in 22 countries«.

Perspectives, stakeholders and political alliances: the case of Austria

Actual programmes and policies, their composition as well as their specific regulations and parameters, reveal political priorities and ideological preferences of governments, political parties and other social forces which have contributed to formulating new or reforming existing policies with a view to child-related benefits. Different balances between the generational gender horizontal and vertical dimensions of distribution may become visible. We will discuss these processes by taking Austria as a case.

The Austrian country report for COST A19 (Beham et al. 2004) shows, that all these measures may even co-exist simultaneously in one country. In addition, the Austrian report elaborates on how specific paradigms of child benefit packages evolve under certain ideological and political constellations. The question of the right balance between vertical and horizontal distribution in particular, has for a long time occupied the two major political parties: the Christian democrats and the Social democrats: should child benefits mainly be seen as part of integrated social policies at large, or rather focus on inequalities between households with and without children with regard to all income classes? Controversial debates were in the end leading towards a general universal and substantial child benefit, which is nowadays widely accepted by all political forces. On the other hand the parental leave benefit (predominantly for mothers), which had been established by a Social democrat government, was recently, under a Centre/ Right government, replaced by a childcare allowance for all mothers, without consideration of previous employment status. This change has so far not been digested fully by Social democrats and Labour Unions.

The Austrian child benefit package, as it stands, is the result of conflicts and compromises. It meets some expectations of some, but not all expectations of all groups. Tax payers without children may complain about their paying too much for others' children; conservative family organisations would prefer a generous tax allowance to the existing tax credit; the women in the Labour Union would prefer a more generous parental leave allowance only for mothers who interrupt employment, to the existing childcare allowance which is universal. However, notwithstanding all these criticisms, according to Bradshaw and Finch (2002), Austria has the most generous child benefit package among 22 OECD countries.

This does not mean, that Austria has the best of all childhood and family policies, and it would be difficult in principle to define what the best of all policies was at all. Behind the different measures contributing to the child benefit package there are different stakeholders: households without and with children, parents, fathers, mothers, working mothers, and eventually also children. If we take children as stakeholders, the evaluation of the Austrian child benefit package is rather positive. It consists of a universal direct child benefit, of a universal tax credit adding to the general child benefit, of a childcare allowance paid up to the third birthday of the child maximum, provided the income of the caring person (usually the mother) is below a certain threshold (notwithstanding the income of the partner). The development of the Austrian child benefit system has been following for a long time (since the Social democrat reform under Bruno Kreisky in the early 1970's) the slogan »For the state each child has the same value« (in the last years this slogan was taken over by the Centre-Right, when extending parental leave allowance for small children also to mothers who had not been employed previously). In the end, this orientation was leading to a general universal and substantial child benefit which comes comparatively close to the idea of a basic income for children, apart from the fact (which is not at all irrelevant), that claimants or recipients are not children themselves, but their parents. This result was not achieved because any of the actors involved had been influenced or inspired by the idea of a basic income for children, but it constituted rather the lowest common multiple of the actors' different and diverging expectations.

The Austrian example confirms also, that in principle universal and substantial child benefits are an adequate measure for reducing child poverty, but not at all a sufficient condition for increasing fertility levels (see both chapters by Bradshaw); other, but financial measures would be needed, too, in particular quantitative and qualitative improvements with a view to child care services and reconciliation of work and family life, issues which will be dealt with in the next section.

Child benefit packages and welfare regimes

In his chapter on »Child benefit packages«, Bradshaw briefly summarises a comparative study on child benefit packages in 22 OECD-countries (all the EU-15 included). Based on a league table according to which the 22 countries are collected in 4 ranks depending on the generosity of their child benefit packages, he concludes that the rankings obtained »bear little relationship to the rankings that would be inferred using Esping-Andersen's regime types«. However, the term »little relationship« needs some interpretation: on one hand, considering that the Nordic countries are spread over ranks 1 and 2, the Conservative countries over ranks 1, 2 and 3, the Anglophone countries over ranks 2, 3 and 4, and the South European over ranks 3 and 4, there seems to be at least some interrelation; on the other hand, the picture is not as clear as if similar welfare regimes were assembled more or less in the same ranks respectively.

Two reasons might be given for this diffuse situation. From the Austrian case we have learnt that a child benefit package given at a certain point in time is the result of a complex historical evolution. Usually new governments do not undo all that has been done by the government before, but rather introduce new policies on top of a given situation. The result is, that welfare states do not correspond fully to Esping-Andersen's regime types, but represent rather a mixture of them. The other reason we addressed already before is that Esping-Andersen's typology is adult-centred; it does not consider welfare from a generational or childhood perspective at all (cf. Pringel 1998). The problem is not only its focus on formal employment, but also when turning the attention to the distributive dimension the question remains of who benefits from redistribution in generational terms, children, adults or elderly persons. In other words, a welfare state that is generous on the whole is – though more likely to be generous to all generations including the young one – not necessarily generous also to the young generation. On the other hand, the British example shows that also a more liberal welfare state with constrained possibilities for income redistribution might be quite successful in reducing child poverty if solving this problem gets high political priority at the level of the government. This underlines again the need for developing a child and generation oriented welfare state theory.

Childcare policy and generational contract

At first glance, the needs and expectations of children seem to be the central issues within the field of childcare. However, a closer look reveals that the interests and perspectives of different groups of adults dominate the debate, whereas the perspective of children only plays a minor role. The childcare question represents a political issue which refers to gender, generational contracts, and to the division of responsibilities between the state and the individual or family.

The demand for public childcare is closely connected to the increasing participation of women in the labour market, especially mothers. With the changeover from the feudal to the modern industrial society the male breadwinner/female homemaker family became the predominant family model: Fathers left the family to work full-time, while mothers stayed at home and took over the responsibility of caring for children and other dependent family members like the elderly. However, working within the framework of this family model, the increasing employment rate of mothers starting with the late 1960's inevitably leads to a »care crisis.« Sweden serves as a good example of this phenomenon. In the early 1970's there was a rising demand for women to join the labour force and an orientation of the Swedish labour market policy towards integrating women into gainful employment. This was supported by the women's movement, which felt that the equal access of women into the labour market was a precondition for gender equality. As a result, in Sweden there was a relatively early and sustainable expansion of public childcare institutions. Other Nordic countries such as Finland and Denmark were the first to follow Sweden's lead, whereas the rest of Europe has been slower to take action.

However, it is not only the goal of integrating women into gainful employment which is connected with the expansion of childcare institutions. There are other interests and expectations at stake. Traditionally, public childcare was also a measure to assist special groups of children, especially those at risk and with special needs. Furthermore, under the rule of the social investment regime, childcare is seen as an institution which prepares children for school as well as for the requirements of a knowledge-based economy. Other associated goals are the increase of the birth rate by improving the possibilities for combining family obligations and work for mothers, and, last but not least, the fight against child and family poverty.

Common questions, different answers

All of the European welfare states are being forced by different challenges to find new solutions to the care problem. The globalisation of the economy, post-industrial modernization, the coming of the knowledge society, demographic and familial change, unemployment, and social exclusion have caused an increase in the importance of childcare policies and the provision of childcare facilities. In spite of the common challenges being faced, each of the European countries has attempted to create its own solutions to the difficulties. When comparing the national childcare systems of the European welfare states the following variations can be identified: (1) the division of responsibility between public sector, market, third sector and families, (2) the definition of childcare as educational institutions or as a care service, (3) the provision rates of public funded childcare for different age groups of children, (4) access, and (5) quality.

(1)   The question »Who cares for the child?« is closely connected with the division of responsibilities among state, market, third sector, and families. With a view to welfare state regimes it could be expected that liberal regimes »tend to favour the market on both demand (parents) and supply (commercial or employer provision) side« (Mahon 2002: 6). This would enforce class inequality by making the accessibility of childcare dependent upon the market capacity of the parents. In contrast, social democratic regimes offer publicly organized and funded childcare, and thus promote class and gender equality as well as post-industrial full-employment. Conservative or »Bismarckian« regimes are characterized by an underdeveloped social service sector and by enforcing the traditional male breadwinner/mother homemaker family model. Under this kind of regime, mothers, grandmothers, and social support networks are seen as central resources in the field of childcare.

THOMAS OLK AND HELMUT WINTERSBERGER

Although this typology can, to a certain extent, explain institutional variations in the childcare field, the value of this approach is limited. For example, Germany and France are commonly seen as prototypes of the conservative welfare state regime. However, whereas France was able to achieve a high degree of government involvement in the field of family policy very early on as well as reach a high level of female participation in the labour market, Germany has an inadequate supply of publicly organised childcare and continues to have a low rate of female participation in the labour market (cf. Jurczyk et al. 2004).

Furthermore, the course of political reforms across different countries can not be completely explained by the »path-dependency« thesis. In fact, the welfare architecture of a given country may undergo dramatic changes capable of overcoming the constraints of a given welfare state regime – a situation which can be currently observed in the UK and Germany. In the UK, which is defined as a liberal welfare state regime, Tony Blair established his Third Way politics at the end of 1990's, and has, since then, implemented new political priorities directed at children and families with programmes such as Sure Start, Children's Fund, etc. However, welfare policies in Germany aimed at children have also experienced a fundamental change. During the 1990's the rate of provision of public day-care for children aged 3-6 was greatly expanded, and currently a new law increasing the supply of day-care facilities for children under the age of 3 to a coverage rate of 25 percent by 2010 is being planned. This demonstrates that new challenges from the economic and social spheres are able to generate the coming of new ideas and political innovations.

However, in the field of childcare policies post-modern welfare states are currently in the process of restructuring, where the relationship between the state and the individual citizen as well as the division of responsibilities among state, market, third sector, and families will see significant changes. Seen from the perspective of class, gender, and generational equality, this process is of the utmost relevance. Firstly, this can be said of the relationship between the state and the individual citizen. The existence and the extent of the social rights of citizens as well as the role of the state in guaranteeing these rights are both crucial to the issue of equality. This is especially true for the field of childcare, because a public guarantee of universal access to high quality childcare promotes class, gender, and generational equality. Secondly, this also holds true for the division of responsibilities amongst state, market, third sector, and families. If we assume that a powerful state takes responsibility for the supply of public childcare, then the accessibility and distribution of these services become part of the political decision making process. This means that the distributional effects of the market would be modified by democratic politics. In contrast, countries where the market mechanism plays a major role in the access to childcare services is made dependent of the market capacity of parents. The result may be a cementing of class inequalities. However, in countries where a relatively autonomous third sector plays an important role in the field of childcare, e.g. parent initiatives and self-organized projects, access to childcare facilities of this kind is made dependent upon the specific competencies of the parents, for instance self-organisation, etc. Finally, in cases where families are seen as the primary childcare institution, the traditional models of a gender specific division of family work will be enforced.

Usually, existing systems of childcare are not exclusively focused on a single institution, but are characterized by a complex mixture of responsibilities divided amongst state, market, third sector, and families. Furthermore, recent political reforms in several countries have proven highly inconsistent, and comprise measures and programmes with conflicting aims and results.

Although political strategies in the field of childcare are by no means coherent and without conflicting elements, it is possible to identify general trends across different countries. In light of changing economic, political, and social conditions, Jenson and Sineau (cf. 2001: 254ff.), have identified five »common patterns of movement in childcare programs«. Taking into account the rise of neo-liberalism, the new public management philosophy, and the financial crisis of European welfare states the following trends can be observed:

1) *Cost Reduction*: In search of less costly services and a reduction of public expenditures in the field of childcare, cut back strategies aim at reducing the costs of the public childcare system as well as reducing the demand for it. Within the public childcare system this means reducing the quality of services and limiting the number of places in publicly funded facilities. However, reducing the demand for childcare services means increasing the incentives for parents, e.g. by giving tax credits for childcare expenditures (private forms of childcare) or childcare allowances (caring for the children themselves).

2) *Decentralization*: In recent years, many countries have delegated the responsibility for childcare to the local authorities (e.g. Belgium, France, and Sweden). This comprises the transfer of financial responsibilities to the local level as well as the delegation of new spaces of policy choices, e.g. which services to provide, to whom, and in what form they should be given.

3) *Diversification*: The decentralization of political choices combined with a greater emphasis on the welfare mix promotes a substantial trend towards the diversity of services in the field of childcare. Whereas in the 1970's and 1980's all across Europe there was a general trend towards expanding publicly funded and provided childcare (e.g. day nurseries and family day care), more recently most countries have shown a preference for a greater variety of measures and programmes in the childcare field. In addition to the public childcare institutions there is a growing number of other options:
   ➢ new forms of non-parental childcare outside the family

> ➢ non-parental childcare within the family home (e.g. babysitters)
> ➢ parental care, supported by parental leaves or by benefits like direct allow-
> ances and respectively tax advantages for the parent who stays at home to
> care for the child(ren).

As previously mentioned, this is critical from a perspective of class, gender, and generational equality: Whereas the decentralization of political choices contributes to a geographical diversification of childcare facilities, measures like low subsidies for day-care nurseries or a privatization of the financial costs for childcare contribute to a class specific diversification as well. In addition, tax credits to finance familial childcare reenforce this trend because tax advantages rise with the incomes of the families.

4) *Flexibility*: This trend is a reaction to the discrepancies between the evermore differentiated demands for childcare by parents, on the one hand, and the rigidities of universal public service facilities, on the other. Some parents prefer childcare allowances because this means they can decide for themselves which kind of childcare they want to have at any given point. Furthermore, there are increasing discrepancies between the temporal differentiated demands for childcare, on one hand, and standardized opening hours of public childcare facilities, on the other. Due to the flexibilisation of working hours and employment relationships, a demand for more flexible childcare arrangements has emerged. Such arrangements apply more flexible opening hours as well as a more precise adjustment of public and private forms of childcare arrangements to the requirements of a deregulated labour market.

5) *Individualization of choice*: The strategy of expanding choices is realized in many different ways. One strategy aims at giving parents more say in choosing childcare programmes and more space for participation on the part of the children. The other strategy aims at enforcing the market mechanisms. This means giving parents more space for individual decisions between a wide range of institutionalised childcare services as well as offering parents the possibility of deciding between institutionalised childcare, on the one hand, and financial subsidies, on the other – thereby enabling them to purchase informal childcare (e.g. nannies) on the market.

As a result of these movements within the childcare programmes the role of the state has changed. In the past the state was seen as guaranteeing the provision of high quality, affordable childcare in the form of a public service. From the perspective of the women's movement this was identified as a precondition for the egalitarian labour market participation of women. This is also relevant from a generational perspective: Only the state is in the position to guarantee every child the right of access to high quality childcare. Influenced by neo-liberal thinking and the philosophy of new public management, individuals and families are now seen not so much as citizens but as consumers. And it is not so much the right of a child to childcare which is at stake but providing parents with more space for choosing which services to get, and which combination of public and private provision are preferred. An emphasis on the market and competition weakens the position of children. Since children are not able to purchase childcare on the market for themselves, their parents – acting as consumers – are the ones demanding childcare for their children. This means that it is the needs and preferences of the parents, and not those of the children, which become relevant in a market model. Under these conditions the responsibility of the state is not so much understood as the provider of childcare facilities but as regulating a market of different childcare institutions and options. This means that within the public debate there is a waning enthusiasm for publicly funded and organized childcare institutions, and a rising emphasis on a greater welfare mix. Therefore, there is a partial withdrawal of European welfare states from a public childcare strategy as well as a strong tendency towards measures and programmes like tax credits and childcare allowances, thereby enabling parents to choose services from a market made up of different public and private childcare institutions.

(2)   There are different concepts regarding childcare institutions. In some countries childcare is primarily seen as an educational institution, in others as a care service, and a third group of countries defines childcare institutions as places, where children can act out their creative potential and can live out their childhood (cf. Wintersberger 1999). Generally, childcare facilities for younger children (aged 0-3) are defined as care services which fall under the jurisdiction of the department of social welfare. With respect to children aged 4-6/7 there is an ever increasing variation: Whereas some countries – one example is Germany as a prototype of the conservative welfare state regime – ascribe care functions to childcare facilities, and define only diffuse educational expectations at best, other countries treat childcare facilities for children in the pre-school age as educational institutions. This is especially true in the case of the »école maternelle« in France and Belgium. In this respect, the age of the child when entering school becomes relevant: In countries like the UK where primary school already begins at the age of 4 or 5 the issue of educational institution versus care service in early childcare is of minor relevance in comparison to countries like Finland, where the entrance age is 7. In recent years under the rule of the social investment principle in many European countries there is a tendency to emphasize the school oriented and curricular character of the educational programmes in the childcare institutions. In many countries this is accompanied by a controversial debate, because it raises fundamental questions of defining the role of childhood and children in society. One such example took place in Finland toward the end of the 1990's, where the pros and cons of a pre-school education for 6 year olds became

the subject of intense discussion. In this debate it was feared (from a child-oriented perspective) that the introduction of a pre-school institution for 6 year olds would dramatically shorten the time for being a child. In the case that »instruction« and »learning« would replace »care« and »play,« the welfare of children would be affected (cf. Alanen et al. 2004: 154f.).

(3)   As mentioned before within the European welfare states the relevance of public childcare has increased enormously in the last decades (cf. Kamerman 1991, Michel and Mahon 2002, Jenson and Sineau 2001). However, the provision rates for different age groups of children vary in different countries. Due to the lack of recent comparative empirical data we revert to the results of the report of the European Community Childcare Network from the mid 1990's (cf. European Commission 1996). The report shows that for children in the age-group 4-6/7 a process of convergence can be seen – one most likely having continued till this day. The provision rates vary between 48 and 99 percent. In contrast, the coverage for children aged 0-3 years is very different – varying from 2 to 48 percent[1]. Also the provision rates for children aged 6-10 years with a range from 0 to 62 percent are quite different. Although there is a general trend towards full-time day-care, nonetheless some countries have fallen behind this standard offering predominantly half-time day care. This is especially true for countries like (Western-) Germany and Austria as representatives of a conservative welfare state regime. In these countries 3 to 4 hours of day-care is typically offered in the morning, which has (ironically) aggravated the problems of reconciling work and family for parents. As a result, many mothers (in these countries) have to restrict their labour market contributions due to the lack of day-care beyond morning hours.

(4)   All across Europe there has been a shift away from defining children as dependent members of the family household towards creating children as subjects in their own right, and guaranteeing their autonomous rights. Whereas this is usually interpreted as a result of the individualization-trend, there are three other aspects mentioned: »a more general recognition of children as agents, an interest in the well-being of children, and concerns about social sustainability.« (Daly 2004: 139) This is also true regarding the citizenship of children in the context of the European Union (cf. Wintersberger 1999: 20). Although this was not the case for some initiatives of the European Council and the European Commission in the past, recent recommendations of the European Parliament as well as of the Parliamentary Assembly of the Council of Europe address children as subjects. A prominent example of this change is the Treaty of Amsterdam, which introduced age as a criterion of discrimination. However, problems and tensions concerning the citizenship and legal entitlements of children still abound, and can be seen in the UN-Convention on the Rights of the Child (for a more extensive discussion see above).

Unfortunately, the undecided status of children's rights in the UN-Convention entails certain problematic consequences. Although there is a tendency towards strengthening children's right to day-care and education at present time, only a few European countries have actually assigned to all children the right to day-care, as can be seen in Sweden and Finland, where there is such a right for all children from 1.5 until entering primary school. In most countries this right is restricted to certain groups of children – mostly elder children from 3 to 6/7 – or limit the number of hours per day as in Germany, where children between 3 and 6 have the right to 4 hours a day. As a consequence, in many local authorities the right of children with unemployed parents to day-care is often restricted to three or four hours a day. This widespread practice is clearly in conflict with Article 2 of the Convention, according to which no child should be discriminated against, irrespective of the child's or his or her parent's race, colour, sex, language, religion, political or other opinion, national, ethnic or social origin, property, disability, birth or other status.

(5) International comparative studies emphasize that the quality of childcare institutions varies between different countries and in some countries internal differences can be identified as well. From an egalitarian point of view such differences may lead to problems. For example, mothers – and this is especially true for highly educated mothers – have a vital interest in high quality care for their children. In the case that mothers valuate existing childcare services as non-satisfactory, they might be forced to interrupt their employment to care for their children. The opposite is also true. An infrastructure providing good care services is one factor in promoting female employment. This is clearly underscored by higher female labour-force rates in the Nordic countries.

In addition to these points there are controversies with regard to the definition of quality. Often quality is constructed as an objective and real entity. From this perspective the analysis is restricted to structural aspects like financial resources, rooms, number of children per educator, qualification of staff, equipment, opening hours, etc. as well as specific outcomes such as child development and school performance. Measuring quality seems to be exclusively a question of the appropriate application of expert knowledge and accurate techniques of measurement. In contrast, it is emphasized that quality is not an objective, technical entity but rather a socially constructed concept of subjective, value-based, relative and dynamic nature »with the possibility of multiple perspectives or understandings of what quality is« (Dahlberg et al. 1999: 5). If we start with the assumption that quality is a relational concept, then it is critical to determine the perspective from which quality is defined. Stakeholders like parents, teachers, decision makers, and experts are interested in different aspects of quality. As a rule, children are the last to be asked because of the widespread prejudice that young children are too difficult to interview.

THOMAS OLK AND HELMUT WINTERSBERGER

However, the issue of quality of public childcare institutions raises fundamental theoretical questions. For example, with the U.K. in mind Hendrick (cf. 2002) argues that the shift of responsibility for childcare from parents to public childcare institutions is flanked by a »commodification« of childcare. Three aspects of commodification are identified: Firstly, the affective and particular informal care work of the family will be transformed into an economic act with the consequence that childcare has to be purchased on the market. By this the unique and individualized mother-child relationship will be transformed into a universal act of exchange – one that can be done by »any« professional to »any« child. Secondly, young children are commodified »in the sense of 'being the object of others' labour'« (ibid.: 278). Thirdly, he identifies a tendency to transform emotional relationships between young children and mothers into affective neutral working relationships between young children and adult employees.

Contrary to this view, Dahlberg et al. (cf. 1999: 74ff.) emphasize the positive potentialities of public childcare institutions. As they see it, childcare institutions are insofar positive places for children in that they are not restricted to the caring function, thereby freeing up the parents to work, but take over the function of community institutions in the civil society which create a democratic culture and which make it possible for children to play an active and creative part in his/her life. Seen from a generational point of view, this approach is of special interest. Children have no say in deciding whether they can stay at home or attend a public childcare institution. As mentioned previously, the increasing demand on public childcare institutions is one result of the modernization of society. The integration of fathers and (increasingly) mothers into gainful employment reduces the time budget which parents can dedicate to their children. Furthermore, things like heavy traffic etc., are making public spaces more and more unsuitable for children. From a generational perspective it would be inequitable if such structural trends would affect the welfare of children. In accordance with this view, it is necessary to create places where children can be creative in their own right. Therefore, the participation of children and the orientation of childcare institutions to child-related needs and expectations are essential features of high quality childcare services. As such, the right of children to live out their creative potential and to structure their environment should not be restricted by educational curricula and programmes, which emphasize the future requirements of the labour market and the knowledge-based economy under the rule of the human capital investment principle.

Childcare and gender policies

As demonstrated above, the issue of childcare is closely connected with gender contracts. Under the hegemony of the male-breadwinner/mother-homemaker model the responsibility of caring for the child(ren) lies exclusively with the mothers, whereas fathers continue their full-time commitment to the labour market. But even the steady increase in female employment starting in the late 1960's did not provoke public debates on reduced labour market participation of men. Moreover, men were not prepared to show a greater commitment to caring for the child at the expense of their labour market participation. Seen from the perspective of gender, it was obvious that the formal right of women to enter the labour market could only be realized under the precondition of access to non-familial childcare. Therefore, access to safe, reliable, and publicly funded childcare was identified by the women's movement as a central measure in the realization of gender equality (cf. Jenson and Sineau 2001).

However, at this point in time, the reconciliation of work and family life was interpreted as a primary issue for women. Because men continued to adhere to the pattern of full-time employment, mothers were compelled to trade gainful employment for the obligation of caring for their children. Yet, with the increasing rates of employed mothers a partial »de-familialisation« was still experienced. This did not mean, however, that the fundamental rules of gender specific division of care responsibilities were suspended: The expansion of public childcare institutions and other services for children and families merely caused a shift in the responsibility for childcare from the mothers to female employees in public childcare institutions and the service sector in general.

Many family-oriented measures and programmes which were introduced to extend choice to mothers and fathers strengthen the traditional gender specific division of labour (cf. Morgan/Zippel 2003). This is especially true for parental leave programmes which were formulated as gender neutral. It is a well known fact that spouses follow an economic rationale by deciding which parent has to stay at home to care for a child. This usually means that the parent who earns more money – and this is the father in most cases – continues to work whereas the other parent – normally the mother – interrupts her employment to care for the child. With this idea in mind, parental leave programmes which offer only small financial compensations for the parent who takes the leave are taken predominantly by mothers. In an effort to avoid such undesirable effects, in recent years counteractive incentives and measures have been gaining influence. For example, in some parental leave schemes the parental allowances are made dependent on the earnings of parents to make it more attractive for full-time employed fathers to take the benefit. Such schemes seem to be very effective but they produce two problems: On the one hand, the costs of these schemes rise with the attempt to introduce incentives for taking the parental leave even for men with high incomes. On the other hand, this would seem to lead to an unjust distribution (from a perspective of vertical inequality), because parents with high incomes would receive higher benefits than parents with lower family incomes.

Another measure aimed at attaining a more just distribution of responsibilities is the introduction of »daddy-quota« in parental leave schemes such as implemented by

Norway and Sweden in the early 1990's, and now planned in Germany. If we look at Norway, for example, fathers are assigned four weeks of the parental leave, which means that the entitlement of this benefit can not be transferred to the mother in the case that the father is not willing to take the leave. The quota can be considered a great success in that nearly 70 percent of the eligible fathers took the »daddy-leave« (cf. Leira 1998: 370). Characteristic of these »daddy-quota« regulations is that they aim at influencing the internal familial share of responsibilities of informal care work. They demonstrate the belief that a policy of gender equality can not produce sustainable effects if it stops at the family's front door. In a normative sense these programmes rely on models of a »new fatherhood« and on the belief that an enhanced contribution of fathers to informal care work not only is a precondition for gender equality but is also positive for both the father and child.

However, contrary to what we have just described, there are trends in family policy that tend in the direction of cementing the traditional gender-related division of labour. This is especially true for all schemes which offer cash transfers and social security benefits for informal carers. In this context the »cash for childcare schemes« introduced in Finland and Sweden in the early 1990's and in Norway in the late 1990's (cf. ibid.: 366ff.) need to be mentioned. According to these schemes the following two goals are to be realized: Firstly, parents shall get more choice with regard to childcare, and secondly, these programmes shall enable parents to spend more time with their children. In some respects these programmes have had unintended effects: For example, many parents take these cash transfers to purchase childcare (especially in the form of nannies and nurseries) and continue their employment. Furthermore, they enforce the traditional gender-oriented division of labour because the financial remuneration is usually lower than the incomes even in the low-wages sector. As a result, »cash-for-childcare« schemes are, in fact, incentives for mothers to stay at home and care for their children. Above and beyond this it is possible that parents' decisions come into conflict with the best interests of the child. This is the case when parents choose the financial benefit even though the attendance of a non-familial childcare institution would have been better for the development of the child.

Childcare from a generational perspective

There have always been relationships of inter-generational solidarity between parents and their children. Such relationships of exchange are currently undergoing a far reaching process of change. The majority of parents invest a great deal in their children – both monetarily and in terms of care. Within traditional societies these investments yielded economic returns because children contributed to the family income by means of gainful employment as well as having taken responsibility for securing an income when their parents reached old age. However, within modern societies this economic function of children has been lost. As a result of the ban on child labour, not only are children unable to contribute to the economic well-being of the family, but additionally became a financial burden on their parents. Furthermore, with the introduction of public pension schemes the responsibility for security in old age has been relocated from one's own children to the welfare state. Conversely, the responsibility for securing the living of the children has remained with the parents. This has problematic consequences with regard to the distribution of income between different population groups. Under such conditions adults having children would constitute a disadvantage, for they have to share their incomes with the child(ren) which means that the per capita income is (*ceteris paribus*) lower than that for adults without children. Furthermore, public pension schemes do not favour those living together with children. On the contrary, those adults who do not need to invest in children are in a much better position to optimize both their financial income and pension entitlements. Seen in these terms, it would be perfectly rational to live without children.

A further consequence of this scheme is the reinforcement of gender-specific inequalities. The value of a pension is dependent on both one's level of income and the duration of employment. Since women are more likely to spend time with their children, their accrued pensions are correspondingly lower than those of men who concentrate on their employment carrier. Public pension systems of this kind, therefore, generate problematic incentives, which undermine their own function. This is the case because public pension schemes rely on an implicit »three-generation-contract«. From the perspective of the individual the entitlement to a pension is based upon one's past, present, and future participation in the labour market. But from a national economic perspective any social benefits, e.g. transfer payments to such members of the non-working population including children and the elderly, have to be deducted from the income of the working population. The sustainability of the public pension system, therefore, depends on a sufficient number of working individuals in relation to the number of people receiving social benefits such as retirees. This is the case only when the fertility rate is high enough to secure a sufficient reproduction of the population. In this respect, the public pension schemes of most European countries are deficient because they ignore the issue of securing the costs associated with raising children.

Most public pension schemes focus on the relationship between the generation of the employed adults and the generation of the elderly. The implicit assumption is that every given generation of adults is motivated enough to have children. Under these conditions there are no positive incentives for adults to live together with children. Furthermore, there is no public guarantee to a standard of living for children that would secure a good childhood in the present as well as the prospect for opportunities in the future. However, from a child-oriented perspective, the generational contract needs to be extended and revised. Whereas the generational contract is usually interpreted as a contract between only two generations, i.e. between the active population of working-age individuals and the elderly population, the proposed revision would involve three generations, namely children, working-age adults, and senior citizens. In this contract not only the issue of social security in old age but also the securing of the costs associated with raising children are included into the collective security system.

However, the prevailing political reform concepts and strategies take a different path. Rather than including children into the public social security system, political strategies aim toward intensifying and expanding the labour market participation of both fathers *and* mothers. Goals such as reducing child and family poverty, enhancing the »employability« of women, and realizing increased gender equality encourage political strategies which lead to a de-familialization of women. Activating social policies increasingly intervene in the division of domestic labour reconstructing parental roles. As a result of this process »the legitimacy of care as a full-time component of motherhood is devalued« (Daly 2004: 139). In the past, it was accepted in most European welfare states that women did not participate in the labour market in order that they could care for their child(ren). Especially mothers with young children had a legitimate claim to public resources without being engaged in gainful employment. In recent times, the dual-income family is becoming the preferred model throughout Europe. Consequently, even single mothers are under increasing pressure to work at least part-time in order to be eligible for social benefits. These changes are based upon the assumption that the state will be taking more responsibility for childcare and caring for the elderly. As a result the inter-generational exchange relationships in the field of childcare are being reconstructed: Previously, inter-generational solidarity meant that parents − especially mothers − cared for their children, who in turn, cared for their parents when they became old. Today, the inter-generational solidarity between father, mother, and children − under the dominance of labour market participation of working-age adults − will concentrate on optimizing the incomes of fathers *and* mothers. This money is necessary in order to secure the material existence of each family member, which includes the costs associated with raising children as well as the public services related to both childcare and care for the elderly.

Conclusion: towards a generational theory of welfare

The following discussion of principles has a different scope: it should be instrumental in characterising the logic of childhood and social policy programmes, in particular with a view to child orientation, and in examining the child impact of programmes. The principles that will by discussed in the following are derived from the previous chapters.

Productivism and distributivism are two concepts referring to the question, to which extent welfare state programmes should be developed around productive contributions, employment biographies, social insurance contributions accrued etc. on the one, and actual needs on the other side. Existing policies are usually based on a mixture of the two principles, the mixtures however may differ among different policy arenas as well as cross-nationally. Although children may be seen as productive members of society, too, their contributions (like a considerable sector of women's contributions) are part of the hidden economy. Therefore we may conclude that a predominant employment orientation of welfare states would be unlikely to favour the child (and female) population.

Children as human beings versus human becomings is a principal dimension, which is connected but not identical with the previous one. The focus on children as human beings emphasises children's needs here and now, underlining in this way a close connection with distributivism. The unterstanding of children as human becomings instead leaves open, whether returns to be expected from »adult children« may entitle to anticipatory claims towards the welfare state here and now or whether generational distributive justice should be achieved only diachronically, in the sense that children will have the same rights as adults only when they eventually become adult.

In recent years all over Europe there has been a shift in the predominant idea of justice from distributivism to productivism (cf. Esping-Andersen et al. 2002). One consequence of this shift has been a change in the public's perception of children as »productive citizen workers of the future«. Conceived in this way, the idea of social investment would legitimate both the cutback of social expenditures for the elderly and passive social protection, while at the same time, investing more in children as human capital. By investing in children both the wealth of the populaton and the competitiveness of the national economy of a given country should increase. From a child-oriented perspective this argumentation is problematic because it makes the potential claims of children to welfare benefits exclusively dependent upon the criterion of future returns. This line of argumentation completely neglects the right of the child to enjoy a good childhood as well as to satisfy his/ her needs and desires in the here an now.

Citizenship could be a concept to combine the two related dimensions as well as to establish balances between divergent scopes and orientations. Citizen's needs have to be considered first of all, but it may include also some productivist elements. Children are to be considered as citizens in their own right with clearly defined rights and responsibilities vis-à-vis society here and now, but also future prospects may be included in such a contract.

The following principles (or principal dimensions) may be discussed in relation to the UN-CRC.

Protection – provision – participation are concepts for structuring and interpreting the CRC. The first refers to the protection of children from detrimental practices and influences, the second to children's access to resources, and the third to children's participation particularly in decisions concerning their own life. For a long period of time protection has been a (may-be too) dominant principle in Western welfare states, and the question may be asked whether in the hidden agenda the purpose was rather control than protection. Western welfare states tend generally to be overprotective with a view to children, and the task is to establish a right balance between the three principles.

The concepts of *individualism, familism and collectivism* define another principal dimension of childhood. Familism used to be the dominant principle in traditional patriarchal society. Ideological conflicts between conservative familism and socialist collectivism characterised the late 19th and early 20th century. Collectivist educational experiments were registered in the post-revolutionary period in the Soviet Union as well as in the beginnings of Israel. At the theoretical level, however, collectivist ideas were much more widespread. The UN-CRC introduces on the one hand the individualism of the child by emphasising children's individual rights, on the other hand it is a comparatively familistic document, avoiding any affinity to collectivist attitudes. Whether this is a principal position or rather an expression of the current »Zeitgeist«, has to be seen.

The concepts of *welfare pluralism and welfare mix* refer to the origin of welfare resources coming from the market, the state and the third sector. With a view to conceptualising the third sector for the purpose of adult-centred research, the family is sometimes included together with institutions of the civil society, in particular non-profit organisations. In connection with a child-centred theory, this would probably not make sense. Or to take childcare as an example: All things being equal – like for instance access to and quality of services – from a child's point of view it is not so important whether the service is provided by a public, market- or social-private in-stitution. It is however more relevant whether childcare is provided within or outside the family.

Finally, also the balance between *cash and care*, between monetary transfers and the provision of social services is often seen as a key criterion of childhood policies. We think however, that this debate is rather driven by adult-centred ideologies (e.g. patriarchal familism and individualist feminism). In both arenas, cash and care, there are possibilities to formulate policies in a more or less child-friendly way. The mere availability of childcare alone is not a sufficient criterion for a child-oriented soci-ety.

Last, but not least, in addition to child-specific principles/ criteria, there are also general problems concerning e.g. *comprehensiveness and coherence* of programmes. Where childhood policies as a whole is rather a by-product of policies for adults (and this is rather the rule than the exception to the rule), we are still in a stage of generational subalternity of childhood. At this stage childhood policies tend to be highly fragmented and incoherent.

In general political debates decision makers often use the term of a *child-friendly society*. In the paragraphs above we tried to give some substantive orientations for conceptualisation. The task of strictly defining the concept as well as of developing operational criteria for measurement is, however, still ahead. This task can only be accomplished by confronting the theoretical instruments with the empirical reality of childhood and social policies in economically advanced societies.

References

Alanen, L., H. Sauli and H. Strandell (2004): »Children and Childhood in a Welfare State: The Case of Finland.« Jensen, A.-M., A. Ben-Arieh, C. Conti, D. Kutsar, M. N. G. Phádraig and H. W. Nielsen (eds): *Children's Welfare in Ageing Europe. Volume 1.* Trondheim: Tartu University Press: 143-209.

Beham, M., H. Wintersberger, K. Wörister and U. Zartler (2004): »Childhood in Austria: Cash and Care, Time and Space, Children's Needs, and Public Policies.« Jensen, A.-M., A. Ben-Arieh, C. Conti, D. Kutsar, M. N. G. Phádraig and H. W. Nielsen (eds): *Children's Welfare in Ageing Europe. Volume 1.* Trondheim: Tartu University Press: 19-79.

Beisenherz, H. Gerhard (2002): *Kinderarmut in der Wohlfahrtsgesellschaft: das Kainsmal der Globalisierung.* Opladen: Leske+Budrich.

Bradbury, B. and M. Jäntti (1999): Child Poverty across Industrialized Nations. Innocenti Occasional Papers n. 71, Florence UNICEF-ICDC.

Bradshaw, J. and N. Finch (2002): *A Comparison of Child Benefit Packages in 22 Countries.* Department for Work and Pensions Research Report No. 174. Leeds: Corporate Document Service.

Dahlberg, G., P. Moss and A. Pence (1999): *Beyond Quality in Early Childhood Education and Care: Postmodern Perspectives.* London/Philadelphia: Falmer Press.

Daly, M. (2000): *The Gender Division of Welfare. The Impact of the British and German Welfare States.* Cambridge: University Press.

Daly, M. (2004): »Changing Conceptions of Family and Gender Relations in European Welfare States and the Third Way.« Lewis, J. and R. Surender (eds): *Welfare State Change. Towards a Third Way?* Oxford: University Press:135-154.

Daniel, P. and J. Ivatts (1998): *Children and Social Policy.* Houndsmills/Basingstoke/ Hampshire/ London: MacMillan Press Ltd.

European Commission Network on Childcare and Other Measures to Reconcile Employment and Family Responsibilities (ed.) (1996): *A View of Services for Young Children in the European Union 1990-1995.* Luxembourg: European Commission Directorate General V.

Esping-Andersen, G. (1990): *The Three Worlds of Welfare Capitalism.* Cambridge: Polity Press.

Esping-Andersen, G., G. Duncan, A. Hemerijck and J. Myles (2002): *Why We Need a New Welfare State.* Oxford/New York: Oxford UP.

Folbre, N. (1994): *Who Pays for the Kids? Gender and the Structure of Constrains*. New York/London: Routledge.

Hendrick, H. (2002): »Conceptualizing Childcare. Early Childhood Education and Care in Post 1945 Britain.« *Zeitschrift für Soziologie der Erziehung und Sozialisation* 22: 265-284.

Hengst, H. (2000): »Die Arbeit der Kinder und der Umbau der Arbeitsgesellschaft.« Hengst, H. and H. Zeiher (eds): *Die Arbeit der Kinder. Kindheitskonzept und Arbeitsteilung zwischen den Generationen*. Weinheim/ München: Juventa: 71-97.

Jensen, A.-M., A. Ben-Arieh, C. Conti, D. Kutsar, M. N. G. Phádraig and H. W. Nielsen (eds): *Children's Welfare in Ageing Europe. Two Volumes*. Trondheim: Tartu University Press.

Jenson, J. and M. Sineau (2001): *Who Cares? Women's Work, Childcare, and Welfare State Redesign*. Toronto/Buffalo/London: University of Toronto Press Inc.

Jurczyk, K., Th. Olk and H. Zeiher (2004): »German Children's Welfare Between Economy and Ideology.« Jensen, A.-M., A. Ben-Arieh, C. Conti, D. Kutsar, M.N.G. Phádraig and H.W. Nielsen (eds): *Children's Welfare in Ageing Europe. Volume 2*. Trondheim: Tartu University Press: 703-770.

Kamerman, S. B. (1991): »Child Care Policies and Programs: An International Overview.« *Journal of Social Issues* 47: 179-196

Kränzl-Nagl, R., J. Mierendorff, J. and Th. Olk (2003): »Die Kindheitsvergessenheit der Wohlfahrtsstaatsforschung und die Wohlfahrtsstaatsvergessenheit der Kindheitsforschung.« Kränzl-Nagl, R., J. Mierendorff and Th. Olk (eds): *Kindheit im Wohlfahrtsstaat. Gesellschaftliche und politische Herausforderungen*. Frankfurt a. M./ New York: Campus Verlag: 9-55.

Leira, A. (1998): »Caring as Social Right: Cash for Child Care and Daddy Leave.« *Social Politics* 5: 362-378.

Lewis, J. (1992): »Gender and the Development of Welfare Regimes.« *Journal of European Social Policy* 2: 159-173.

Mahon, R. (2002): »Child Care: Towards What Kind of »Social Europe«?« *Social Politics* 9: 343-379.

Michel, S. and R. Mahon (eds) (2002): *Child Care Policy at the Crossroads. Gender and Welfare State Restructuring*. New York/London: Routledge.

Morgan, K. J. and K. Zippel (2003): »Paid to Care: The Origins and Effects of Care Leave Policies in Western Europe.« *Social Politics* 1: 49-85.

Olk, Th. (2004): »Kinder und Kindheit im Wohlfahrtsstaat – eine vernachlässigte Kategorie?« *Zeitschrift für Sozialreform* 1-2: 81-101.

Pringel, K. (1998): *Children and Social Welfare in Europe*. Buckingham/Philadelphia: Open University Press.

Qvortrup, J., M. Bardy, G. Sgritta and H. Wintersberger (eds) (1994): *Childhood Matters. Social Theory, Practice and Politics*. Aldershot: Avebury.

Qvortrup, J. (1995): »From Useful to Useful: the Historical Continuity in Children's Constructive Participation.« *Sociological Studies of Children*, 7: 49-76.

Wintersberger, H. (1999): »Work Viewed from a Childhood Perspective.« *Family Observer*: 18-24.

Wintersberger, H. (2005): »Work, Welfare and Generational Order: Towards a Political Economy of Childhood.« Qvortrup, J. (ed.): *Studies in Modern Childhood. Society, Agency, Culture*. Basingstoke/ New York: Palgrave Macmillan: 201-220.

Notes

1 It has to be mentioned that in most European countries new born children are due to parental leave schemes, usually with one of their parents (in most cases their mothers) until they are 1 to 1.5 year(s).

THOMAS OLK AND HELMUT WINTERSBERGER

MEASURING CHILDREN'S WELFARE

SOME PROBLEMS IN THE INTERNATIONAL COMPARISON OF CHILD INCOME POVERTY

Jonathan Bradshaw

Introduction

Child poverty is probably the most important indicator of child well-being and this has been recognised (perhaps belatedly) by the European Union (EU) in that child poverty rates are published as one of the nine primary indicators of Social Inclusion. Indeed they are the only child-based indicator included in the set of primary and secondary indicators.

The availability of comparative data on child poverty has been much improved in recent years. The Luxembourg Income Study (LIS) has enabled a comparison of child poverty rates on a consistent basis for now 31 countries and also how these have changed over time. The LIS website enables easy access to this data (http://www.lisproject.org/keyfigures/povertytable.htm). UNICEF have used this data for their excellent League Tables of child poverty in rich nations. The latest League Table (UNICEF 2005) spawned an extensive analysis of child poverty in a series of working papers by Corak (2006) and others available on from the UNICEF website (http://www.unicef-icdc.org/publications/). Independently of LIS, the OECD has gathered child poverty rates from member states national sources on a consistent basis and published the analyses – the most recent version is Mira D'Ercole and Forster (2005). Then there is the data for the EU countries that has emerged from the European Community Household Panel Survey and is the vehicle for the child poverty estimate for the Laeken indicators but the data has also been exploited independently by Ritakallio and Bradshaw (2006). The ECHP which covered only the EU12 is being replaced by the Survey of Income and Living Conditions covering the EU25. In addition to these sources there are the Euroquol surveys run out of the European Foundation for the Improvement of Living and Working Conditions in Dublin which has begun to publish household poverty rates (www.eurofound.eu.int/publications/htmlfiles/ef0593.htm), the European Social Survey now with the second sweep available. Both those surveys collect income data grouped into bands and the reliability of the poverty estimates based on this data is somewhat untested.

Despite this rich variety of sources there are a number of serious problems with this data. In this chapter I will identify these problems in no particular order.

Timeliness

The data available is all very out of date. The latest LIS data is for around 2000 though for some of the countries it is earlier. The Mira D'Ercole and Forster (2005) OECD data is for around 2000. The latest and last ECHP was 2001 but the income data was for 2000. The replacement for the ECHP, the SILC survey is being introduced progressively but data will not be available for all countries until 2007. Meanwhile Eurostat have been publishing child poverty rates for some countries for 2003 based either on SILC or national estimates. The general point is that these surveys take a considerable time to be processed at a national level let alone at a comparative level. The result is that they are out of date. Really too out of date to draw lessons about current national performance. To illustrate this Chart 1 shows how the child poverty rates derived from the ECHP have changed over time. Until the 2000 survey the UK had the highest child poverty rate in the EU12 but the 2001 survey found that its position in the league table had got better and the UK had the fifth highest child poverty rate. But that is 2000 income; only one year after the UK Prime Minister committed his government to abolishing child poverty and before most of the policy measures had come on stream. We know from national data available up to 2004/5 that the child poverty rate in the UK has been declining since 2000. For national governments comparative data that is five or six years old is only of historical interest.

Income

All these child poverty rates are based on income and income is only an indirect indicator of living standards. Further there are reasons to be anxious about the reliability of income data collected in surveys. The information on income in household surveys is generally provided by one informant who may not be informed about the income of all adults in the household. There may be a systematic tendency to under-report income especially at the bottom end of the distribution if the respondent is anxious about the risks to the receipt of benefits or tax credits. Also the reporting of income by the self employed, farmers and students is notoriously inaccurate. Also income fluctuates and the different surveys record income over different time periods. Current income may be very different from normal income and vice versa – as a result of changes in employment status or family structure and as we shall see this is one reason for the weak relationship which exists between current income poverty and deprivation.

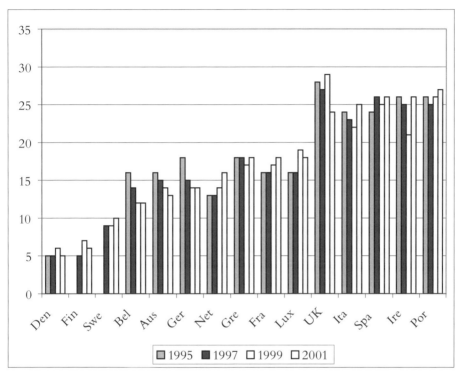

Chart 1: % children 0-15 living in households with equivalent income less than 60% of the median before housing costs (Source: Eurostat)

So income is unreliable but even more seriously it may be invalid. It is generally agreed that expenditure is a better measure of current command over resources. Expenditure can take account of dissavings, borrowings in a way that income cannot. Income does not take account of gifts or of domestic consumption. Further what income can buy varies between countries according to relative prices and though we can attempt to control for this by using Purchasing Power Parities they are not an entirely satisfactory method. Also what income needs to buy varies between countries according the availability of subsidised services – for example Sweden and Finland provide free school meals for all children while in other countries parents have to pay – out of their income. The National Health Service in the UK provides free treatment for children, while in many other countries there are user charges for health care. The

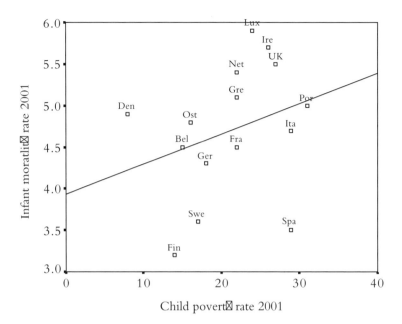

Chart 2: Child poverty by infant mortality. Mid 2001.

cost of childcare varies considerably between countries. So the same income does not imply equivalent living standards in different countries and it does not achieve the same level of well-being.

This is illustrated in chart 2 which plots the child poverty rate in the mid 1990s against a key measure of health outcomes for the same period. There appears to be a positive relationship but the correlation coefficient is only r=0.35 and not statistically significant and Spain has a substantially lower infant mortality rate than you would expect given its poverty rate while Denmark's is higher than it should be.

The ECHP enables us to compare income child poverty rates with two other measures of poverty and deprivation among children. Chart 3 plots the income child poverty rate as at 2001 against the proportion of children in families having difficulty or great difficulty managing in 2001 (there is not data for Germany and Sweden). There appears to be a positive relationship but the correlation coefficient is r=0.4 and not statistically significant. Greece have much higher rates of difficulty making ends meet than their relative child poverty rate would suggest and the UK and the Netherlands much lower rates.

JONATHAN BRADSHAW

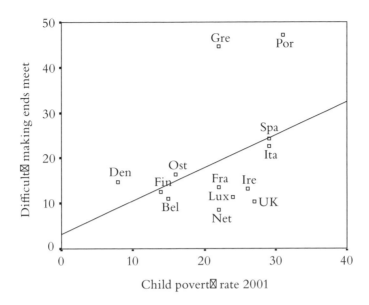

Chart 3: Child income poverty by child subjective poverty. ECHP 2001.

There are set of questions in the ECHP which can be used to form an index of child deprivation. They are

1. Can the household afford keeping its home adequately warm?
2. Can the household afford paying for a week's annual holiday away from home?
3. Can the household afford replacing any worn-out furniture?
4. Can the household afford buying new, rather than second-hand, clothes?
5. Can the household afford eating meat, chicken or fish every second day, if wanted?
6. Can the household afford having friends or family for drink or meal at least once a month?
7. Has the household been unable to pay scheduled rent for the accommodation during the past 12 months?
8. Has the household been unable to pay scheduled mortgage payments during the past 12 months?
9. Is there normally some money left to save (considering household's income and expenses)?

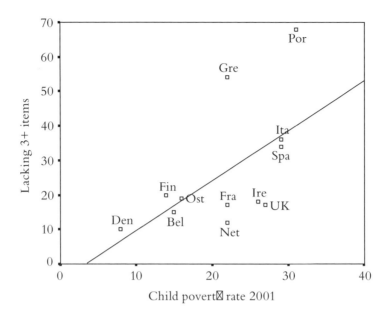

Chart 4: Income child poverty by % children living in household lacking three of more items

Chart 4 plots the percentage of children living in households lacking three or more of these items (data on Luxembourg, Germany and Sweden is missing) against the income child poverty rate. There is a positive relationship r=0.58 and it is just statistically significant. Again Greece and Portugal have much higher proportions of deprived children than their income poverty rates would indicate.

However what is very important is that there is a much closer relationship between the subjective poverty rate and deprivation than there is between income poverty and deprivation or subjective poverty. This is shown in Chart 5 the correlation is r=0.97 and statistically significant. This disjunction between child income poverty, subjective poverty and indicators of deprivation has led us to argue (Bradshaw and Finch 2003) that when measuring poverty it is best to examine overlaps. Children living in families who are poor on more than one dimension are more likely to be reliably poor.

Jonathan Bradshaw

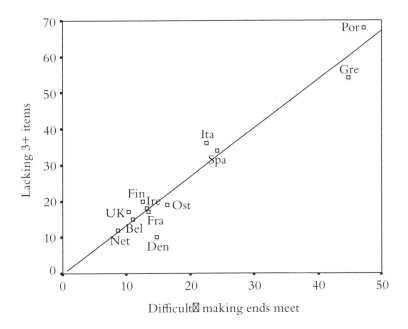

Chart 5: Subjective child poverty by % children lacking three or more necessities.

Relative measures

One of the reasons for this disjunction is that the child income poverty measure being employed here is a relative one – equivalent income less than 60 per cent of the median. However the actual income of those families living below this threshold is very different in different countries. Further the point on the income distribution that this threshold comes is determined by the income distribution – it will be relatively higher in countries with a less dispersed income distribution. This issue has become more salient with the expansion of the EU to include a larger number of countries with very much lower living standards. Chart 6 gives the distribution of relative child income poverty for the EU24 (data for Malta is missing). Slovenia has the lowest relative child poverty rate at the less than 60 per cent of median equivalent income threshold but this does not mean the living standards of children in Slovenia are the highest in the EU. Take Portugal and the UK their child poverty rates are fairly similar 27 and 23 percent respectively. However the threshold of 60 per cent of the median in Portugal is 4273 Euros per annum whereas the threshold for the UK is 7821 Euros per annum (in ECHP 2001).

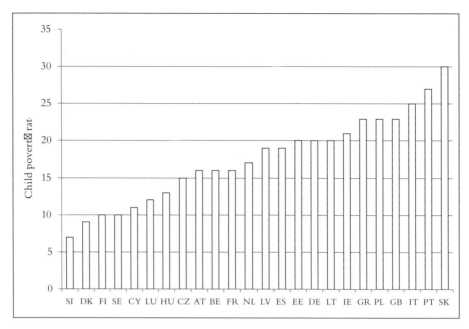

Chart 6: Child poverty rate. <60% median circa 2003. Eurostat 2005 Living Conditions and Welfare

Thus the relative income thresholds used in EU comparisons of poverty do not present a picture of real living standards and in particular the countries among the EU 10 with low child poverty rates would, if a more absolute poverty measure was used all end up with higher child poverty rates. Eurostat and the Social Protection Committee of the EU have so far resisted publishing a more absolute indicator of poverty but in Chart 7 we show the distribution of child poverty rates that would be obtained if for the EU 12 based on ECHP analysis if a threshold of 60 per cent of the EU median is used. The child poverty rates in Italy, Greece, Spain and Portugal are much higher than those shown in chart 1 using a relative threshold.

Equivalence scale

In order to take account of the relative needs of different household type when using income data to measure poverty, equivalence scales have to be used. A variety of different equivalence scales are used in the literature. The OECD originally settled on a scale which weighted the first adult in a household as 1.0, the second adult as 0.7 and each child at 0.5. This scale had no scientific basis; it was derived from a negotiation between national governments to produce a consensus. It was then decided that the scale was too generous to families with children and the modified OECD equivalence

JONATHAN BRADSHAW

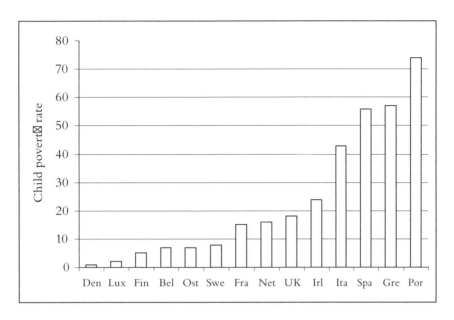

Chart 7: Child poverty rate s obtained using a threshold of 60 per cent of the EU median. Own analysis of the ECHP 2001.

scale was introduced which weighted, the first adult in a household as 1.0, the second adult as 0.5 and each child as 0.3. Then someone recognised that the modified OECD equivalence scale was very similar to the square root of the number in the household and so many analysts began to adopt the square root of N as their equivalence scale, which effectively weighted the first adult as 1.0, the second adult as 0.4 and the first child as 0.3. The trouble with all this is that although which equivalence scale is used does not make a big difference to overall poverty rates, it can make a big difference to the composition of the poor. This is illustrated in Chart 8 which is based on work by Ritakallio (2002). It shows the relative risk in older people and child poverty rates that would be obtained using the OECD and modified OECD for couples with children and people aged 65 plus. It can be seen that for almost all countries (the Netherlands is the exception) moving from the OECD to the modified OECD scale increases the proportion 65+ defined as poor and reduces the proportion of couples with children defined as poor, often by large amounts. This might have an effect on the perception of the problem by EU policy makers.

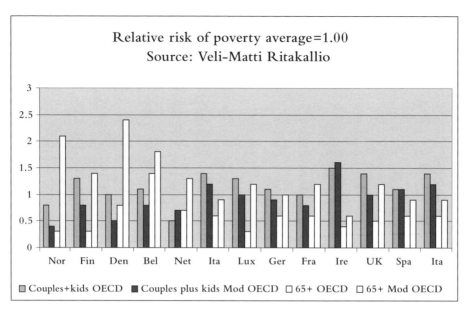

Chart 8: Changes in the relative risk of poverty using OECD and Modified OECD equivalence scales.

Arbitrary income threshold

It is inevitable that a relative income poverty measure involves using a threshold. The choice of threshold varies 40, 50 or 60 per cent of the mean or median income. Analysis based on the LIS has tended to use 50 per cent of the median including the UNICEF Report Cards. The EU has come to adopt a threshold of 60 per cent of the median – on the grounds, it appears from the Atkinson et al (2002) report, that 50 per cent produces too many farmers, the self employed and students in the poor group! These thresholds are arbitrary in the sense hat they are completely unrelated to any notion of adequacy or budget standards. The threshold that is used can make a difference to the relative position of countries as is shown in Chart 9. The countries are ranked by their child poverty rates at 50 per cent of the median. At 60 per cent of the median they would have had a rather different rank order with for example Luxembourg four places lower in the league table. This is particularly problematic if by chance the threshold coincides with the point on the income distribution where many households are receiving very similar incomes, an experience not unusual in analyses of pensioner's incomes.

JONATHAN BRADSHAW

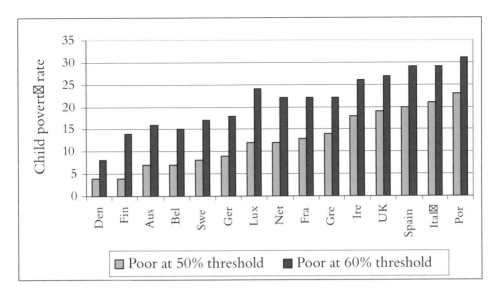

Chart 9: Child poverty rates obtained using different thresholds. ECHP 2001.

Poverty gaps

Most child income poverty is analysed using rates – the proportion of children below a threshold. However there is an argument that at least as much attention should be paid to gaps – how far below the threshold children are. There is an argument to be had about whether it is better for a country to have a large number of children a little below the threshold or a smaller number of children a long way below the threshold. As can be seen in Chart 10 although there is a relationship between rates and gaps there are some countries – GB and Portugal who have relatively lower gaps than their rates and others – Denmark and Slovenia who have relatively higher gaps than rates. There are a variety of ways of estimating gaps, in this example it is the average percentage difference from the poverty line. In income surveys there tend to be respondents with nil incomes or sometimes negative income and these cases can have a big impact on average poverty gaps, which is a reason why they are not used very often.

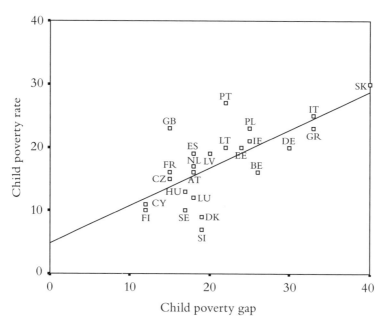

Chart 10: Child poverty rates compared with child poverty gaps. Circa 2003. Eurostat data.

Persistent child poverty

Similarly there is a debate to be had about whether those countries with high but dynamic/short term child poverty are better or worse than those countries with lower but more persistent child poverty. It is probably a more damaging experience for a child to be poor for years than to have a short episode of living in poverty. It can be seen in chart 11 that there is actually a very close relationship between the child poverty rate in one year 2001 and the proportion of children who have lived in poverty for all of the last three years.

Factors influencing variations in child poverty

Child poverty varies within and between countries according to a variety of factors associated with the characteristics of families – the family composition, the number of children, the employment status of parents, the educational level of the parents, age of youngest child and age of parents. Ritakallio and Bradshaw (2006) have explored these variations using the ECHP. When all these variations are taken into account residual variation in child poverty can be ascribed to the effectiveness of policy. Rita-kallio and Bradshaw (2006) built a model which controlled for the socio economic

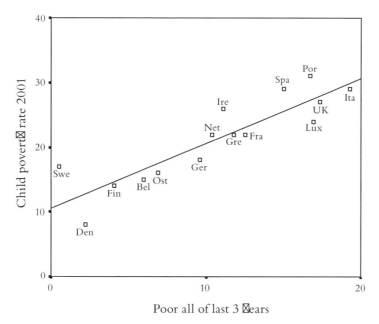

Chart 11: Child poverty rate in 2001 by percentage of children poor in the three years 1999, 2000 and 2001.

characteristics of each country and then compared the actual child poverty rate with the expected child poverty rate. Their results are reproduced in Chart 12. Sweden is taken as the base case for comparison. Compared with Sweden only Austria had a lower child poverty rate than predicted on the basis of their characteristics. That means that only Austria's social policy package is achieving better results than Sweden and Ireland and the Netherlands packages are particularly ineffective. It is significant that in this volume in my other chapter we found Austria with the most generous child benefit package and the Netherlands with one of the least generous.

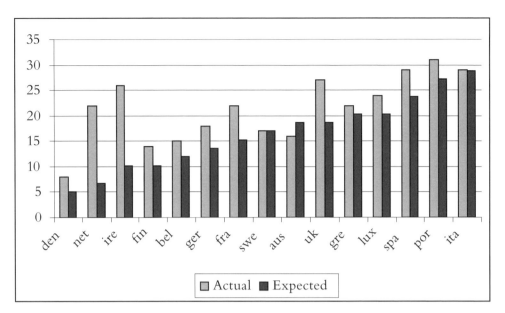

Chart 12: Actual and expected child poverty rates given the population characteristics. ECHP 2001. Ritakallio and Bradshaw (2006)

Conclusion

This chapter has sought to demonstrate some of the problems in using income as a measure of child poverty. Income poverty measures have become the dominant way in which child poverty is represented and compared. This is likely to continue in the EU given the commitment to the Laeken indicators of social inclusion, given that SILC and other surveys are designed for that purpose and given the strong support of economists for that approach. However in my view we should be developing a wider repertoire of measures. There is potential for the use of deprivation indicators and subjective measures and indeed using overlapping measures, there is potential for exploring other indicators of child well-being and indeed UNICEF in its Innocenti Report Card series has already made a distinguished start. My view is that we should move away from income poverty measures in comparative research and operationalise indicators of child well-being – some of which could be income measures.

JONATHAN BRADSHAW

References

Atkinson, T., B. Cantillion, E. Marlier and B. Nolan (2002): *Social Indicators. The EU and Social Indicators*, Oxford: Oxford University Press.

Bradshaw, J. and Finch, N. (2003): *A Comparison of Child Benefit Packages in 22 Countries*, Department for Work and Pensions Research Report No.174, Leeds: Corporate Document Services.

Chen, W-H. and M. Corak (2005): *Child poverty and changes in child poverty in rich countries since 1990*, Innocenti Working Paper 2005-02, Florence: UNICEF Innocenti Research Centre.

Corak, M. (2006): *Principles and practicalities for measuring child poverty*, International Social Security Review, 59, 2/2006, 3-35.

Mira d'Ercole, M. and M. Förster (2005): *Income distribution and poverty in OECD countries in the second half of the 1990*s, DELSA/ELSA(2004)7/ANN Paris: OECD.

Ritakallio, V-M. and Bradshaw, J. (2006): Family Poverty in the European Union, in Bradshaw, J. and Hatland, A. (eds) Social Policy, Employment and Family Change in Comparative Perspective, Cheltenham: Edward Elgar.

Ritakallio, V-M. (2002): 'New recommendations for compilation of statistics will change the cross-national picture of poverty in Europe', Paper presented at the EU COST A15 meeting in Urbino, 25 October 2004.

UNICEF (2005): *Child poverty in rich countries 2005*, Innocenti Report Card 6, Florence: UNICEF Innocenti Research Centre.

CHILD POVERTY IN THE U.S: A NEW FAMILY BUDGET APPROACH WITH COMPARISON TO EUROPEAN COUNTRIES

Donald J. Hernandez, Nancy A. Denton, and Suzanne E. Macartney

This chapter presents a new poverty measure for the U.S. using Census 2000 data, and interprets results vis-à-vis extant internationally comparable estimates. These results are important because children who live in poverty and lack access to high quality early education and health care experience negative consequences compared to other children (Duncan and Brooks-Gunn 1997; Edmunds and Coye 1998; McLoyd 1998; Shonkoff and Phillips 2000; Takanishi 2004. See http://mumford.albany.edu/children/index_sg.htm).

Unofficial U.S. Poverty Measures Prior to 1960

The first U.S. publication to use the term »poverty« referring to a specific dollar value threshold was the 1870-1871 report of the Massachusetts Bureau of Statistics of Labor, followed by *The Philadelphia Negro* (W.E.B. DuBois 1899) (For a detailed history see Fisher 1994 1997). The nineteenth-century term »pauperism« pertained to persons receiving public relief from the state or private charity assistance. Early twentieth century social workers, economists, and sociologists increasingly defined poverty as »insufficient income regardless of source«, providing the basis for the idea of a poverty line or threshold (Fisher 1993:10). This paradigm shift involved »the view that poverty was mainly due to economic and other institutional and social factors rather than to 'drunkenness…moral depravity…laziness…shiftlessness'« (Fisher 1997: 10).

In 1949, the Congressional Joint Economic Committee formed the Subcommittee on Low-Income Families (SLIF) which designated families with a cash-income below $2,000 as worthy of intensive study (Gordon 1997: 39-41). Although there was no official or quasi-official poverty line, U.S. Census Bureau practice was consistent with the SLIF reports. As early as 1948 the Census Bureau reported on families with incomes under $2,000, and beginning in 1958 on families with incomes under $3,000. A year later, in July 1959, Michael Harrington wrote an article later expanded as *The Other America: Poverty in the United States* (1962), which brought an explosion of public and government interest to the problem of poverty.

Official Poverty and Unofficial Views: 1965-1980

President Lyndon Johnson announced his War on Poverty in January 1964, and the annual report of his Council of Economic Advisors (CEA) designated a poverty threshold of $3,000 (in 1962 dollars) for families and $1,500 for unrelated individuals, values nearly the same as the inflation-adjusted nonfarm thresholds published by Mollie Orshansky in 1963. In May 1965 the U.S. Office of Economic Opportunity (OEO) adopted the Orshansky economy food plan thresholds to define poverty for statistical, planning, and budget purposes (Orshansky 1965; Gordon 1997: 54). Various scholars, including Orshanky, favored higher thresholds. In fact, »(a) May 10, 1965, internal OEO briefing memorandum on the new poverty definition noted that while Orshanky's higher poverty thresholds derived from the low-cost food plan 'cannot be characterized as excessive,' the lower thresholds derived from the economy food plan had been selected as the OEO's poverty definition 'on the premise that the first order task of the War Against Poverty is to get at the hard-core poor'« (Gordon 1997: 85, ftnt 290).

Meanwhile, others offered alternative approaches. Rose Friedman presented a quite conservative view in an American Enterprise Institute (AEI) pamphlet published in February 1965, proposing a threshold of $2,220 for a four-person household in 1963 dollars, only 71% of the Orshansky level. Victor Fuchs, also in 1965, proposed a relative poverty measure setting the threshold at one-half of median family income, arguing »(t)oday's comfort or convenience is yesterday's luxury and tomorrow's necessity. In a dynamic democratic society how could it be otherwise? The foregoing discussion suggests that a meaningful definition of poverty can best be found by setting relative standards« (Fuchs 1965: 74).

In the same year, despite her conservative approach, Rose Friedman argued in the American Enterprise Institute pamphlet for a relative poverty concept, »(i)f the trend in growth of real income of the past 35 years were to continue....one of its manifestations will be a rise in what is regarded as the standard of poverty....All groups will continue to share in economic progress and the people then [at the end of the twentieth century] labeled poor will have a higher standard of living than many labeled not poor today« (quoted in Gordon 1993: 53).

Fuchs was the first in the U.S. to propose a relative measure based on one-half median family income, although Peter Townsend in Britain proposed a similar measure in 1962, but the underlying idea has a long history. Emphasizing poverty must be defined compared to current living standards, Adam Smith defined economic hardship as being unable to consume commodities that »the custom of the country renders it indecent for creditable people, even of the lowest order, to be without« (Smith 1776: 691; see also Hernandez 1993: 240). John Kenneth Galbraith echoed two centuries later that poverty is relative, arguing »[p]eople are poverty-stricken when their income, even if adequate for survival, falls markedly behind that of the community. Then they cannot have what the larger community regards as the minimum necessary for decency, and they cannot wholly escape, therefore, the judgment of the larger community that they are indecent. They are degraded for, in a literal sense, they live outside the grades or categories which the community regards as respectable« (Galbraith 1958: 323-324).

A decade later in 1974, Lee Rainwater comprehensively reviewed public opinion surveys, family budget studies, and family-budget expert evaluations, finding that Americans from the Great Depression onward regarded a »low« or »poverty« level income as equal to less than 50% of median family (disposable) income in a given year (Rainwater 1974; see also Hernandez 1993; 241). Culminating this line of research in 1980, the U.S. Bureau of Labor Statistics convened an Expert Committee, chaired by Harold W. Watts, which developed and recommended an approach specifying the lowest, »social minimum« standard, set at 50 percent of the prevailing (median) family standard, to mark the boundary indicating deficiency and deprivation (Expert Committee on Family Budget Revisions 1980).

More than a decade later, General Social Survey data for 1993 indicate that on average Americans viewed a »poverty level« income for a four person family to be $17,658 (in 1993 dollars), that is, 48% of median family income ($36,959) (Citro and Michael 1995; U.S. Census Bureau 2005a). Thus from 1937 through the early 1990s, public perceptions regarding poverty tracked the value of one-half median family income.

The relative poverty threshold for a family of four set equal to one-half of median family income is also consistent both with the best-known statement about U.S. poverty during the Great Depression and with the official U.S. measure when it was adopted. In his Second Inaugural Address on January 20, 1937, President Franklin Delano Roosevelt portrayed poverty in the United States, declaring, »I see one-third of a nation ill-housed, ill-clad, and ill-nourished« (Barlett 1968: 971). A relative poverty measure using one-half of median family income as the threshold for a family with two parents and two children and implemented using 1940 census data indicates that 32% of the U.S. population was poor in 1939, essentially identical to the level cited by President Roosevelt two years earlier (Hernandez 1993).

A quarter century later, the threshold developed by Orshansky and officially adopted was set at essentially one-half of median family income, although the relative poverty concept apparently was not an explicit consideration (Gordon 1997). Because the official threshold is unchanged since 1963, except for annual adjustment for inflation, and insofar as real median income increased by 70% between 1963-1999, the (inflation-adjusted) official threshold had fallen to 31% below one-half of median family income by 1999.

The National Academy of Sciences Panel: 1995

Responding to public controversy, the U.S. Congress asked the National Research Council of the National Academy of Sciences to convene a Panel on Poverty and Family Assistance to address rising concerns about the official poverty measure. The panel's »… major conclusion is that the current measure needs to be revised: it no longer provides an accurate picture of the differences in the extent of economic poverty among population groups or geographic areas of the country, nor an accurate picture of trends over time« (Citro and Michael 1995: 1).

The panel recommended that new poverty thresholds »… represent a budget for food, clothing, shelter (including utilities), and a small additional amount to allow for other needs (e.g., household supplies, personal care, non-work-related transportation)« (Citro and Michael 1995: 4). The Panel recommended, as a reasonable range, initial thresholds for a two-adult two-child family set 15%-25% less than one-half median family income in 1992 (Citro and Michael 1995; U.S. Census Bureau, 2005a). For comparative purposes it suggested a midpoint value, that is, a threshold 20% below one-half of median family income (Citro and Michael 1995: 262; U.S. Census Bureau 2005a).

The Panel also recommends a revised family income measure defined »…as the sum of money income from all sources together with the value of near-money benefits (e.g., food stamps) that are available to buy goods and services in the budget, minus expenses that cannot be used to buy these goods and services. Such expenses include income and payroll taxes, child care and other work-related expenses, child support payments to another household, and out-of-pocket medical care costs, including health insurance premiums« (Citro and Michael 1995: 5). Thus, »nondiscretionary expenses« would be deducted from family incomes for families with such expenses in calculating poverty, because these funds are not available to pay for discretionary consumption (Citro and Michael 1995: 102). The extent to which recommended changes in the family income measure lead to poverty estimates closer to a relative (one-half median income) standard depends on how they are implemented.

Two additional Panel recommendations are that the poverty threshold »… should be adjusted to reflect the needs of different family types and to reflect geographic differences in housing costs« (Citro and Michael 1995: 5). The need for family-type adjustments result from the lesser consumption of children than adults and from economies of scale available to larger families, while the need for geographic adjustments reflects the substantial variation across the nation in costs for shelter (Citro and Michael 1995: 7-8).

Finally, regarding annual updating, the Panel states »(w)e believe a preferable approach is one that updates the thresholds in a conservative or quasi-relative manner—one that drives the thresholds by changes in spending on necessities that pertain to a concept of poverty rather than by changes in spending on all kinds of consumption« (Citro and Michael 1995: 143). Thus, the Panel does not fully accept the idea that poverty levels should be set or updated to reflect the prevailing standard of living.

The NAS Panel calculated a child poverty rate of 21.9% using the official measure in 1992, but 26.4% using their proposed measure. The rate would be 28.2% using a relative poverty measure. (See Hernandez (1993) for method of calculation). Thus, as of 1992, the Panel recommendations would have eliminated seven-tenths of the gap separating the official measure from a relative measure centered on one-half median family income.

Responding to the NAS Panel's report, the U.S. Census Bureau developed experimental poverty measures for 1990-1997 (and more recently 1998-2002) (Short, Garner, Johnson, and Doyle 1999). The Bureau's experimental measure with the highest value for children in 1992 was 25.6%. This measure reflects many Panel recommendations, but not geographic differences in the cost of living. This experimental measure would eliminate about six-tenths of the gap separating the official and relative poverty rates in 1992. However, because more recent Census Bureau results adjust experimental thresholds only for inflation, they do not account for increases in median family income, and therefore are falling further behind the relative standard (U.S. Census Bureau 2005c 2005d).

Basic Family Budgets of the Economic Policy Institute: 2000-2001

Pursuing an alternative approach during the late 1990s, the Economic Policy Institute (EPI) in Washington, D.C. was developing »basic family budgets« for more than 400 U.S. communities including most components recommended by the NAS Panel, but using a somewhat different and generally more generous set of procedures (Bernstein, Brocht, and Spade-Aguilar 2000; Boushey, Brocht, Gundersen, Bernstein 2001). Two primary differences between EPI calculations and NAS Panel recommendations are as follows (Citro and Michael 1995: 9-11, 56-57, 70-71).

First, the EPI did not estimate the value of near-money (non-cash) income, such as food stamps or housing assistance program benefits. Second, the EPI defines some major budget costs (food, shelter, transportation for work, child care) to reflect minimum standards, while the NAS Panel focuses on actual expenditures among low income families as a baseline starting point (Citro and Michael 1995: 56-57, 70-71). In addition, EPI budgets are calculated for six family types, one-parent or two-parent families with one, two, or three children under age 12, and do not account for income or consumption of other family members living in the home.

The new family budget approach to measuring poverty presented here uses the broad framework recommended by the NAS Panel, setting thresholds based on the cost of food, housing, and other necessities, and calculating family resources based on a measure of family income that has been decreased by an amount equal to non-discretionary expenses work, health care, and federal taxes. It does so taking account of income of all family members in the home, where cohabiting parents both are counted as family members. Our specific estimates use or adapt the EPI procedures using Census 2000 data (IPUMs 5% microdata file prepared by Ruggles, et al 2004). (Contact authors for detailed procedures),

Basic Budget Poverty Thresholds: The New Approach

Food budgets for individual families were estimated by the EPI using the U.S. Department Agriculture's (USDA) »low-cost food plans« which are calculated to reflect the costs of nutritionally adequate diets. We adopt their approach, but develop estimates based on all family members of all ages. The U.S. Department of Housing and Urban Development (HUD) estimates »fair market rents« (FMRs) that measure the cost in particular metropolitan and non-metropolitan areas of renting housing with specific numbers of bedrooms that is decent, structurally safe, and sanitary. We follow the EPI in using these data for housing costs, but also estimate costs for larger families.

The NAS Panel recommends further that new poverty thresholds include the cost of clothing and additional needs such as household supplies, personal care, and non-work-related transportation. Based on data from the U.S. Consumer Expenditure Survey and Federal Communications Commission, the EPI estimates the cost of »other necessities« as equal to 31% of food and housing costs. These other necessities include the cost of clothing, personal care items, household supplies, bank fees, union dues, telephone, television, school supplies, reading materials, music, and toys. We follow the EPI, calculating »other necessities« as 31% of the food and housing cost estimate for specific families.

Summing costs of food, housing, and other necessities for individual families produces a Basic Budget Poverty threshold for each family. Our median threshold is $18,414 for children in two-parent, two-child families in 1999, and $16,625 for children in one-parent, two-child families, compared to an official threshold of $13,423 (U.S. Census Bureau 2005b). In addition to thresholds, however, disposable family income is the other side of the equation in measuring poverty.

Disposable Family Income: The New Approach

To calculate disposable family income we start with the total value of money income for all family members in the household. From this we subtract the dollar value of federal taxes, transportation for work, child care, and health insurance coverage. We also take into account likely effects of food stamps and other near-money income, based on separate analyses of the U.S. Census Bureau's Current Population Survey (CPS).

Using an approach somewhat different than the EPI to estimate income taxes, we developed a random-assignment procedure to map CPS 2000 federal income tax estimates onto the Census 2000 sample (U.S. Census Bureau 1993), and applied rules for federal Social Security and Medicare payroll taxes and the federal Earned Income Tax Credit (EITC) to estimate the effects on family income for specific families.

(Social Security taxes fund the national retirement system, disability and survivors benefits to workers and their families, and cash payments for food, clothing, and shelter to help aged, blind, and disabled persons with little or no income, while Medicare taxes fund the national health insurance program for persons age 65 or older, helping pay for health care but not covering all medical expenses or most long-term care (U.S. Social Security Administration 2006). The Earned Income Tax Credit (EITC or EIC) results in a tax refund when the EITC exceeds the amount of federal taxes owed. It was approved by the U.S. Congress in 1975 partly to offset social security taxes and as an incentive to work (U.S. Internal Revenue Service 2006)).

The EPI estimated costs of transportation for work based on owning and operating a car, according to the size of the metropolitan area, and whether the child lives in a non-metropolitan area, assigning the costs to each parent, regardless of whether the parent worked. We have adopted the EPI estimates for one and two parent families but limit the costs to the number of parents (or other persons 18 years and older in the family) who worked last year. The NAS Panel recommends the cost be assigned on a weekly basis for workers, but because most commuters depend on automobiles which must be owned and operated on a continuing basis, we assign transportation costs to workers on an annual basis. Lack of access to an automobile can act as a barrier to obtaining reasonably well-paid work by parents, because of the costs and complications associated with lengthy commutes between home and work via public transit (Ihlanfeldt and Sjoquist 1998; Pugh 1998; Raphael and Stroll 2002; Waller, 2005).

The NAS Panel recommended that child care expenses be assigned to all parents who were working or in school and had a child under age 15. The EPI relied for child care cost estimates mainly on results from the Children's Defense Fund (CDF) study. We calculate three sets of estimates for child care. The first, similar to the NAS Panel, sets child care expenses at the weekly limit allowed by the Internal Revenue Service (IRS) in 1999, equivalent to as much as $2,400 per year for one child, and $4,800 per year for two or more children. Following the NAS Panel, these estimates apply only to working parents for the weeks all parents in the home are working, and are capped at the annual values indicated, or the lowest annual income of the working parent, whichever is less. As a guiding principle, the NAS Panel recommended that the dollar value be set to »…represent a reasonable level of expenses necessary to hold a job, excluding additional expenses that parents may elect to provide enrichment for their children« (Citro and Michael 1995: 242).

Our second set follows the EPI, setting child care costs equal to local costs of center-based child care as estimated from a survey conducted by the Children's Defense Fund, and including child care costs only if all parents in the family are employed, but reducing the cost by one-half if a parent worked no more than one-half of the year (Boushey, Brocht, Gundersen, and Bernstein 2001). Thus, contrary to the NAS Panel, EPI estimates include expenses that involve enrichment for their children in center-based programs. This approach is similar to the NAS Panel in assigning child care costs only if parents are working, but different from the NAS Panel by assuming that parents are interested in enrolling children in educationally enriched programs, and that this requires enrollment at least six months continuously, rather than enrolling children in care only for the precise weeks during which parents are employed.

Our third set of estimates apply child care costs as estimated by the Children's Defense Fund to all children, regardless of parental work, reflecting the assumption that child care is necessary for parents to work, but also reflecting an important additional dimension in the case of child care, namely the enrichment or educational needs of children. One rationale for assigning child care costs to all children is that past research has found that many not-employed mothers would seek employment and many employed mothers would work more hours if child care were available at reasonable cost. This is especially true for mothers who are young, single, and with low education or little income (Presser and Baldwin 1980).

But at least as important, high quality early education programs have been found to be beneficial for children, particularly those with disadvantaged family circumstances, and to have salutary consequences for the broader society (Haskins and Rouse 2005; Lynch 2004). The range of estimates developed here does not, however, directly address the cost implications of differences between typical center-based care and high quality center-based programs. Recent research has found that there is considerable room for improvement in the quality of many early education programs in the U.S. (Clifford et al 2005, Pianta et al 2005; Clifford, Bryant, and Early 2005; Early, et al

2005). Costs vary by whether the programs are half-day or full-day, the qualifications of the teachers, whether the programs are provided in public schools or community-based organizations, whether »comprehensive services« are provided, etc. However, insofar as a recent estimate suggests that a quality preschool program may cost $8,000 per child, and our locality based estimates of actual costs range from $3,540 to $7,848, our approach may substantially underestimate the costs of high quality preschool in most localities across the U.S. (Haskins and Rouse 2005).

In addition, many U.S. preschool age children are not in formal day care settings. In 1997, for example, among children under age 5, only 21% were cared for in an organized care facility, and 30% with employed mothers were cared for in such facilities (U.S. Census Bureau 2002). Many parents in the U.S. may not be able to afford center-based care, and federal spending on child care programs is small compared to European countries (Bergmann 1996; Kamerman and Kahn 1995; Waldfogel 2001).

In sharp contrast, a study of 11 rich European nations and Australia found the following. »Most European countries have recognized the role of government in expanding access toward full coverage of the 3-to-6-year-old age group … to benefit from at least two years of high-quality ECEC (Early Childhood Education and Care) … all children have a legal right to attend *free* school-based provision from age 30 months in Belgium … age 3 in Italy, and age 4 in the Netherlands and UK. These education-based programmes are viewed as good for children and are widely accepted by the public. Indeed over 95% of children attend regardless of family income or employment status« (Neuman and Bennett 2001: 49-51). In addition, for younger ages, »(p)arental leave measures are an important part of the ECEC systems….With the exception of Australia and the U.S., mandatory job-protected paid *maternity leave* policies exist for working mothers … Statutory, job-protected *parental leave* … exists in all 12 countries …« (Neuman and Bennett 2001: 31). Thus, our third measure of costs for Early Childhood Education and Care is intended to reflect European standards for universal parental leave and early education, although our cost estimates are at least somewhat, and perhaps substantially, below the funding levels in European countries for ECEC and paid parental leave.

Turning to medical expenses, the NAS Panel recommended that the family resource measure should deduct the value of out-of-pocket medical care expenses, including health insurance premiums (Citro and Michael 1995: 11). In the European context, such information would be unnecessary, because all rich countries other than the U.S. provide universal access to government-funded national health care systems (In the U.S. such a program exists only for persons age 65 and older). The approach taken by the EPI to address health care costs is to create a weighted average of costs across three sets of children (no coverage, private coverage, government coverage), based the state-specific cost of obtaining private health insurance for those without insurance, and the employee cost of premiums for families with employer-sponsored insurance, combined with out-of-pocket costs as reported by the Consumer's Union.

The CPS indicates that 23% of children below 200% of the official poverty threshold are uninsured, compared to 8% for children in higher income families. Therefore, the »weighed average« approach may understate the costs of full coverage for all low income children and therefore the health component of basic budget poverty.

The NAS Panel recommended that the value of near-money benefits from programs such as food stamps be included with the value of money income as a family resource. The EPI did not develop such estimates, but we have calculated estimates from the CPS for food stamps, and also indicating the approximate effect on basic budget poverty of the federal housing assistance, energy assistance, and the free or reduced-price school meals programs.

Basic Budget Poverty Rates and Alternative Measures

To assess the implications for U.S. child poverty of various costs to families, we begin by focusing on the costs of food, housing, other necessities, and transportation for work. Next, we compare these results to the measure commonly used in international comparisons across rich countries, as well as to the official poverty measure and a measure based on one-half median family income.

Census 2000 data indicate, for income year 1999, that 11.4% of U.S. children lived in families with incomes too low to cover the local costs of food and housing (Table 1), and 17.6% of children lived in families that could not afford the combined local costs of food, housing, and other necessities.

By comparison, the official poverty rate using Census 2000 data for children was 14.8%, only 3.4 percentage points above the »food and housing« measure and 2.8 percentage points below the measure including »other necessities«. Thus, the official measure is equivalent to the cost of food and housing and a bit more, but not enough to fully cover other necessities, such as clothing, personal care expenses, household supplies, reading materials, school supplies, telephone, television, toys, etc. But these »basic budget measures« do not include the costs of transportation to work, child care, or health care. Taking into account transportation costs, 21.3% of children in 1999 are counted as poor, two-fifths greater than the value of 14.8% suggested by the official measure.

To compare poverty levels across rich countries, researchers from the Organization for Economic Cooperation and Development (OECD), the United Nation's Children's Fund (UNICEF), and others have for nearly two decades relied on a measure based on 50% of national median post-tax and transfer income using data from the Luxembourg Income Study (LIS) and other sources (Oxley, Dang, Antolin 2000;

Bradbury and Jantti 2001; Smeeding and Torrey 1988; UNICEF 2005). The estimate most comparable to the basic budget approach based on LIS and OECD indicates a U.S. child poverty rate of 21.9% in 2000 (UNICEF 2005).

The UNICEF results require two adjustments to be comparable to our basic budget approach. First, insofar as official child poverty in the U.S. was 0.9 percentage points greater in 1999 than in 2000, the comparable UNICEF rate for 1999 would be 0.7 percentage points greater in 1999 than in 2000, at about 22.6% (assuming the proportionate changes for children in the UNICEF and official poverty rates between 1994-2000 also hold for 1999-2000 (UNICEF 2005; Bradbury and Jantti 2001).

Second, the UNICEF measure is based on household, not family, income. Research by Hernandez has shown for the official U.S. poverty measure that as of 1997 the shift from a household definition, to a family definition counting cohabiting couples as two-parent families, to the official U.S. family definition involves a shift in the estimated level of poverty from 11.5%, to 12.7%, to 13.3% (reported on pp. 13 to 14 and C-23 to C-26 in Short, et al 1999). The corresponding shifts for children are from 18.2% to 19.1%, to 19.9% (Hernandez 1998). Insofar as the current basic budget approach classifies cohabiting parents as a two-parent family, the UNICEF measure should be adjusted upward by about 0.9 percentage points (19.1% − 18.2 % = 0.9%) for the shift from the household to the cohabiting-couple family definition. Thus, the adjusted UNICEF value is about 23.5%.

Our basic budget measure taking into account the cost of food, housing, other necessities, and transportation for work of 21.3% for U.S. children in 1999 is within 0.6-2.2 percentage points of the unadjusted and adjusted UNICEF estimates of 21.9%-23.5%. The close correspondence of results using these two measures indicates that, at the national level, they are quite similar in their assessment of U.S. child poverty. In remaining sections of this chapter we designate as »Baseline Basic Budget Poverty« this measure comparing after-tax income to the family budget which includes the costs of food, housing, other necessities, and transportation for work.

But neither the Baseline Basic Budget Poverty measure nor the UNICEF measure explicitly takes into account the cost of child care, an expenditure which the NAS Panel highlights as important for working parents with young children. Moreover, these estimates fall 3.5-5.7 percentage points below the relative child poverty rate of 27.0% calculated from the CPS using one-half median family income as the standard (for method of calculation, see Hernandez, 1993). Attention now turns to the costs of early care/education and health care.

Costs of Early Childhood Education and Care and of Health Care

Children in European countries, as noted above, generally have access to and participate in formal Early Childhood Education and Care (ECEC) arrangements supported by the national government, or if they are infants or toddlers they have parents who can care for them at home because of government-guaranteed, job-protected, paid maternal or parental leave arrangements. Similarly, children in Europe and other rich countries have access to government-funded national health coverage. Table 1 presents four additional basic budget estimates.

These calculations indicate the following. The Baseline Basic Budget Poverty rate of 21.3%, rises to 24.8% accounting for child care costs for working parents at the levels recommended by the NAS Panel, to 27.8% accounting for center-based care costs for working parents based on estimates by the Children's Defense Fund, and further to 32.4% accounting for center-based care costs for all children based on CDF estimates. Because parents of some low income children in the U.S. receive at least partial subsidies for child care or early education, more refined estimates would be slightly lower. Taking account of health care costs, the poverty rate rises from the baseline of 21.3% to 27.4%. In the case of health care, however, because the cost estimate is a weighted average across those with private coverage, government funded coverage, and no coverage, the estimates may be too low, perhaps by several percentage points. Simultaneously taking account both of early care/education and health care costs, the poverty rate rises from the baseline of 21.3% to 34.1% counting ECEC for children with working parents based on FCD costs, and to 38.3% counting ECEC for all children based on FCD costs.

In view of the stark differences between the U.S. and many other rich countries in government support for child care/early education and health care, a poverty measure going beyond the UNICEF approach to incorporate these costs shows much larger differences than indicated by the UNICEF measure. The UNICEF poverty rates for six countries with near universal maternal/parental leave, preschool and national health insurance range from 2.4% in Denmark to 10.2% in Germany. The UNICEF measure for the U.S. is at least double these rates at 21.9% (UNICEF 2005), and the Basic Budget Poverty Rate taking into account child care/early education and health care is three times greater counting child care (CDF measure) for working parents (34.1%) and nearly four times greater counting child care for all children (CDF measure) than in any of these six countries at 38.3%. The large gaps between the U.S. and other rich countries reflect vividly the consequences of living in nations with very different levels of government financial commitment to the early care/education and health of their children.

Food Stamps and Other Non-Cash Benefits

Beyond components of Basic Budget Poverty discussed above, the NAS Panel also recommends that a new U.S. poverty measure add to after tax income »…the value of near-money nonmedical in-kind benefits, such as food stamps, subsidized housing, school lunches, and home energy assistance (Citro and Michael 1995: 10). These near-money benefits are not directly included in our estimates, because relevant measures are not collected in Census 2000. However, we have conducted analyses of the CPS to assess how these programs reduce Basic Budget Poverty, calculating a series of rates using the official approach but with thresholds equal to 100%, 150%, and 200% of the official threshold (See Table 2). Because of conceptual differences, measures of poverty based on the official and basic budget approaches will count as poor somewhat different sets of children, but the overlap is 85-95%.

Measures setting the thresholds at 150% and 200% of the official threshold yield poverty rates of 28.2% and 38.7%, respectively, compared to the 100% official threshold measure at 16.9%. Thus, the Baseline Basic Budget Poverty measure of 21.3% is somewhat closer to the official 100% measure than the 150% measure, and the most comprehensive Basic Budget Poverty estimate (38.3%) is quite close to the 200% estimate (38.7%). Thus, results for the 100%, 150%, and 200% poverty measures provide a reasonably good guide to the impact of various near-cash benefit programs on various basic budget measures. The results for food stamps indicate that this program acted to reduce the 100% official poverty rate by 0.8 percentage points, to reduce the 150% official poverty rate by 0.3 percentage points, and that it had no measurable effect on the 200% official poverty rate. Results regarding the effects on official poverty measures for three additional programs--federal housing assistance, energy assistance, and free/reduced school meals programs--indicate that taken together, these three programs reduced the 100%, 150%, and 200% poverty measures by no more than 0.9 percentage points.

Program participation rates for children range from 3.2% for energy assistance, to 5.8% for housing assistance, 10.8% for food stamps, and a very large 56% for free/reduced school meals. The value of these benefits is substantial, especially food stamps and housing assistance, and quite important for children receiving them. Nonetheless, the dollar values of these four near-money benefit programs are such that they act to lift no more than 2% of children out of Baseline Basic Budget Poverty, regardless of the measure used.

Poverty among Children, Parents, and other Adults

Children are much more likely than adults to live in poverty, and this also is true of parents compared to other adults, and of mothers compared to fathers (Table 3). Children experience the highest poverty rates. The poverty gap between children and adults is 5 percentage points (15% vs. 10%) according to the official measure, but 8 percentage points (21% vs. 13%) using the Baseline Basic Budget measure. The gap expands to 16 percentage points (32% vs. 16%) taking into account the costs of Early Child Education and Care (for all children), and still further to 18 percentage points (38.3% vs. 20.5%) also taking health insurance costs into account.

The poverty gaps separating children from adults who are not caring for their own dependent children in the home are even larger, because poverty rates for these non-parental adults are lower than for parents. The gap between parents and non-parents is only 1-3 percentage points using the official measure, and slightly larger at 3-6 percentage points using the Baseline Basic Budget measure. But parents are 11-14 percentage points more likely than other adults to live in poverty taking account of Early Childhood Education and Care, and this remains constant or increases slightly further to 11-16 percentage points taking health insurance costs into account.

Thus, according to the basic budget measures, children are 6-11 percentage points more likely than parents to live in poverty, because children are more concentrated than parents in poor families. But children are 10-22 percentage points more likely than adults without their own children in the home to live in basic budget poverty. Important differences also exist among parents. Mothers caring for children in their homes are most similar to children in their poverty rates. The basic budget poverty gaps separating children from mothers are only 3-5 percentage points, compared to 9-12 percentage points for the gaps between children and fathers.

Thus, while it has long been known that children are more likely than adults to live in poverty, and that mothers caring for children are more likely than fathers to live in poverty, budget-based poverty measures demonstrate that the poverty gaps separating children from adults without children in the home, and mothers from fathers as of 1999 are larger than previously suggested by the official poverty measure.

Child Poverty across U.S. Geographic Areas

National estimates are important for assessing overall levels of economic need among children (and adults) in the U.S., but many federal and state policies are focused at the local level. The NAS Panel recommended taking account of the local cost of living, especially with regard to housing, in calculating poverty rates, and our approach does so. A thorough analysis of differences in poverty rates across U.S. localities is not possible in this chapter, but Table 4 presents estimates for the 10 Consolidated Metropolitan Statistical Areas (CMSAs) with the largest number of children, many of which have a high cost of living, as well as for an additional 11 localities (both smaller metropolitan areas and the rural regions of selected states) that have comparatively low costs (Table 3 estimates do not count the value of near-cash benefits). Not surprisingly, comparisons across localities in basic budget poverty can lead to very different conclusions than comparisons based on official poverty, because the latter does not take into account differences in the local cost of living. (See http://mumford.albany.edu/children/index_sg.htm).

Child Poverty, Race-Ethnicity, and America's Future

Children in various race-ethnic and immigrant origin groups often differ enormously both in the economic resources available to their families and in where they live (Hernandez and Charney 1998; Hernandez 1999; Hernandez 2004). The new basic budget approach to measuring poverty allows us to present a summary measure of the implications of these differences across groups (See Table 5).

The large differences in Basic Budget Poverty among race-ethnic and immigrant origin groups, and the much higher rates experienced by many race-ethnic (non-white) minorities has potentially profound implications for America's future. Census Bureau projections indicate that children in the U.S. are leading the way toward the creation of a new American majority. The proportion of children who are white, non-Hispanic is projected to fall steadily, dropping below 50% after 2030, only 25 years from now. This transformation does not reflect the emergence of a single numerically dominant group, but instead a majority consisting of a mosaic of diverse race-ethnic groups from around the world.

Immigration and births to immigrants and their descents are the forces driving this historic transformation, and children in immigrant families are the fastest growing group within the child population. In 2030, the baby-boom generation born between 1946 and 1964 will be in the retirement ages of 66-84 years old. The Census Bureau's projections indicate that by 2030, 72% of the elderly will be white, non-Hispanic, compared to only 56% for working-age adults, and 50% for children. As a result, as the growing elderly population of the predominantly white baby-boom generation reaches the retirement ages, it will increasingly depend for its economic support during retirement on the productive activities and civic participation (that is, voting) of working-age adults who are members of racial and ethnic minorities. Many of these workers will, as children, have grown up in immigrant families.

Table 5 shows that among children in native-born families, only Asians have comparatively low poverty, while Native Hawaiian and other Pacific Islanders experience medium poverty levels, and comparatively high levels are experienced by blacks,

Mexicans, mainland-origin and island-origin Puerto Ricans, other Hispanics, and Native Americans. Among children in immigrant families, some white groups also have very high poverty rates, namely those from Albania, former Yugoslavia, former USSR, and the West Asian nations of Afghanistan, Bangladesh, Pakistan, Iraq, Saudi Arabia, and Yemen Arab Republic. But children in immigrant families from Mexico, from four Central American countries, from four Indochinese countries, and from the Dominican Republic and Haiti, which account for 54% of all children in immigrant families, also all experience very high poverty rates, as do blacks from Africa. Because children from these countries represent a majority of children in immigrant families, their circumstances and prospects are especially consequential for the future of America. (See http://mumford.albany.edu/children/index_sg.htm).

Conclusion

Poverty measurement in the U.S. has a long and controversial history. Perhaps the most important conceptual advance in the evolution of poverty measurement was the paradigm shift from »pauperism«, which focused only on persons dependent on the state for public relief or on charities for assistance, to the modern social science concept of »poverty« based on a subsistence budget reflecting the amount that a family must spend in order to live at a minimally adequate level. Not until May 1965 did the U.S. government adopt an official poverty measure, but during the same period, scholars revived the notion dating back at least to Adam Smith that poverty must be defined in »relative« terms, that is, in comparison to contemporary standards of living in a given society at a given time, a perspective which is consistent with historical family budget estimates and public opinion polls in the U.S. since the 1930s. These scholars argue that an appropriate poverty measure is one that sets a threshold equivalent to one-half median family, and this is the standard used by the OECD, UNICEF, and scholars conducting major international comparisons across rich countries.

When it was adopted in 1965, the official U.S. threshold was set at a level essentially identical to one-half median family income, though not as a matter of principle. But over time the U.S. measure has lagged further and further behind the one-half median family income standard, because it has been adjusted only for inflation, not for increases in the real standard of living. The official measure also has come under increasing criticism, which culminated in 1995 in a report of a National Academy of Sciences Panel recommending that the official measure be revised to take account of profound changes that have occurred in the American society, economy, and public policy since the 1960s. The NAS Panel recommendations focused on four key issues.

Six years later in 2001 the Economic Policy Institute published family budgets for each of more than 400 localities in the U.S. for each of the major components identified by the NAS Panel with the exception of near-money public benefits. The EPI estimates are conceptually consistent with, but generally more generous than, the NAS Panel recommendations and procedures. We have adapted and extended the EPI approach to develop new Basic Budget Poverty rates for the U.S. using Census 2000 data and other sources. The results indicate that our Baseline Basic Budget Poverty rate for children in 1999 was 21.3%, only slightly lower than the 22.6% estimated by UNICEF based on median family income, and the appropriately adjusted UNICEF measure which is 23.5%. The Baseline Basic Budget Poverty measures and the unadjusted and adjusted UNICEF measures are 3.5-5.7 percentage points less than the 27.0% estimate using a relative poverty concept setting the threshold at one-half of median family income, and they do not explicitly account for the cost of early care/education or health care.

Insofar as children in Europe and other rich countries generally have access to government funded national health insurance, and formal child care or early education arrangements, and, if they are infants or toddlers, to parents who can care for them at home because of government-guaranteed, job-protected, paid maternal or parental leave arrangements, and insofar as federal support for these services in the U.S. lags far behind, a more comprehensive approach to comparing the circumstances of children in the U.S. and other rich countries requires an adjustment for child care/early education and health coverage.

Our most comprehensive measure incorporating these factors yields a Basic Budget Poverty rate of 38.3% for U.S. children, compared to 2-10% in a variety of European countries. The Basic Budget Poverty rates are especially high for race-ethnic minority children in native-born families who are black, Hispanic, Native American, or Native Hawaiian or other Pacific Islander, and for those in immigrant families, particularly those from Mexico, Central America, Dominican Republic, Haiti, Indochina, Albania, former Yugoslavia, former Soviet Union, Afghanistan, Pakistan, Bangladesh, Iraq, Jordan, Saudi Arabia, Cape Verde, Sudan, Senegal, Somalia, Ethiopia, Eritrea, Yemen, Kenya. These high poverty levels and large race-ethnic differentials merit increasing public policy attention because it is projected that race-ethnic minority children will constitute a majority of U.S. children by 2030. The current circumstances and future prospects of U.S. children do not compare favorably to their European peers.

Acknowledgements

We are indebted to Jared Bernstein and his colleagues at the Economic Policy Institute for providing their results in electronic format and for their path-breaking research, Charles T. Nelson for his indispensable advice in navigating the Current Population Survey data collection, files, and tax estimates, and Ruby Takanishi for her wise counsel. For computer assistance we thank to Hui-Shien Tsao. Finally, we gratefully acknowledge the William and Flora Hewlett Foundation for supporting research that provided a basis for this chapter, as well as the Russell Sage Foundation and the Population Reference Bureau. The authors are responsible for any errors of fact or interpretation.

References

Bartlett, J. (1968): *Familiar Quotations.* 14th ed. rev. and enl. E.M. Beck (ed). Boston: Little Brown.

Bergmann, B.R. (1996): *Saving Our Children from Poverty: What the United States Can Learn from France.* New York: Russell Sage Foundation.

Bernstein, J., C. Brocht, M. Spade-Aguilar (2000): *How Much is Enough? Basic Family budgets for Working Families.* Washington, D.C., Economic Policy Institute.

Boushey, H., C. Brocht, B. Gundersen, and J. Bernstein (2001): *Hardships in America: The Real Story of Working Families.* Washington, D.C., Economic Policy Institute.

Bradbury, B. and M. Jantti (2001): »Child poverty across twenty-five countries«. Bradbury, B., S.P. Jenkins and J. Micklewright (eds): *The Dynamics of Child Poverty in Industrialized Countries.* Cambridge: Cambridge University Press, under copyright of UNICEF: 62-91.

Citro, C.F. and R.T. Michael (eds) (1995): *Measuring Poverty: A New Approach.* Washington D.C.: National Academy Press.

Clifford, R.M., O. Barbarin, F. Chang, D. Early, D. Bryant, C. Howes, M. Burchinal, and R. Pianta (2005): »What is Pre-kindergarten? Characteristics of public pre-kindergarten programs« *Applied Developmental Science* 9(3): 126-143.

Clifford, Richard M., Donna Bryant, and Diane M. Early (2005): »What we know about pre-kindergarten programs. *Principal* September/October: 21-24.

Duncan, G.J. and J. Brooks-Gunn (eds) (1997): *Consequences of Growing Up Poor.* New York: Russell Sage foundation.

Early, D., O. Barbarin, D. Bryant, M. Burchinal, F. Chang, R. Clifford, G. Crawford, W. Weaver, C. Howes, S. Ritchie, M. Kraft-Sayre, R. Pianta, and W.S. Barnett (2005): »Pre-kindergarten in eleven states: NCEDL's multi-state Study of pre-kindergarten & study of state-wide early education programs (SWEEP). Chapel Hill: NCEDL working Paper, May 24.

Edmunds, M. and M. J. Coye (eds) (1998): *America's Children: Health Insurance and Access to Care.* Washington, D.C.: National Academy Press.

Expert Committee on Family budget Revisions (1980): *New American Family Budget Standards.* Madison, WI: Institute for Research on Poverty.

Fisher, G. (1994): »From Hunter to Orshansky: An overview of (unofficial) poverty lines in the United States from 1904 to 1965 – SUMMARY« downloaded March 11, 2005, from http://aspe.os.dhhs.gov/poverty/papers/htrssmiv.htm.

Fisher, G. (1997): »From Hunter to Orshansky: An overview of (unofficial) poverty lines in the United States from 1904 to 1965«, revised version of paper presented October 28, 1993 at the Fifteenth Annual Research Conference of the Association for Public Policy analysis and

Management in Washington, D.C. downloaded March 11, 2005, from http://www.census. gov/hhes/poverty/povmeas/papers/hstorsp4.html.

Fuchs, V. (1965): »Towards a theory of poverty«. *The Concept of Poverty*. Washington, DC: Chamber of Commerce of the United States: 71-91.

Galbraith, J.K. (1958): *The Affluent Society.* Boston: Houghton Mifflin.

Harrington, M. (1962): *The Other America: Poverty in the United States.* New York: The Macmillan Company.

Haskins, R. and C. Rouse (2005): »Closing achievement gaps«. *The Future of Children, Policy Brief, Spring 2005.* Princeton, N.J.: Princeton-Brookings.

Hernandez, D.J. (1993): *America's Children: Resources from Family, Government, and the Economy.* New York: Russell Sage foundation.

Hernandez, D.J. (1998): »Official poverty in the U.S.: Re-conceiving the unit of analysis« Unpublished paper prepared for the U.S Census Bureau.

Hernandez, D.J. (1999): »Socioeconomic and demographic risk factors and resources among children in immigrant and native-born families: 1910, 1960, 1990«. D.J. Hernandez (ed) *Children of Immigrants: Health, Adjustment, and Public Assistance.* Washington, D.C.: National Academy Press: 19-125.

Hernandez, D.J. (2004): »Demographic change and the life circumstances of immigrants«. *The Future of Children, Special Issue on Children of Immigrants* 14(2):16-47 (Fall 2004)

Hernandez, D.J. and E. Charney (eds) (1998): *From Generation to Generation: The Health and Well-Being of Children in Immigrant Families.* Washington, D.C.: National Academy Press.

Ihlanfeldt, K, and D. Sjoquist (1998): »The spatial mismatch hypothesis: A review of recent studies and their implications« *Housing Policy Debate* 9(4): 842-892.

Kamerman, S.B. and A.J. Kahn (1995): *Starting Right: How America Neglects Its Youngest Children and What We Can Do About it.* Oxford: Oxford University Press.

Lynch, R.G. (2004): *Exceptional Returns: Economic, Fiscal and Social Benefits of Investment in Early Childhood Development,* Washington, DC: Economic Policy Institute.

McLoyd, V.C. (1998): »Socioeconomic disadvantage and child development,« *American Psychologist* 53(2): 185-204.

Neuman, M., and J. Bennett (2001): *Starting Strong: Early Childhood Education and Care.* Paris, Organization for Economic Co-operation and Development.

Orshansky, M. (1963): »Children of the poor« *Social Security Bulletin* 26(7): 3-13, July 1963.

Orshansky, Mollie (1965): »Counting the poor: Another look at the poverty profile« *Social Security Bulletin* 28(1): 3-29, January 1965.

Oxley, H., T.T. Dang, and P. Antolin (2000): »Poverty dynamics in six OECD countries« *Economic Studies* No. 30, 2000/I

Pianta, R., C. Howes, M. Burchinal, D. Bryant, R. Clifford, D. Early, and O. Barbarin (2005): »Features of pre-kindergarten programs, classrooms, and teachers: Do they predict observed classroom quality and child-teacher interactions?« *Applied Developmental Science* 9(3): 144-159.

Presser, H.B. and W. Baldwin (1980): »Child care as a constraint on employment: prevalence, correlates, and bearing on the work fertility nexus«. *American Journal of Sociology* 18(5): 1202-1213.

Pugh, M (1998): »Barriers to work: the spatial divide between jobs and welfare recipients in metropolitan areas« Washington, DC: Brookings Institution.

Rainwater, L. (1974): *What Money Buys: Inequality and the Social Meanings of Income*. New York: Basic books.

Raphael, S. and M.A. Stoll (2002): »Modest Progress: The narrowing spatial mismatch between blacks and jobs in the 1990s«, Washington, DC: Brookings Institution.

Ruggles, S., M. Sobek, T. Alexander, C.A. Fitch, R. Goeken, P.K. Hall, M. King, and C. Ronnander (2004): *Integrated Public Use Microdata Series: Version 3.0* [Machine-readable database]. Minneapolis, MN: Minnesota Population Center [producer and distributor], 2004. Accessed at the IPUMS site, http://www.ipums.org.

Shonkoff, J.P. and D.A. Phillips (eds) (2000): *From Neurons to Neighborhoods: The Science of Early Child Development*. Washington, D.C.: National Academy Press.

Short, K., T. Garner, D. Johnson, and P. Doyle (1999): *Experimental Poverty Measures: 1990 to 1997*. U.S. Census Bureau, Current Population Reports, Consumer Income, P60-205, Washington, D.C., U.S. Government Printing Office.

Smeeding, T.M. and B.B. Torrey (1988): »Poor Children in Rich Countries,« *Science* 42 (November): 873-877.

Smith, A. (1776): *Wealth of Nations*. London, Everyman's Library. As cited in »Alternative Measures of Poverty« A staff Study Prepared for the Joint Economic Committee (of the U.S. Congress), October 18, 1989, p. 10 and Patricia Ruggles, *Drawing the Line*. Washington, DC: Urban Institute, p. 20.

Takanishi, R. (2004): »Leveling the playing field: Supporting immigrant children from birth to eight«. *The Future of Children, Special Issue on Children of Immigrants*, 14(2):61-79.

UNICEF (2005): *Child Poverty in Rich Countries, 2005*. Innocenti Report Card No. 6. Florence, Italy: UNICEF Innocenti Research Centre.

U.S. Census Bureau (1993): Current Population Reports, Series P60-186RD, *Measuring the Effect of Benefits and Taxes on Income and Poverty: 1992*. U.S. Government Printing Office, Washington, D.C.

U.S. Census Bureau (2002): Current Population Reports, Series P70-86, *Who's Minding the Kids? Child Care Arrangements: Spring 1997*. U.S. Government Printing Office, Washington, D.C.

U.S. Census Bureau (2005a): »Historical Income Tables – Families« (Revised May 12, 2004) Table F-6. Downloaded April 15, 2005, http://www.census.gov/hhes/income/histinc/f06.html.

U.S. Census Bureau (2005b): »Poverty Thresholds in 1999, by Size of Family and Number of Related Children« (Last Revised August 22, 2002). Downloaded April 16, 2005, http://www.census.gov/hhes/poverty/threshld/thresh99.html.

U.S. Census Bureau (2005c): »Standardized and Unstandardized Experimental Poverty Rates: 1990 to 1999, Downloaded April 26, 2005, http://www.census.gov/hhes/poverty/povmeas/exppov/suexppov.html.

U.S. Census Bureau (2005d): »Experimental Poverty Measures, 1999-2001, Downloaded June 6, 2005, http://www.census.gov/hhes/poverty/povmeas/exppov/99_01expovmeas.html.

U.S. Internal Revenue Service (2006): downloaded January 30, 2006, http://www.irs.gov/individuals/article/0, id=96406,00.html.

U.S. Social Security Administration (2006): downloaded January 30, 2006, from http://www.ssa.gov/SSA_Home.html, http://www.ssa.gov/notices/supplemental-security-income/, and http://www.ssa.gov/pubs/10043.pdf.

Waldfogel, J. (2001):»International policies toward parental leave and child care«, *The Future of Children, Special Issue on Caring for Infants and Toddlers*, 11(1): 99-111.

Waller, M. (2005): »High cost or high opportunity cost? Transportation and family economic success« Washington,« *The Brookings Institution, Policy Brief, Center on Children & Families #35*, DC: Brookings Institution

Table 1 – Official, Relative, and Basic Budget Poverty: Children Ages 0-17, United States, Census 2000. (See http://mumford.albany.edu/children/index_sg.htm)

Poverty		Percent
(1)	**Official Poverty**	14,8
(2)	**Relative Poverty**[a]	27,0
(3)	**Basic Budget Poverty**[b] – based on cost of food and housing	11,4
(4)	**Basic Budget Poverty**[b] – based on cost of food, housing, and other necessities	17,6
(5)	**Baseline Basic Budget Poverty**[b] **based on cost of food, housing, other necessities,** **and transportation for work**	**21,3**
(6)	**Baseline Basic Budget Poverty**[b] *plus* NAS child care costs	24,8
(7)	**Baseline Basic Budget Poverty**[b] *plus* the cost of child care for working parents	27,8
(8)	**Baseline Basic Budget Poverty**[b] *plus* the cost of child care for all children	32,4
(9)	**Baseline Basic Budget Poverty**[b] *plus* cost of health care	27,4
(10)	**Baseline Basic Budget Poverty**[b] *plus* cost of child care for working parents, and health care	34,1
(11)	**Baseline Basic Budget Poverty**[b] *plus* cost child care/early education for all children, and health care	38,3

[a] Calucated from the Census Bureau's Current Population Survey, 2000.

[b] All Basic Budget Poverty measures compare costs to after-tax income.

Table 2 (a). Effect of Noncash Benefit Programs on Official Child Poverty, Current Population Survey (CPS), 2000

	Child Poverty Rate	100% Official Poverty	150% Official Poverty	200% Official Poverty	250% Official Poverty
	Child Poverty Rate	16,9%	28,2%	38,7%	48,6%
(1)	+ Food stamps	16,1%	27,9%	38,7%	48,6%
(2)	+ Housing Assistance	16,5%	28,1%	38,7%	48,6%
(3)	+ Energy Assistance	16,9%	28,2%	38,7%	48,6%
(4)	+ School Meals	16,4%	27,8%	38,5%	48,5%
(5)	+ Housing Assistance, Energy Assistance or School Meals	16,0%	27,7%	38,5%	48,4%
(6)	+ Food Stamps, Housing Assistance, Energy Assistance, or School Meals	15,0%	27,3%	38,4%	48,4%

	Effect on Poverty Rate (absolute reduction)	100% Official Poverty	150% Official Poverty	200% Official Poverty	250% Official Poverty
(7)	+ Food Stamps	-0.8%	-0.3%	-0.1%	0.0%
(8)	+ Housing Assistance	-0.4%	-0.1%	-0.1%	0.0%
(9)	+ Energy Assistance	0.0%	0.0%	0.0	0.0%
(10)	+ School Meals	-0.5%	-0.4%	-0.2%	-0.2%
(11)	+ Housing Assistance, Energy Assistance or School Meals	-0.9%	-0.6%	-0.3%	-0.2%
(12)	+ Food Stamps, Housing Assistance, Energy Assistance, or School Meals	-1.9%	-0.9%	-0.4%	-0.2%

Table 2 (b). Program Participation Rates and the Dollar Value of Programs for Children, Current Population Survey (CPS), 2000

		Participation Rate	Dollar value for child at 25th Percentile	Dollar value for child at 50th Percentile (median)	Dollar value for child at 75th Percentile	Dollar value for child at 90th Percentile
(13)	Food Stamps	10,8%	$1.120	$2.112	$3.360	$4.764
(14)	Housing Assistance	5,8%	$1.380	$1.812	$3.324	$4.176
(15)	Energy Assistance	3,2%	$120	$200	$300	$469
(16)	School Meals Low Price/Free	56,0%	$60	$179	$709	$1.063

Table 3. Official and Basic Budget Poverty for Children, Working Age Adults, and the Elderly, by Sex, Census 2000

	Official Poverty			Baseline Basic Budget Poverty			Baseline Basic Budget Poverty Plus Child Care/ECE for All Children			Baseline Basic Budget Poverty Plus Health Care & Child Care/ECE for All Children		
	Total	Male	Female	Total	Male	Female	Total	Male	Female	Total	Male	Female
Total (all ages)	**10,5**	9,4	11,5	**14,9**	13,7	16,1	**20,1**	18,7	21,4	**24,9**	23,5	26,3
Children ages 0–17	**14,8**	14,7	14,9	**21,3**	21,2	21,3	**32,4**	32,4	32,5	**38,3**	38,2	38,3
Adults ages 18+	**8,9**	7,4	10,3	**12,9**	11,1	14,6	**16,1**	14,0	18,0	**20,5**	18,3	22,6
Adults ages 18–64	**8,9**	7,6	10,2	**13,0**	11,4	14,5	**16,7**	14,7	18,7	**21,8**	19,6	24,1
Adults ages 65+	**9,1**	6,3	11,1	**12,5**	9,3	14,8	**12,8**	9,5	15,0	**13,9**	10,8	16,1
Parents ages 18+	**10,2**	7,6	12,4	**15,5**	12,4	18,1	**24,4**	20,9	27,2	**30,0**	26,1	33,1
Non-parents ages 18+	**8,3**	7,3	9,2	**11,7**	10,5	12,8	**12,3**	11,1	13,4	**16,2**	15,0	17,3
Non-parents ages 18–44	**8,9**	8,6	9,3	**12,6**	12,1	13,3	**13,5**	13,0	14,2	**19,0**	18,4	19,7
Non-parents ages 45–64	**7,1**	6,3	7,7	**9,9**	8,9	10,9	**10,0**	9,1	11,4	**14,4**	12,7	15,9
Non-parents ages 65+	**9,0**	6,2	11,1	**12,5**	9,2	14,7	**12,7**	9,4	15,0	**13,8**	10,6	16,1

*Parents defined as persons with at least one of their children ages 0–17 in home.

*Non-parents defined as persons with none of their children ages 0–17 in home.

Table 4. Poverty for Children Ages 0–17: Ten Largest Metropolitan and Select Areas, Census, 2000

Area	Baseline Basic Budget Poverty (*plus* cost of health care & child care for all children)	Baseline Basic Budget Poverty (*plus* cost of health care & child care for children with working parents)	Baseline Basic Budget Poverty (based on cost of food, housing, other necessities, & transportation to work)	Basic Budget Poverty (based on cost of food, housing & other necessities)	Basic Budget Poverty (based on cost of food & housing)	Official Poverty	Total Children
New York CMSA	43,1	38,3	28,4	25,3	17,6	16,2	4.750.750
Los Angeles CMSA	52,0	47,1	34,6	29,8	19,2	20,3	4.143.216
Chicago CMSA	35,4	30,2	20,3	17,6	11,7	13,0	2.261.063
Washington–Baltimore CMSA	28,7	24,6	16,1	13,5	8,8	8,9	1.750.803
San Fransisco–Oakland CMSA	35,2	31,3	22,7	19,7	12,6	9,6	1.659.380
Philadelphia CMSA	33,0	28,7	20,0	17,4	11,7	12,8	1.451.777
Boston CMSA	35,3	29,5	17,6	15,2	10,0	9,9	1.113.606
Detroit CMSA	29,8	26,0	18,3	15,7	10,8	13,3	1.288.271
Dallas–Ft.Worth CMSA	38,9	32,7	22,6	18,7	11,2	12,8	1.339.543
Houston CMSA	42,2	35,8	25,2	21,0	13,2	16,4	1.276.168
Binghamton, New York	41,1	34,7	17,2	14,2	9,9	14,3	59.478
Muncie, Indiana	33,8	28,3	16,1	11,3	7,5	13,8	25.392
Baton Rouge, Louisiana	37,1	31,3	21,0	16,8	11,4	17,8	154.781
Las Cruces, New Mexico	61,7	53,4	34,9	28,8	17,6	30,5	48.853
Pensacola, Florida	37,9	30,6	21,8	18,1	11,7	18,1	94.003
Arkansas rural	41,5	34,6	24,1	18,4	12,1	23,3	375.472
Iowa rural	29,4	23,7	10,7	7,7	4,7	9,1	453.126
New Mexico rural	56,1	46,8	30,8	24,5	15,6	27,4	220.866
Mississippi rural	46,9	38,9	28,0	22,5	15,7	27,4	470.741
Oregon rural	39,9	31,9	20,6	15,4	9,0	14,1	281.169

CHILD POVERTY IN THE U.S: A NEW FAMILY BUDGET
APPROACH WITH COMPARISON TO EUROPEAN COUNTRIES

Table 5. (Part 1 of 7) Children Ages 0-17, by Immigrant Country or Race/Ethnic Origin,

	% Asian (non-Hispanic)	% Black (non-Hispanic)	% Hispanic	% White (non-Hispanic)	Mother Bachelor's Degree or More	Mother Some College	Mother 0-11 Years of School	Mother 0-8 Years of School	Mother Limited English Proficient (LEP)	Baseline BB Poverty plus child & health care	Baseline Basic Budget Poverty	Official Poverty
Total Percent	4,2	14,7	16,6	62,9	22,5	54,9	17,7	5,8	11,4	38,3	21,3	14,8
Total Native Born	0,7	16,4	8,0	73,2	23,4	58,6	12,2	1,7	1,7	34,4	18,2	13,4
Total Immigrant	18,7	7,8	52,2	20,7	19,1	39,8	40,1	22,6	50,9	54,3	34,1	20,7
Low Poverty -- 0-9.9% Native-Born families												
Asian	100,0	0,0	0,0	0,0	38,6	73,8	6,3	1,2	2,6	26,8	13,7	7,7
White	0,0	0,0	0,0	100,0	27,5	62,9	8,6	1,2	0,7	26,2	11,4	8,1
Low Poverty -- 0-9.9% Immigrant families												
Paraguay	5,2	1,6	72,7	19,8	43,6	68,9	11,9	6,1	32,6	26,6	8,8	2,4
Ireland	1,0	1,5	1,6	95,8	33,5	69,5	5,5	0,4	2,0	20,7	7,6	2,9
New Zealand	4,0	3,1	2,5	75,0	40,7	73,3	6,8	1,1	1,3	22,7	7,5	2,9
North Ireland	2,7	0,0	0,0	97,3	45,2	82,4	2,6	0,2	1,4	22,4	6,7	3,7
Azores	1,7	0,9	3,1	92,0	3,9	26,6	35,5	17,9	20,3	37,0	13,9	4,8
South Africa, U of	5,1	7,6	0,8	86,3	51,3	78,6	5,1	0,9	4,3	20,0	9,8	4,8
Netherlands	5,1	3,7	2,6	87,7	42,9	78,1	4,2	0,0	7,7	18,0	10,6	4,9
Australia	6,9	2,4	2,5	87,4	42,1	71,9	11,0	0,4	4,7	21,4	9,4	4,9
Philippines	83,8	3,2	3,9	8,3	46,8	77,1	8,0	3,1	24,8	25,6	11,6	5,1
United Kingdom	5,2	9,8	2,5	82,1	37,5	75,2	4,1	0,3	2,1	19,7	9,1	5,3
Cyprus	2,1	0,0	1,5	96,3	41,1	74,5	9,9	2,2	17,2	22,5	11,9	5,4
Sri Lanka (Ceylon)	84,0	4,2	4,3	5,7	38,4	69,5	7,7	0,3	21,4	21,3	10,2	5,5
Other N/W Europe	2,7	2,5	3,0	91,0	49,2	83,1	3,3	0,8	9,6	17,9	9,2	5,6
Poland	0,6	0,5	1,8	97,0	24,7	55,5	12,1	2,3	48,4	28,1	12,9	5,7

Table 5. (Part 2 of 7) Children Ages 0-17, by Immigrant Country or Race/Ethnic Origin, Census 2000[a]

Low Poverty -- 0-9.9% — *Immigrant families (cont'd)*

	% Asian (non-Hispanic)	% Black (non-Hispanic)	% Hispanic	% White (non-Hispanic)	Mother Bachelor's Degree or More	Mother Some College	Mother 0-11 Years of School	Mother 0-8 Years of School	Mother Limited English Proficient (LEP)	Baseline BB Poverty plus child & health care	Baseline Basic Budget Poverty	Official Poverty
Canada	5,1	3,3	2,4	87,5	38,2	75,5	6,1	1,3	4,7	21,8	10,1	6,0
Austria	2,2	2,5	1,6	93,2	3 6,7	67,3	10,3	2,1	11,0	20,8	11,6	6,4
Uruguay	0,9	0,3	60,9	37,9	22,3	54,6	21,9	2,9	27,7	34,3	14,5	6,4
Italy	0,9	1,5	2,7	94,7	23,3	50,1	14,6	5,3	15,7	27,2	13,1	6,4
Zimbabwe	3,7	40,5	3,3	52,6	53,8	85,8	1,4	0,0	4,7	18,0	9,8	6,6
India	94,1	0,9	0,6	3,3	62,5	78,6	11,4	2,7	30,8	23,5	12,9	6,9
Taiwan	94,6	0,4	0,8	3,7	66,8	86,3	3,1	1,2	57,4	20,5	11,9	7,0
Portugal	0,6	1,6	4,5	92,8	10,8	34,4	34,1	17,3	31,4	31,2	14,7	7,1
Cameroon	0,0	96,1	1,3	2,6	47,3	83,2	4,2	0,8	17,1	46,5	25,2	7,2
Czechoslovakia	0,7	1,4	1,9	95,7	42,1	76,5	4,8	1,0	22,9	24,6	14,0	7,5
Japan	72,6	4,9	3,8	17,3	39,5	77,4	4,2	0,7	45,3	25,4	12,1	7,5
France	4,1	4,7	2,6	88,1	48,9	79,8	5,3	1,9	17,5	22,1	11,5	7,6
Liberia	0,6	95,7	0,6	2,9	30,6	68,2	11,4	2,2	10,6	47,9	24,7	7,7
Greece	0,5	0,8	1,4	97,0	31,3	58,5	14,7	7,4	19,5	30,8	17,8	7,9
Hong Kong	93,7	0,4	1,4	3,9	44,4	67,5	17,8	7,4	47,2	26,0	16,1	8,2
Fiji	56,6	1,9	2,2	2,8	9,5	37,1	29,3	6,6	23,0	39,9	23,0	8,2
Tanzania	48,7	30,8	3,3	10,2	51,2	80,5	6,4	0,7	17,4	23,1	11,8	8,8
Burma (Myanmar)	91,4	0,6	3,1	3,9	39,9	61,0	26,3	7,4	59,9	34,0	17,1	9,2
Hungary	1,2	0,6	1,1	97,1	40,7	69,6	6,8	0,4	14,6	28,6	15,3	9,3
Germany	1,7	9,2	4,8	83,4	28,7	62,5	8,6	1,3	8,6	27,2	13,2	9,3

Table 5. (Part 3 of 7) Children Ages 0-17, by Immigrant Country or Race/Ethnic Origin, Census 2000[a]

	Official Poverty	Baseline Basic Budget Poverty	Baseline BB Poverty plus child & health care	Mother Limited English Proficient (LEP)	Mother 0-8 Years of School	Mother 0-11 Years of School	Mother Some College	Mother Bachelor's Degree or More	% White (non-Hispanic)	% Hispanic	% Black (non-Hispanic)	% Asian (non-Hispanic)
Low Poverty -- 0-9.9% Immigrant families (cont'd)												
Ghana	9,3	19,0	40,2	20,0	3,7	12,8	60,5	24,3	1,0	1,2	97,1	0,4
Singapore	9,4	15,8	25,4	27,0	2,8	7,8	72,0	51,4	21,3	1,3	2,8	74,3
Iran	9,6	15,3	25,1	29,3	1,3	5,3	77,0	47,1	92,2	2,0	0,5	5,0
Korea	9,9	18,1	31,5	54,5	2,4	7,9	66,6	39,9	6,9	1,2	2,4	89,2
Medium Poverty -- 10-19.9% Native-Born families												
Native Hawaiian-Pacific	17,1	29,3	48,2	4,9	1,7	12,5	50,7	12,6	0,0	0,0	0,0	0,0
Medium Poverty -- 10-19.9% Immigrant families												
Chile	10,3	21,0	34,6	37,6	2,8	13,2	65,2	31,1	29,0	69,3	1,0	0,6
Barbados	10,5	26,9	44,2	2,4	2,4	14,4	56,9	20,8	3,8	0,8	95,0	0,4
Bolivia	10,6	27,1	48,9	51,8	5,8	16,0	60,3	23,1	17,3	81,5	0,6	0,4
Spain	10,8	16,7	30,3	28,0	3,6	15,2	65,7	35,8	40,9	53,6	3,1	1,9
Belgium	11,6	18,2	24,0	12,6	1,8	9,4	70,6	46,7	91,4	3,1	4,5	1,1
Peru	12,0	26,2	44,5	51,5	3,0	13,6	58,3	23,3	18,3	80,2	0,5	0,8
Argentina	12,2	20,1	35,5	32,1	3,3	13,2	64,2	34,1	43,9	53,5	0,7	1,7
Nigeria	12,2	21,2	39,9	10,5	1,6	4,9	81,7	44,0	1,6	1,2	96,5	0,7
Uganda	12,3	17,5	31,1	11,0	3,6	7,7	83,1	56,2	7,9	0,0	50,9	40,4
Romania	12,4	20,9	35,9	36,7	3,9	17,8	55,2	32,3	96,7	1,8	0,6	0,8
Cuba	12,7	22,5	36,4	32,2	3,8	19,8	57,2	24,4	26,9	71,9	1,0	0,2
Guyana/Bri Guiana	13,0	25,1	45,1	2,5	7,0	22,7	44,4	16,1	5,1	4,2	58,9	27,4
Egypt/UnArabRep	13,1	20,5	36,4	34,5	1,8	5,7	78,9	56,5	92,6	2,1	3,6	1,4

Table 5. (Part 4 of 7) Children Ages 0–17, by Immigrant Country or Race/Ethnic Origin, Census 2000[a]

Medium Poverty -- 10-19.9% Immigrant families (cont'd)

	% Asian (non-Hispanic)	% Black (non-Hispanic)	% Hispanic	% White (non-Hispanic)	Mother Bachelor's Degree or More	Mother Some College	Mother 0-11 Years of School	Mother 0-8 Years of School	Mother Limited English Proficient (LEP)	Baseline BB Poverty plus child & health care	Baseline Basic Budget Poverty	Official Poverty
Panama	1,1	25,0	54,6	18,8	23,8	62,6	12,6	2,7	23,4	39,9	22,0	13,2
China	97,0	0,3	0,6	2,0	43,1	58,5	25,0	13,7	63,5	39,8	26,5	13,3
St. Lucia	0,0	96,2	3,2	0,6	17,8	49,3	19,4	4,7	6,9	66,8	37,4	13,4
Malaysia	86,1	2,2	0,8	10,2	42,1	63,5	16,2	5,7	34,3	33,3	22,0	13,5
Brazil	2,6	3,7	10,3	82,9	30,8	55,7	18,1	8,1	44,6	44,3	25,6	13,5
Turkey	4,9	2,1	1,2	91,3	40,1	60,0	17,0	7,8	38,1	37,2	20,8	13,6
Indonesia	73,8	1,4	1,8	22,1	43,1	73,8	10,1	3,8	40,5	33,9	23,8	13,8
Bulgaria	0,3	0,9	0,3	98,1	54,9	74,7	4,6	2,7	41,1	38,9	22,6	13,8
Jamaica	0,5	95,1	1,7	2,4	18,4	55,4	18,8	2,3	1,9	48,4	27,8	13,9
Grenada	0,9	97,0	0,9	1,1	21,2	55,7	15,6	2,7	0,4	48,9	28,3	14,5
Venezuela	1,5	0,7	71,6	25,9	36,4	66,2	15,2	5,5	48,5	43,9	25,9	14,6
Morocco	1,4	6,5	4,2	87,5	34,3	60,8	18,0	4,3	25,2	46,7	29,2	15,1
Trinidad & Tobago	8,2	80,1	4,0	6,0	17,8	53,5	16,6	4,1	1,4	47,5	27,0	15,3
Oth IndSubcon/MidEast	32,5	1,1	1,1	64,7	33,3	64,7	13,8	4,5	30,4	44,8	26,2	15,4
Lebanon	3,4	0,7	2,1	93,7	32,0	62,3	15,9	3,8	24,6	39,3	22,8	15,5
Colombia	0,2	0,6	82,7	16,2	22,2	51,1	21,6	6,8	57,1	48,9	29,8	15,8
Syria	3,7	0,3	1,3	94,4	30,1	57,5	23,2	8,4	40,9	46,6	31,2	15,9
Costa Rica	0,4	5,4	77,0	17,1	13,9	47,5	24,6	10,6	47,2	49,6	27,5	16,9
Nicaragua	0,3	0,9	86,3	12,3	11,3	37,4	34,4	11,2	58,0	57,7	35,0	17,2
St. Vincent	1,7	94,3	1,4	2,6	14,9	44,7	24,3	3,4	2,7	54,4	35,8	17,8

Table 5. (Part 5 of 7) Children Ages 0-17, by Immigrant Country or Race/Ethnic Origin, Census 2000[a]

	% Asian (non-Hispanic)	% Black (non-Hispanic)	% Hispanic	% White (non-Hispanic)	Mother Bachelor's Degree or More	Mother Some College	Mother 0-11 Years of School	Mother 0-8 Years of School	Mother Limited English Proficient (LEP)	Baseline BB Poverty plus child & health care	Baseline Basic Budget Poverty	Official Poverty
High Poverty -- 20.0+% Native-Born families												
Ecuador	0,5	0,7	87,1	11,5	12,1	43,0	30,9	13,9	59,2	56,4	35,0	17,8
Algeria	0,4	9,0	2,4	87,3	39,6	67,2	9,7	3,1	40,6	35,2	27,2	18,0
Vietnam	94,7	0,8	1,1	3,1	13,8	36,2	43,6	21,4	72,6	46,7	30,3	18,2
Belize/Brit Honduras	1,1	68,7	19,8	8,9	13,1	50,8	17,0	5,3	8,9	51,4	32,5	18,2
Antigua-Barbuda	0,0	96,1	2,0	1,9	20,6	54,1	21,0	1,5	0,9	50,4	30,1	18,4
Israel/Palestine	2,5	1,0	1,0	95,0	38,8	63,4	15,0	3,2	25,2	39,4	26,1	18,6
St. Kitts-Nevis	0,0	97,7	1,1	1,3	18,5	51,0	19,1	1,8	0,3	57,0	41,6	19,7
Jordan	4,9	0,9	2,1	92,0	24,1	53,5	16,7	3,3	33,1	54,0	33,8	19,7
Africa, non-specified	6,0	70,8	2,5	20,1	26,6	59,7	18,3	8,0	28,2	49,7	31,3	19,7
Ethiopia	0,5	95,9	0,9	2,6	19,4	53,9	21,0	9,7	38,9	54,8	32,6	19,8
Other Hispanic	0,0	0,0	100,0	0,0	10,9	44,3	24,5	4,7	8,7	50,3	29,1	20,7
Native American	0,0	0,0	0,0	0,0	11,5	48,3	19,7	2,6	4,9	52,2	31,1	24,1
Puerto Rican Mainland	0,0	0,0	100,0	0,0	10,7	44,0	24,6	3,5	7,9	58,8	38,9	27,6
Black	0,0	100,0	0,0	0,0	11,4	46,6	21,1	1,8	0,8	60,1	39,9	31,4
Puerto Rican Isl-Origin	0,0	0,0	100,0	0,0	9,6	35,9	37,2	10,7	39,1	65,9	47,1	34,2
High Poverty -- 20.0+% Immigrant families												
Cape Verde	0,0	75,1	7,2	16,1	7,8	30,0	47,6	21,0	53,9	63,2	36,5	20,0
Former USSR	1,0	0,4	0,6	97,8	44,1	69,7	10,1	1,9	58,0	45,1	29,6	20,1
Other Oceania	3,4	4,0	1,2	3,5	9,3	40,1	21,0	3,8	31,1	62,2	36,5	20,2
Pakistan	90,8	0,8	1,0	6,2	43,1	60,1	21,5	8,1	47,3	52,7	35,3	20,4

Table 5. (Part 6 of 7) Children Ages 0-17, by Immigrant Country or Race/Ethnic Origin, Census 2000[a]

High Poverty -- 20.0+% Immigrant families (cont'd)

	% Asian (non-Hispanic)	% Black (non-Hispanic)	% Hispanic	% White (non-Hispanic)	Mother Bachelor's Degree or More	Mother Some College	Mother 0-11 Years of School	Mother 0-8 Years of School	Mother Limited English Proficient (LEP)	Baseline BB Poverty plus child & health care	Baseline Basic Budget Poverty	Official Poverty
Yugoslavia	0,6	0,6	1,3	97,3	16,8	37,1	26,9	15,0	54,9	48,0	29,5	20,5
Kenya	22,4	69,9	0,5	7,0	36,2	75,1	10,9	6,2	17,5	47,7	30,3	20,8
Albania	0,1	0,5	1,0	97,5	22,7	36,1	20,5	11,7	70,4	62,9	36,9	21,9
Senegal	1,4	91,5	3,1	4,0	22,9	43,3	35,3	12,8	33,7	61,7	39,3	21,9
El Salvador	0,3	0,6	93,4	5,4	4,3	17,5	63,3	35,8	70,0	68,2	43,0	22,7
Indochina, non-specified	23,3	2,0	1,7	72,4	25,7	48,0	26,3	7,8	48,8	58,2	38,6	22,9
Haiti	0,2	96,6	1,8	1,0	11,5	38,0	36,5	12,2	51,0	65,3	42,4	23,2
Other Caribbean	1,5	76,8	11,7	9,1	19,8	52,7	22,4	7,1	10,5	55,6	38,2	23,3
Guatemala	0,4	0,8	92,1	6,1	7,9	22,4	58,9	38,0	67,5	66,7	44,1	23,9
Iraq	6,7	0,1	1,7	91,2	17,1	36,3	39,7	22,1	55,1	52,9	34,5	26,3
Bangladesh	93,4	1,4	0,8	2,2	32,5	49,2	30,7	10,3	67,0	62,5	44,9	27,6
Honduras	0,2	2,1	88,5	8,9	8,1	25,8	50,8	28,2	63,5	67,6	44,5	27,6
Afghanistan	34,1	0,0	0,3	65,0	18,8	47,3	28,8	12,9	57,8	64,2	43,8	28,5
Dominican Republic	0,7	67,0	30,6	0,9	15,6	44,2	30,5	5,6	24,2	56,1	41,9	28,9
Eritrea	0,0	99,0	0,0	1,0	13,2	32,8	35,1	16,7	57,6	62,3	39,6	29,7
Mexico	0,1	0,3	97,3	2,2	3,5	14,7	67,6	42,3	68,2	73,1	47,2	30,0
Thailand	87,8	2,5	1,3	7,2	14,0	29,7	53,1	41,9	65,8	61,1	40,6	30,4
Laos	96,0	0,5	0,7	1,6	4,0	19,0	59,8	43,4	73,2	69,4	42,5	31,4
Dominican Republic	0,3	2,0	92,8	4,6	9,8	35,2	40,6	16,6	65,8	72,5	51,6	31,9
Saudi Arabia	30,6	6,0	0,9	62,1	40,3	61,6	14,6	5,5	51,6	60,6	41,9	32,2

Table 5. (Part 7 of 7) Children Ages 0-17, by Immigrant Country or Race/Ethnic Origin, Census 2000[a]

High Poverty -- 20.0+% Immigrant families (cont'd)	Official Poverty	Baseline Basic Budget Poverty	Baseline BB Poverty plus child & health care	Mother Limited English Proficient (LEP)	Mother 0-8 Years of School	Mother 0-11 Years of School	Mother Some College	Mother Bachelor's Degree or More	% White (non-Hispanic)	% Hispanic	% Black (non-Hispanic)	% Asian (non-Hispanic)
Cambodia (Kampuchea)	33,7	46,1	63,9	72,9	40,4	59,6	22,2	5,5	1,6	1,2	1,6	94,6
YemenArabRep(N)	42,0	53,9	72,5	65,3	52,6	60,1	20,9	9,2	80,0	1,0	2,3	16,6
Sudan	43,9	51,2	76,2	56,1	23,2	33,2	45,2	30,0	13,1	0,5	85,9	0,5
Somalia	60,9	74,2	90,2	75,0	37,2	51,5	24,7	8,5	1,2	0,1	97,7	0,6

[a] See http://mumford.albany.edu/children/index_sg.htm for additional results for about 200 child indicators by detailed age of children, country of origin, immigrant generation, and geographic locality in the U.S.

CHILD BENEFIT PACKAGES IN 22 COUNTRIES

Jonathan Bradshaw

Introduction

Every industrial country has a 'package' of tax allowances, cash benefits, exemptions from charges, subsidies and services in kind, which assist parents with the costs of raising children. This package plays a part, along with labour market income, in tackling market driven child poverty. Parts of the package assist parents in employment: by subsidising low earnings, subsidising childcare costs, creating or structuring financial incentives or disincentives to be in employment or to work part-time or full-time or, in couples, have one parent or two parents working. Other parts of the package assist parents to stay out of the labour market, enabling them to stay at home to care. The package may influence the number of children a women will have and the birth spacing. It may also have an impact on family form making it more or less easy for a parent to separate or bring up a child alone.

This chapter is an investigation of variations in the structure and level of this package in 22 countries as at July 2001[1]. The data was obtained by national informants who provided data on family demography and labour supply and details of their tax benefits, cash benefits and services in their countries. They also completed a matrix, which simulated how *model families* would be treated by the child benefit package in their country. The analysis updates earlier work on the child benefit package undertaken in a series of studies (Bradshaw and Piachaud 1980, Bradshaw et al 1993, Bradshaw et al 1996, Ditch et al 1995, 1996 and 1998).

The model family method is an attempt to compare social policies on a systematic basis. The procedure is to identify a specific range of model families. In this project we included couples with 1–3 children and lone parents with 1–2 children. The children's ages ranged from under 3 to 17. This choice enables us to compare childless couples and families with children; the treatment of childcare costs for a lone parent and variations in the package for couples by the number of children. For each family a variety of income cases have to be specified. In this project we included earnings at half average, average and twice average and covered one and two earner families. There was also a »base« case without earnings and living on social assistance. The policies that are taken into account in the package are tax benefits, income related cash benefits, non income related cash benefits, social insurance contributions, rent/housing benefits, local taxes/benefits, child care costs/benefits, social assistance, guaranteed child support and other support (such as food stamps in the US). We also took account of any charges (and benefits such as free school meals) for schooling and a standard package of health care.

Housing costs are particularly difficult to handle in this kind of comparative research and there is no good solution. We have opted to follow the OECD method of assuming that our families are tenants and that rent is 20 per cent of average earnings and does not vary with family size and type. There is further discussion of these problems in (Kuivalainen (2003), Bradshaw and Finch (2002) and Bradshaw and Finch (2004)).

There is of course scope for argument about these assumptions. The method is designed to ensure that like is being compared with like. The results are illustrative not representative. They present a formal picture of how policy **should** operate given the law and regulations, not necessarily how it **does** operate. In particular no allowance is made for non take-up of income-tested cash benefits or tax benefits. Also after the impact of the package, families have to pay different prices for commodities, and in some countries they have to pay for services that are free or subsidised in other countries. We have taken some account of variation in the costs of living by expressing the value of the package in terms of purchasing power parities.

Of course policies that help parents with the costs of child rearing operate in the context of varying national family patterns, varying labour market conditions and variations in the level of earnings from employment.

Tax benefit and cash benefits for children

In most countries the most important parts of the child benefit package are tax benefits and cash benefits, income-related and non-income related. Countries use different mixes of these mechanisms for delivering help to families and the value of that help varies by family type and size, the age of the child and by earnings level. Chart 1 summarises the value of tax benefits and cash benefits for a couple plus two children for one earner on half average male earnings. Chart 2 is for the same family type but for two earners on average male and half average female earnings. In Chart 1 at this low earnings level it is the Anglophone countries that tend to make most use of tax benefits, however among the EU countries Belgium, Germany and the Netherlands also have tax benefits. At this level of earnings, perhaps surprisingly the package in the USA, Luxembourg and the UK are the most generous. In the USA a two-child family at this income level receives more than £600 per month more than a child less couple with these earnings – in Food Stamps and Earned Income Tax Credit. Spain has no child benefit package at this earnings level.

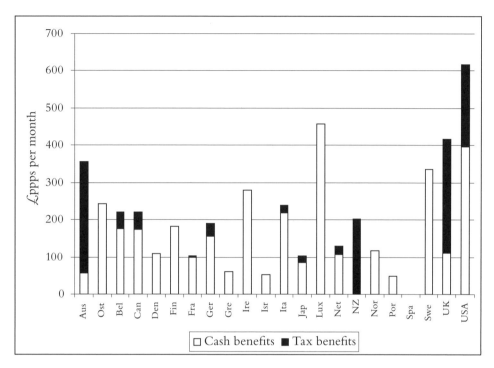

Chart 1: Cash benefits and tax benefits for children: Couple plus two children aged 7 and 14 July 2001. One earner half average earnings.

The family in Chart 2 has two earners and is much better off. Now New Zealand no longer pay any child benefit, generally the Anglophone countries have lower support than in the previous chart and some of the EU countries, Belgium, France, Germany and Luxembourg have the most generous support. More countries also have tax benefits at this level of earnings – child tax allowances that only benefit tax payers and are of most benefit to higher earning families.

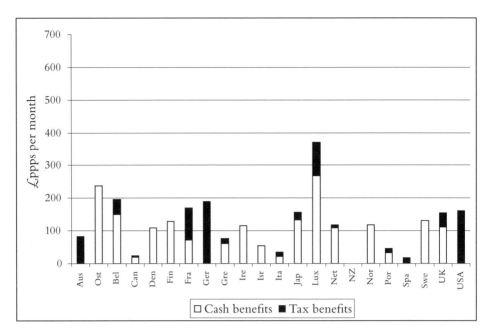

Chart 2: Cash benefits and tax benefits for children: Couple plus two aged 7 and 14. July 2001. Two earners average male and half average female.

Housing costs

So far we have only compared the cash benefit and tax benefit parts of the package. Housing costs are an important element of the child benefit package. The majority of countries (all but six) have a demand side subsidy or housing benefit scheme that reduces the gross rent paid by low income households and in the majority of these the amount of rent reduction is greater when there are children in the household. So housing benefits are an important component of the child benefit package but also one, which is very difficult to deal with in comparative studies (Bradshaw and Finch 2004, Kuivalainen 2002). It can be seen in Chart 3 that housing benefit systems make a substantial contribution to reducing housing costs for a low income couple with two children in Australia, Austria, Denmark, Finland, France, Germany, Ireland the Netherlands, New Zealand and the USA and they make a smaller contribution in Greece, Luxembourg, Norway, Sweden and the UK.

JONATHAN BRADSHAW

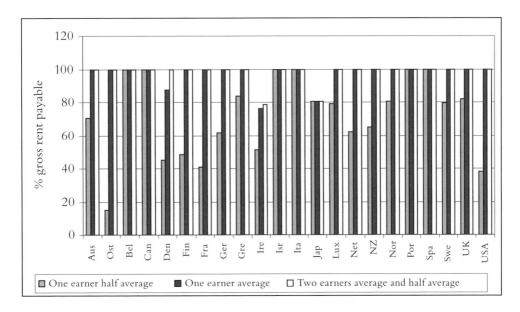

Chart 3: % gross rent paid by family type: Couple plus two children. July 2001

Childcare

Subsidies towards the costs of childcare are also important. The study took account of the costs of full-time, formal pre-school childcare of the most prevalent type in each country. The costs of preschool childcare are shown in Chart 4[2] which shows the net costs of pre–school childcare for a lone parent with one preschool child at low and average earnings and for a couple who are both earning average earnings. For two earner couples, the cost of childcare falls heavily upon the parents and more than wipes out the value of the child benefit package for some families in some countries. Countries use a variety of different methods for helping parents with the costs of preschool childcare. Only Ireland, Israel and Spain have no subsidy of any kind towards these costs. The level of help depends on income in many countries. For the better off couple the highest levels of net childcare costs are found in the Ireland, New Zealand, the Netherlands, UK and the USA.

Out of school provision for children with working parents has not been a policy priority for most of the countries in this study. However, demand is high and countries are beginning to acknowledge this, especially for the younger age groups. In many countries fees are being reduced in much the same way as for pre-school childcare.

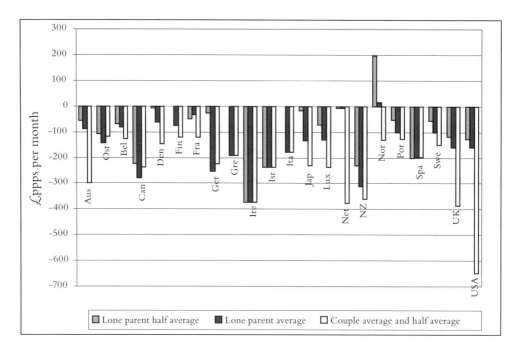

Chart 4: Costs of fulltime childcare after subsidies per month. July 2001

The costs of schooling (and value of benefits like free school meals) were explored in the original study but where they exist do not have a major impact on the child benefit package and they will not be the focus of analysis here although they are taken into account in the analysis below.

The study also included the costs of a standard package of health care. Most countries have either free health care for children or they mitigate charges at low earnings levels. There are only two countries in which health charges represent a substantial drain on the child benefit package – the USA and the Netherlands. In Australia, Canada and Ireland they represent a lesser yet significant drain on the child benefit package.

Maternity leave, paternity leave, parental leave and leave to care for sick children are all important parts of the child benefit package and closely linked to childcare policy for the under threes. However although such provision was covered in the original study it will not be dealt with here.

Social assistance

The package discussed so far is what is paid to families with earnings. To obtain a perspective on the value of benefits paid to families out of employment we compare the level of social assistance paid in our 22 countries. There is considerable variation between countries in what they consider to be the appropriate level of their social assistance benefits and also in how they evaluate the relative needs of families of different sizes and types. It can be seen from Chart 5 that after housing costs and services the overall level of the social assistance package is highest for lone parents with one child in Austria, Denmark, Netherlands, Norway, and the UK and lowest in Portugal and Spain (there is effectively no social assistance in Greece). For couples with three children it is highest in Austria, Australia, Luxembourg, and Sweden and lowest in Spain and Italy.

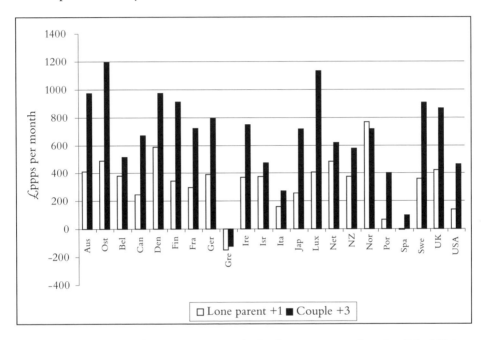

Chart 5: Net income on social assistance per month after housing costs and services. July 2001.

The structure and level of the child benefit package

In our previous study based on the situation in 1992 (Bradshaw et al. 1993), the main vehicle for delivering the child benefit package was non-income related child benefits. At that time the contribution of income related child benefits had grown in importance, but child tax benefits had diminished in importance, and were being employed by fewer countries – perhaps because they tended to be of most benefit to better off families in the countries that had them.

In this study (which includes more countries) non income-related child benefit is still the most popular vehicle for delivering the child benefit package. Only seven countries do not have any non-income related child benefits – Canada and Germany have abandoned theirs, and the Australian scheme, which was effectively universal, is no longer so except for lone parents. In addition to these New Zealand, Portugal, Spain and the USA lack a non income-related child benefit.

One country, the UK, has abandoned its income-related child benefit and now 13 countries have income related child benefits or social assistance for employed families.

The main shift has been towards using the income tax system to distribute resources to families with children. The Anglophone countries have all introduced or developed tax credits for children. For low-income families they are now an important element of the package. Out of all the countries only Austria, Denmark, Finland, Ireland, Israel, Norway, Portugal and Sweden have no recognition of the needs of children in their income tax arrangements.

Housing benefits are an important component of the package at low-income levels in some countries. Education costs and health costs in most countries reduce the value of the package but only by modest amounts. As long as childcare costs are not involved the child benefit package is a positive contribution to family incomes in most countries. Chart 6 presents a summary of the structure of the package for a couple with two school age children with one earner on average male earnings.

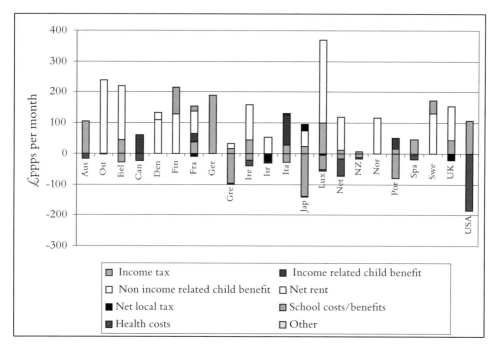

Chart 6: Structure of the child benefit package for a Couple plus two children with one earner on average earnings. July 2001

However this is for just one family and the most important conclusion of the comparisons of the levels of the child benefit package is that they vary within and between countries by family size and type, by earnings and by whether the comparison is made of the tax and cash benefit system only or after housing and service costs and benefits. This is illustrated for selective cases in Charts 7 to 9. Chart 7 shows how the package varies by family size. France for example comes well down the league table in its child benefit for small families but is much more generous to families with three or more children. The UK in contrast is unusual in having a package that benefits one child families relatively more generously and Finland does not pay anything extra for the third and subsequent child in a family.

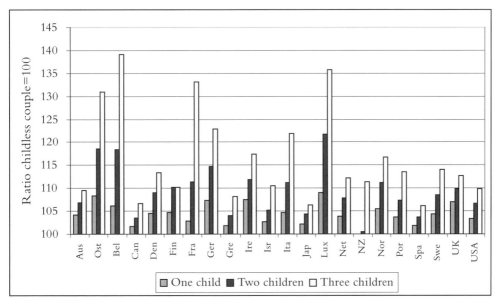

Chart 7: Value of the child benefit package by number of children. One earner on average earnings. July 2001.

Chart 8 takes a standard family and shows how the child benefit package varies by earnings. The Anglophone countries have considerably larger packages for low earning families, a number of countries have a standard amount regardless of earnings and in France, Greece and Japan the value of the package increases with earnings.

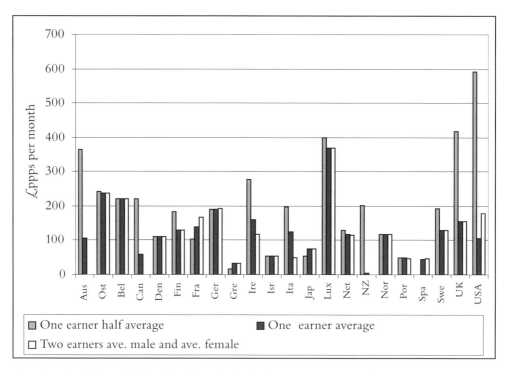

Chart 8: Value of the child benefit package by level of earnings. Couple with two children. July 2001.

Chart 9 shows how the package varies by family type. Luxembourg for example has the most generous child benefit package for couples with children but it does not have the most generous package for lone parents. Some countries are neutral to lone parents including Australia, Canada and the UK, others favour lone parents over couples – Austria is most generous to lone parents and most of the Nordic countries are also, Denmark is the exception. Others favour couples over lone parents including many of the continental EU countries with the notable exception of the Netherlands.

JONATHAN BRADSHAW

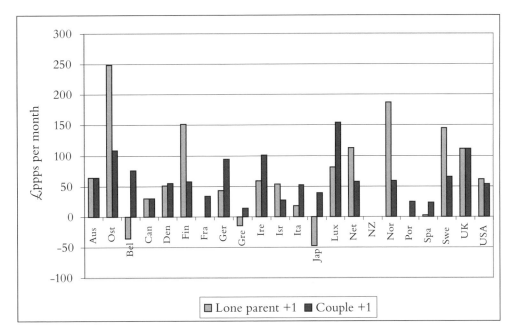

Chart 9: Value of the child benefit package by family type. One earner average earnings. July 2001.

The implications of these variations is that it is unsafe to take one or a few standard families to represent a country's child benefit package. This is one of the drawbacks of the OECD series Benefits and Wages (OECD 2004) that includes only couples and single parents with two children.

Replacement rates[3] and marginal tax rates[4]

The data on the tax benefit package for families in work and on social assistance can be used to assess replacement rates and marginal tax rates. Some countries have very high replacement rates and they do not tend to be the countries that are most anxious about incentives to work. It can be seen in Chart 10 that Australia, the UK, the USA and Canada have comparatively low replacement rates for couples. They are higher for lone parents who need childcare in Canada, Ireland New Zealand. However there are countries like Denmark, Germany, Israel, Luxembourg, New Zealand and Norway, who are managing with very high replacement rates.

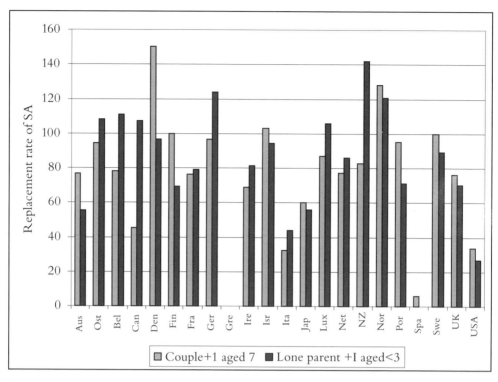

Chart 10: Notional replacement rates – net income in employment at half average earnings as a % of net income on social assistance.

The Anglophone countries, which are most anxious about the impact of work incentives on labour supply, do have comparatively high marginal tax rates at the lower end of the earnings distribution. This is because they rely more than other countries on income related benefits and tax credits, which are withdrawn as earnings increase. The loss of childcare benefits is a particular cause of high marginal tax rates for lone parents as can be seen in Chart 11.

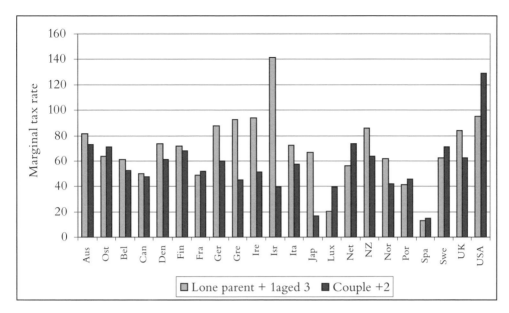

Chart 11: Marginal tax rates on moving from half average to average earnings

Summary rankings

Given the finding that there is considerable variation in the child benefit package by family type, number of children, level of earnings and whether the comparison is made before or after housing costs, and the costs and benefits of services it was not easy to produce an overall comparison of the level of the child benefit package. Chart 12 presents the overall ranking of the average child benefit package paid to a 'representative' sample of families. The selection is of course not representative in the real sampling sense because the mix of family types and earnings levels varies from country to country. Ideally we would like to be able to adjust the child benefit package to the general pattern of family types/earnings levels of each country – but that is a considerable challenge for comparative work, though the European Social Survey may be an excellent basis for it in the future, at least for European Countries.

Austria has a package, which is considerably more generous than any other country. The negative child benefit package for some countries is because housing costs and charges for services cancel out the values of tax and cash benefits for children. There appear to be four groups:

Leaders: Austria, Luxembourg, Finland.
Second rank: France, Sweden, Germany, Belgium, UK, Denmark, Norway, Australia.

Third rank: Ireland, Israel, Canada, USA, the Netherlands and Italy.
Laggards: New Zealand, Portugal, Spain, Japan, and Greece.

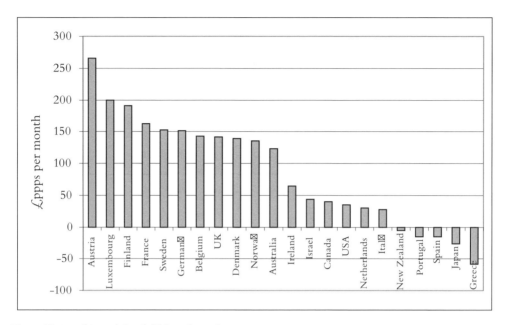

Chart 12: Ranking of the child benefit package.

This ranking is expressed in purchasing power parities and it is somewhat different if it is expressed as a proportion of average earnings. Chart 13 does this and it can be seen that there are some rerankings. France moves up the league table for example and the UK moves down. However in broad terms the classification is sustained – Austria is an outlier at the top of the distribution, Finland is very good, and many of the EU countries have generous child benefit packages. The Netherlands does not given its circumstances and resources and Italy and the southern European countries are clearly laggards.

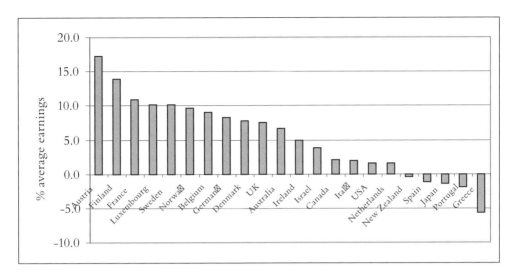

Chart 13: Rankings of the child benefit package as % average earnings.

Conclusion

The countries with the most generous overall child benefit package are not those countries which employ a substantial element of targeting, either through tax credits, or income related benefits. They are the countries that deliver most if not all their value as a non-income related child benefit.

The rankings that have been obtained bear little relationship to the rankings that would be inferred using Esping-Anderson's (1991) regime types. The social democratic (Nordic) welfare states tend come in the top half of the table but they are not the leaders and Denmark and Norway are well down the rankings. The liberal (Anglophone) welfare states are distributed throughout the rankings with the UK and Australia in the second rank. New Zealand is consistently towards the bottom of the rankings. The conservative (corporatist) countries tend to be found in the upper half of the table but the Netherlands is a big exception. Austria is something of an outlier with considerably more generous child benefit package than any other country after housing costs and services. The southern EU countries are in the bottom half of the table but spread, with Italy somewhat above the others. Japan, our only representative of the Pacific Rim/Confucian model, is found towards the bottom.

In the original study we undertook some analysis which sought to explain the variation in the rankings. There is scope for further work on the association between the child benefit package and the characteristics of countries – both their inputs and their outcomes. There may also be potential for some multivariate analysis, though the number of countries is a constraint on this. It appears that it is not the level of the wealth of a nation, nor the character of its labour market, nor the level of earnings but rather its social expenditure and especially the share of its social expenditure going to families, as against the elderly, that determines the child benefit package. The level of the child benefit package achieved is also associated with success in reducing market-generated levels of child poverty and it is also possibly associated with higher fertility rates. Those countries that make most effort to transfer resources horizontally have the most generous child benefit packages. Nations make choices. The policies that they choose have an impact on the financial burdens born by parents raising children.

This is not the only way in which the effort of welfare states to support families with children can be compared. Comparisons of inputs can be made by comparing social expenditure on families. Comparisons of outcomes can be compared using micro social data on child poverty (see my other chapter). The two can be combined in studies using micro simulation techniques such as Euromod. The advantages of the model family method is that it can produce up-to-date comparisons, fairly easily, which give insights into how different family types are treated within and between countries by their tax and benefit systems.

References

Bradshaw, J. and N. Finch (2002): *A Comparison of Child Benefit Packages in 22 Countries*, Research report 174, London: Department for Work and Pensions, www.dwp.gov.uk/asd/asd5/rrep174.asp, 30 April 2005.

Bradshaw, J. and N. Finch (2004): 'Housing benefits in 22 countries', *Benefits*, **12** (2), 87-94.

Bradshaw, J. and D. Piachaud (1980): *Child Support in the European Community*, London: Bedford Square Press.

Bradshaw, J., S. Kennedy, M. Kilkey, S. Hutton, A. Corden, T. Eardley, H. Holmes and J. Neale (1996): *Policy and the Employment of Lone Parents in 20 Countries, The EU Report*, European Observatory on National Family Policies, York: EU/University of York.

Bradshaw, J., J. Ditch, H. Holmes and P. Whiteford, (1993): *Support for Children: A Comparison of Arrangements in Fifteen Countries*, Department of Social Security Research Report 21, London: HMSO.

Bradshaw, J., N. Finch and E. Mayhew (2005): 'Financial incentives and mothers' employment: a comparative perspective', in P. Saunders (ed.), *Welfare to Work in Practice: Social Security and Participation in Economic and Social Life*, International Studies in Social Security, Volume 10, Aldershot: Ashgate Publishing.

Ditch, J., H. Barnes and J. Bradshaw (1996): *A Synthesis of National Family Policies in 1995*, York: European Observatory on National Family Policies, CEC.

Ditch, J., H. Barnes, J. Bradshaw and M. Kilkey (1998): *A Synthesis of National Family Policies*, European Observatory on National Family Policies, EC/University of York.

Ditch, J., H. Barnes, J. Bradshaw, J. Commaille and T. Eardley (1995): *A Synthesis of National Family Policies in 1994*, York: European Observatory on National Family Policies, CEC.

Kuivalainen, S. (2003): 'How to compare the incomparable: an international comparison of the impact of housing costs on levels of social assistance', *European Journal of Social Security*, **5** (2), 128-149.

OECD (2004): 'Purchasing Power Parities, Main Economic Indicators, April 2004', www.oecd. org/std/ppp, 30 April 2005.

OECD (2004): 'Income distribution and poverty in OECD countries in the second half of the 1990s', Mimeo.

OECD (2004): *Benefits and Wages*, Paris: OECD.

Notes

1 This chapter is a summary of a study originally published as Bradshaw, J. and Finch, N. (2002) *A Comparison of Child Benefit Packages in 22 Countries*, Department for Work and Pensions Research Report No.174, Corporate Document Services: Leeds http://www.dwp.gov.uk/asd/asd5/rrep174.asp Data for Ireland and the Netherlands has been corrected since the original data was produced. The countries were Australia (Aus), Austria (Ost), Belgium (Bel), Canada (Can), Denmark (Den), Finland (Fin), France (Fra), Germany (Ger), Greece (Gre), Ireland (Ire), Israel (Isr), Italy (Ita), Japan (Jap), Luxembourg (Lux), Netherlands (Net), New Zealand (NZ), Norway (Nor), Portugal (Por), Spain (Spa), Sweden (Swe), United Kingdom (UK), United States (USA).

2 Net childcare costs here are represented as positive amounts. Norway shows a negative childcare costs because of benefits paid for a preschool child.

3 Here the proportion of net in-work income that would be »replaced« by social assistance.

4 The proportion of extra earnings that would be foregone in extra direct taxes, loss of income related benefits and extra charges.

Negotiating Childhood and Children's Welfare

Negotiating childhood poverty: Children's subjective experiences of life on a low income

Tess Ridge

This chapter takes a subjective approach to understanding the lives and experiences of low-income children, and draws on children's accounts and discourses to explore how they negotiate their lives and manage their relationships in the context of restricted social, material and structural environments. In general, children living in poverty have been seen as passive victims of poverty and disadvantage, rather than as reflexive social agents whose lives are organised by the constraints of a poor childhood. To understand how children who are poor make sense of the presence of poverty in their lives we must engage directly with them through mediums that privilege their accounts and are grounded in their subjective realities. Only by respecting children's meanings and listening to their experiences and concerns we can gain some deeper insight into how children interpret the presence of poverty in their childhoods. The chapter draws on findings from a range of qualitative studies and includes a comparative analysis of data from Country Reports[1] produced for the COST A19 programme of research, which examined child welfare across a range of European countries. Where possible these reports will be used to provide a contextual insight into a range of childhoods experienced in a variety of cultural settings, and to illuminate commonalities and differences in children's experiences.

The main focus of the chapter will be children's subjective experiences of poverty, however, in general in Europe there has been very little qualitative research carried out with low-income children. The country reports reveal that children *per se* have rarely been the central focus of data generated about their lives, and this especially so with low-income children. The chapter draws most heavily on the reports from Estonia, Ireland and the UK, which have, to differing degrees, been able to report findings from qualitative research carried out with low-income children, and these studies, with others, will be used to provide an insight into how low-income children negotiate their lives.

Each of these three countries have significant levels of child poverty. In Estonia, in 2002, children formed the largest part of the population living under the absolute poverty line, and they were the population group most at risk of experiencing poverty (Kutsar and Trumm, 1999). The Estonian report draws on a survey of children's perceptions of their economic, social and emotional well-being (Kutsar, 2000). In Ireland although child poverty rates are dropping, in 1998, one in eight children were still consistently poor[2]. The report draws on a range of qualitative insights from children, and in particular Daly and Leonard's (2002) study of low-income family life, which included interviews with children. In the UK, as elsewhere, poverty is a generational issue and children are disproportionately more likely to experience poverty than any other generational groups. During the late 1990s the proportion of children living in poverty peaked at 35 per cent, and although poverty rates are now slowly falling, poverty is still an enduring factor in the lives of a substantial number of the UK's children. The report profiles a range of studies that include findings from low-income children (Middleton et al., 1994; Davis and Ridge, 1997; Shropshire and Middleton, 1999; Roker, 1998). These studies are employed alongside findings from my own research with children living in low-income families, whose voices are used here to give depth and insight to our understanding of children's lives (Ridge, 2002).

To understand something of the impact of poverty in childhood it is first important to examine how child poverty is approached in public discourse and to highlight the images and representations of poverty that are dominant. A poor childhood does not happen in isolation and children are particularly vulnerable to images and discourses, which are shaped without any reference to the meanings and realities of their lives. In general our understandings of childhood poverty and disadvantage have developed largely in isolation from children themselves. Both as children and part of the constituency of the 'poor' their lives and experiences have tended to be obscured from the public gaze and their voices remain absent from poverty discourse (Ridge, 2002). Common perceptions of children who are poor have often been informed by media representations and public discourse, or by statistical measurement. Each of these has contributed towards generating constructions of childhood that have tended to dominate and shape public perceptions of child poverty.

Public discourse and media representation of 'poor' children

Public discourses and media representations of children who are poor are habitually simplistic, ambiguous and contradictory. What are presented are often exaggerated constructions of a 'poor' child. However, polarised accounts of 'poor' children can carry a powerful social and cultural charge. Children are often portrayed as helpless victims, passively suffering from impoverished lives (Scraton, 1997; Davis and Bourhill, 1997). Central to this discourse are also attendant notions of poor parenting. Thus the dominant framework for understanding children's experiences of poverty and its problems becomes the family setting, and hence the solution to child poverty lies within it (Scraton, 1997). The 'poor' family is then pathologised and deemed the province of expert intervention and the drive towards 'responsibilisation' of parents (Alanen, et al., 2004). These constructions simultaneously excite our protective instincts whilst obscuring the lived experience and meanings of poverty for children themselves. This construction of child poverty as a family failing is apparent across a range of different countries. Even in Finland where child poverty rates are in general low, the discourse of 'moralising familism' and the associated 'responsibilisation of parents' has meant that even the *direct* effects of poverty on children's material well-being and choices are treated indirectly, from the viewpoint of the protective influence of good parenting' (Alanen, et al., 2004). Privatising poverty within the family obscures the disproportionate generational impact of many government policies on poverty in childhood, especially during periods of recession as in the 1980s in the UK and in the early 1990s in Finland (Oppenheim and Harker, 1996; Alanen et al., 2004). Conversely, 'poor children' have also been portrayed as dangerous beings, children out of control, representing both an immediate and a future threat to society, stability and social order (Davis and Bourhill, 1997; Lee, 2001). These representations and attendant 'behavioural' discourses set up powerful cultural and symbolic notions of poverty which can rebound into all areas of low-income children's lives, generating bigotry, ignorance and in some cases fear. They are ordered and given substance through prejudice and the specificities of class, ethnicity, age and gender (Goldson, 1997; 2001; Lee, 2001). Such images and constructions can have a significant social, cultural and structural impact on the everyday lives of poor children among their peers, nourishing the potential for stigma, difference and social exclusion.

Statistical accounting

Statistical accounting has also been a key site in which childhood poverty has been constructed and reconstructed over time. Statistical measurements of all aspects of children's lives have played a central role in how children's lives have been portrayed (Qvortrup et al., 1994). Historically statistics have tended to obscure rather than reveal children's lives, and there has been an absence of data relating to the well-being of children which put the child at the centre of the inquiry (ibid.). This is particularly so in relation to child poverty. Low-income children have rarely been the focus of poverty studies and their disproportionate vulnerability to poverty has often emerged only as an adjunct to the study of adult poverty (Saporiti 2001; Ridge, 2002). In effect, in the past, children were more likely to be highlighted as a cause of adult poverty than recognised as a generational group that was itself highly vulnerable to poverty. The traditional focus on household measures, and the 'familialisation' of childhood has meant that lives and experiences of low-income children have tended to be concealed both within the family and by adult-centred statistical accounting and research methodologies (Qvortrup, 1997). The Italian report highlights how the intensely privatised nature of Italian childhood has meant that the experiences of children who are poor are easily obscured by their status as subordinates within their families. In Italy, as in other countries, information on children's lives has often been drawn from proxy sources. In this way children's lives are unveiled only as a by-product of interviews with parents or other adults with their care.

However, the measurement and monitoring of the economic well-being of children has greatly improved and there is now a considerable body of statistical knowledge which explores the dynamics and consequences of child poverty (see among others the COST A19 Country Reports: Jensen et al., 2004, Ruxton, 1996; Bradshaw, 2000). As a result we know an increasing amount about which children are vulnerable to experiencing poverty, and under what circumstances. These studies provide a valuable insight into the possible consequences for children of experiencing poverty in childhood. However, statistical data is also often used as an authoritative social and political tool for driving policy interventions in the lives of children and their families. Research, which purports to 'know' about children and the experiences of childhood, can be instrumental in informing social policies and public perceptions. Theories and ideas about experiences in childhood of which children themselves have had little or no input can directly infringe on how children experience their childhoods (James, 1993).

Children who are experiencing poverty are vulnerable to research findings that may distort their lives and render their childhood experiences insignificant, particularly in relation to their future adult selves. From statistical research, we know substantially more about the outcomes of child poverty in adulthood than we do about the experience of poverty in childhood. Therefore, the child becomes the project for the future, rather than the agent of the present. Children who are poor are often seen as the most likely to fail as 'satisfactory' adult citizens, as a consequence 'poor children' easily become conceptualised as future 'poor adults'. Especially when situated in the context of statistical accounts that present the spectres of unemployment, illiteracy, teenage pregnancy and family instability as the heritage that awaits them. Clearly the outcomes of childhood poverty are critical and significant in their own right, but a dominant conception of children as future citizens and workers rather than children experiencing poverty in the immediacy of childhood, leaves us without any textural insight into childhood itself. The future well-being of children as adult citizens and workers is the key priority of a 'child-centred social investment strategy' as outlined by Esping-Andersen (2002). However, positioning the child as the 'citizen-worker' of the future rather than the 'citizen-child' of the present has profound implications for children's lives (Lister, 2003). As Prout (2000) argues government policies which draw heavily on poverty studies linking childhood poverty with poor adult outcomes are focused primarily on 'the better adult lives that will, it is predicted, emerge from reducing child poverty. ...not on the better lives that children will lead as children' (pp 305).

Engaging with children

In general we remain largely ignorant of how children might interpret their experiences of poverty and how those experiences may be mediated through their differences and become embedded in a range of social and structural environments. When setting out the theoretical and practical challenges of engaging meaningfully with children we need to 'adopt practices which resonate with children's own concerns and routines', furthermore 'attention must be given to the wider discourses of childhood, to the power relations, organisational structures and social inequalities which in large part, shape children's everyday lives' (Christensen and James, 2000:7). As Qvortrup (1990) argued, if we are serious about improving the life conditions of children then at the minimum we must ensure that children's own voices are heard. Research which does not give children voice and power in the research process and treats them as 'objects' of study, rather than active subjects in their own right, risks marginalising children's lives and experiences, and leaving them vulnerable to social and political representations which others impose upon them (Grover, 2004).

The realities of poverty as a lived experience in childhood are hard to capture, and measure; they are diffuse and particular. Children do not experience poverty in isolation from their peers, friends, families and neighbourhoods; poverty is experienced in a diversity of social and cultural settings. However, some children are at much greater risk of experiencing poverty than others and the risks factors, which heighten the likelihood of children experiencing poverty in childhood, are remarkably similar across all the country reports. Children who live in families where there is unemployment or low wages are at risk, as are children who have many siblings or live in lone-mother households. Minority ethnic groups, Travellers and children of refugees and asylum-seekers, who may already be at the margins of mainstream society, are also especially vulnerable to being in poverty. Refugee children are often positioned as the 'other' and this can be especially formidable in a school situation where children are trying to fit in and make friends. The intra-generational contract between peers is strained because children are 'starting from outside of its boundaries, and as one of a group that is often negatively viewed in the wider society, the child's status is low, and the social distances to be negotiated in order to be allowed into peers groups can be great' (Candappa and Egharevba, 2002:169).

Comparative dimensions of children's economic welfare

Poverty can permeate every area of children's lives from the personal and familial to the economic, social and cultural. Children's economic status is an important indicator of their overall well-being and a crucial factor in their capacity to access material goods and participate in shared leisure activities with their peers. In this section of the chapter findings from qualitative studies and cross-country reports are used to explore the everyday lives and experience of children in different countries and compare them with those of low-income children.

In general children are not independent financial actors. As a generational group they are excluded from key economic domains such as the labour market, financial services and the property market. Their financial status is intimately bound up with their dependent status within their families. Therefore children's access to economic resources are contingent on their families' capacity to generate external funds and the inter-generational contracts between parents and children structured around economic values, resource distribution, and notions of equity which reside within their individual family settings. Parental endowment of economic resources to children in the forms of pocket money, allowances and spending money bestows semi-autonomous economic power and status on children, albeit in a limited fashion.

On the whole, children's access to economic resources is increasing and they are now perceived as major consumers in their own right (Gunter and Furnham, 1998). This commodification of childhood has generated considerable concern about the 'loss of childhood' and the rise of the 'child-consumer' and 'Kinder culture' (Steinberg and Kincheloe, 1997). Childhood has its own social and cultural demands, and the need to stay connected and identified with the prevailing trends and fashions of their peers are a driving force behind much of children's consumer behaviour. Children's need for financial resources and their desire to attain certain commodities reflect not just the 'common culture of acquisition' (Middleton et al., 1994; Daly and Leonard, 2002), but also the significance of consumer goods as a means of communication between young people (Willis et al., 1990; Miles, 2000; Hengst, 2001). In the country reports, studies that engage directly with children's patterns of consumption show that in each country children are becoming increasingly significant and often sophisticated and discerning consumers. In general the country reports identify three key areas of economic consumption for children; spending related to image maintenance and social identity, such as clothes and shoes; spending related to shared peer group activity, such as leisure goods and services, sports activities, clubs and movies; and spending on media and the development of real and virtual identities, such as magazines, videos, CDs, and mobile phones.

Children's access to autonomous incomes

For children living in poverty and disadvantage the increasing commodification of childhood and the real and symbolic nature of childhood consumption and identity creates considerable economic and social pressures. Therefore the issue of access to adequate financial and material resources to ensure the maintenance of secure social identities has profound implications for children in poverty who are experiencing constraints on intra-familial redistribution engendered by financial insecurity. A central issue therefore for many low–income children is their lack of access to their own autonomously controlled income in the form of pocket money or allowances. In the restricted environment of a low-income household the needs and concerns of children may come a poor second to the pressing concerns of day to day maintenance of the household. Access to money becomes an insecure and transient luxury, often linked to changes in family employment status or family structure (Ridge, 2002).

In general the reports showed that the majority of children in the different countries gained access to autonomously controlled income from three primary sources; pocket money; extra payments for birthdays, academic success etc; and earned income from work. The Irish report highlights a study of childhood poverty using an Index of Deprivation, which revealed that children who were shown to be 'consistently poor'[3], had very high deprivation levels in relation to pocket money (Cantillon et al., 2003). Similarly in Norway, Sandbæk (2004) found access to pocket money constrained among low-income children. A further study of children in low-income families in Ireland also shows that a quarter of children in the study did not receive pocket money and were very conscious of their low-income status and the need to live within their families' means (Daly and Leonard, 2002). Studies with low–income children featured in the UK report also reveal the difficulties children have in gaining access to regular pocket money (Middleton et al., 1994; Shropshire and Middleton, 1999; Roker, 1998; Ridge, 2002). When children do receive some pocket money they identify it as an important element in maintaining their social status and social acceptance. In Ridge's (2002) study children were using their pocket money to stay socially connected, for transport, school activities, buying clothes and meeting up with friends. For these children, pocket money was a vital source of autonomous income that allowed them to share in part in the everyday activities and culture of their friends. Here is Nicole explaining what she uses her pocket money for:

'Bus fares going into town, sometimes I save it and like try and like save enough money to get like a new pair of trousers and that takes me ages'
Nicole 13 years old (Ridge 2002:42)

The Estonian report draws on a study by Kutsar (2000) which explored children's perceptions of their household's economic performance and its impact on their lives and well-being. This showed that children who viewed the economic performance of their households as poor felt that they received less pocket money than their friends. They were also more likely to feel excluded from social events with their peers, and disadvantaged across a range of social and economic indicators. Poverty in childhood is not experienced in isolation and Kutsar's study highlights the importance of understanding and acknowledging children's subjective perceptions of their own economic and social well-being in relation to their status and standing apropos other children. It is unlikely that the provision of pocket money for children as a secure and autonomously controlled resource would be seen as a key issue for low-income children by policy makers. Adults may not value or understand the real or symbolic value of such issues for children themselves. Pocket money is important for children as it gives them some autonomous access to material goods and other opportunities. However, pocket money depends on gifts and favours and ultimately on family resources, so many children move towards greater financial autonomy through part-time paid employment.

Paid work

Country reports reveal a range of employment experiences for children, and as would be expected employment was age dependent with older children undertaking the most work. Although in Denmark it is common for children from the age of 11-12 to supplement their pocket money with income from employment. Employment patterns across countries were also ordered by gender and differing urban and rural spatial configurations. Adult 'ownership' and control of working space means that children's access to employment is legally restricted. Yet, as the German report highlights, pressures to acquire consumer goods and mobile phones can lead to increasing transgressions of employment law. In countries like Austria and Finland where the legal age for employment is 15 opportunities to earn income from part-time work are diminished, however, under these circumstances, children may well be driven to find work in the hidden economy. In Bulgaria there are signs that almost all working children are employed illegally and often during school time. Although we know that a high percentage of children and young people work, the situation of children on a low income is less clear. Low-income children are particularly at risk of undertaking illegal employment, however, across all countries there is generally a lack of data relating to low-income children's experiences of employment and without a subjective insight into children's work strategies we cannot know. The Irish report confirms the trend towards increasing employment amongst children, including research evidence of significant levels of employment among 12 year olds in Dublin (Whyte, 1995). The Irish report also reveals the link between receiving no pocket money and working. This was also apparent in a study of low-income children in the UK where low-income children who were not receiving pocket money, were likely to be in part time employment, or looking for employment (Ridge, 2002). Qualitative studies with low-income children in Ireland, Estonia and the UK all confirm the importance of employment for children who are poor. However, their opportunities for employment can be severely restricted by their neighborhood environment and the chances available to them. In general children's motivations for working 'express a relationship between choice and constraint, freedom and necessity' (Mizen et al., 2001). Furthermore, as Hengst (2001: 23) argues although children's employment is 'primarily an expression of their drive to consume, it is equally an expression of their striving for autonomy and (social) identity'. This is particularly apparent in low-income children's rationalisations about work.

> 'I just want to have my own money. I'd like to be able to have a bit of pocket money to go out and buy my own stuff and not have to ask for money all the time, and be able to say I've worked for that money, and spend it because I feel good about it'
> Lisa 15 years (Ridge 2002:49)

Employment represents an opportunity for freedom and independence, it also represents a key strategy in children's negotiations of their limited economic, social and environmental worlds. Income from employment frees them, to some degree, from the economic constraints of their family environment and renders them economic agents in their own right.

Image maintenance and social identity

A key area in which children and young people attempt to construct their own identities and lifestyles is through consumption and the diversity of ways in which meaning can be endowed upon consumer goods (Miles, 2000). For younger children the need to 'fit in' and feel part of the prevailing peer culture is strong, and research with children has shown that they are under considerable pressure to wear 'acceptable' clothes from an early age (Middleton et al., 1994; Ridge, 2002). As children get older the relationship between peer inclusion, and individually becomes more complex (Miles, 1996). Clothing, bags, shoes and personal accessories become culturally and symbolically powerful markers of both individuality and belonging. Young people use fashion and clothing as a means of making and expressing their identities (Willis et al., 1990). Research with teenagers exploring consumption and lifestyle also reveals the key role played by peer friendship groups as arbiters of identity, providing the context, and parameters, in which teenagers construct and reconstruct their identities (Miles, 2000) Evidence from the cross-country reports shows considerable commonality between children in different cultures about the importance of clothes and the consumption of image and lifestyle items. For example the Norwegian report highlights a study of children's consumption patterns that shows clothing and shoes as key purchases particularly for girls (Brusdal, 2001). For low-income children, however, the challenge of conforming to childhood norms and expectations written onto clothing and other lifestyle image goods is particularly acute. Inadequate resources and restricted opportunities affect their capacity to engage in socially and culturally appropriate behaviour. The construction and maintenance of appropriate image is considered to be an essential prerequisite for chosen peer group inclusion and the formation of secure social identities.

Children who are poor identify clothing norms and expectations as particularly important for maintaining their social status. In the Irish report, Daly and Leonard's (2002) study of children in low-income families found that clothing was the most frequently mentioned form of spending and children were often saving what little money they had over time to ensure that they could buy the 'right' forms of clothing. Where children were working their earnings went largely on either clothing or to help in household economies. In common with low-income children in the UK, Norway and Estonia, low-income children in the Irish report were struggling to be included in their peer groups and fearful of being bullied or rejected by their peers if they were unable to fulfill the requirements of accepted norms.

> Look at these crap runners [trainers] I'm wearing. My ma can't afford to get me the
> right ones and it's terrible when you can't afford the right ones. You have no choice
> but we couldn't afford it so I was the one that got picked on.
> Susan (Daly & Leonard, 2002: 137)

In the UK, children's fear of being left out or seen as different by other children fuelled their desire to have the 'right' clothes and image (Ridge, 2002). Children were very conscious of the costs of purchasing adequate clothing and were sensitive to their parent's inability to afford them. 'Those children without pocket money or other access to economic resources were particularly vulnerable and concerned about their group image and identities. (Ibid.)

Children in school

The scholarisation of children has meant that children spend a significant part of their lives within the institutional bounds of school. Listening to low-income children's subjective accounts of their school lives reveals to us areas of concern and disequilibrium which are easily obscured, overlooked or undervalued in a setting which is primarily concerned with pedagogical performance and academic outcomes. Image and identity is shaped and made meaningful in a diversity of spatial and temporal settings and the school space generates considerable social challenges for the low-income child. In Bulgaria there are growing numbers of children dropping out of school; with over one third dropping out for family – mainly financial – reasons. Roma children in particular are increasingly likely to never attend school at all (Raycheva et al., 2004). The UK report reveals that a key concern of low-income children at school is the fear of isolation and bullying within school. This is chiefly engendered by children's apprehensions about being seen as 'other' coupled with their inability to conform to institutionalised rules and expectations, especially those embedded in clothing codes. In Ridge's study (2002) low-income children expressed concerns that they were unable to participate equitably in school life across a range of different areas including school trips, extra curricular activities and resourcing materials and equipment needed for lessons and examination projects. Some children, like Martin were acutely conscious of the qualitative differences between their school experiences and those of their peers:

> I don't usually go on trips 'cos they are expensive and that … At our school they do loads of activities and they go to loads of different places … I don't bother asking'
> Martin 11 years (Ridge 2002: 77)

Whilst the focus of policy and discourse is invariably on improving low-income children's academic performances, children's own subjective accounts of their school lives reveal the sometimes overt but more often covert and subtly embedded institutional barriers that children face on a daily basis. Structural and institutional exclusion *within* school prevents children from enjoying secure, engaging and inclusive educational experiences; it also impinges on children's social presence and undermines their endeavors to construct satisfactory social identities with their school peers.

Shared peer group activity and social participation

The second key area of children's spending identified in cross-country reports was spending associated with shared peer group activity and social participation. The commodification of childhood is particularly apparent in the area of leisure activities.

The reports reveal a range of different social and leisure experiences for children in each country. However, the overall impression is of a change in children's free and leisure time and a growth in commodified leisure consumption. There has also been an increase in large corporate leisure concerns such as theme parks in Denmark and Norway and in Cyprus the growth of expensive private summer schools offering sports and leisure activities. Even in Italy where children's lives have been significantly 'privatised' within the family setting, and children's experiences of social engagement outside of the family have been severely restricted, there is a growing trend towards 'new' meeting spaces, where paying for 'access' is increasingly the norm. In Austria children's leisure interests are changing and the traditionally strong framework of institutionalized leisure opportunities for children is declining as children increasingly see commercial opportunities as more attractive. The Austrian report also highlights a key element in children's perceptions of leisure time. 'Social contacts with friends are an important component of children's own definitions of leisure time' (Beham et al., 2004:52). Children place high value on their friendships, and social relationships with like and unlike others play a vital role in children's lives. Friendship for children, as for adults, creates an entry point into wider social relationships. It plays a role as a social asset and a source of social capital, both in childhood and in the future. Conversely, difficulties in maintaining social relationships can leave children vulnerable to social exclusion (see Ridge and Millar, 2000). Difficulties in meeting friends and sharing in social activities with their peers leads to fears of social isolation, dislocation and bullying (Ridge, 2002). Therefore, while country reports show a growing trend in childhood towards leisure consumption, subjective insights from low-income children in the UK and Ireland reports reveal a different story, exposing the impact that the growing commercialisation of childhood is having on children who are poor and unable to follow the trend towards commodified social participation.

In the UK, as elsewhere, children's engagement with commodified leisure experiences are increasing with the growth of private leisure centres, expensive sports complexes, bowling alleys, multi-screen cinema complexes and so on (Mizen, 2001). However, the costs of participating and sharing in these experiences are often expensive and children who are poor find it hard to gain access to them. The problems children reported were the costs of engagement and participation, including entrance fees, transport costs and difficulties conforming to appropriate clothing and equipment codes. These are issues that may not be of concern to more affluent children and their parents, and are easily overlooked or undervalued by policy makers. Significantly, many of the children interviewed in the UK studies showed a resigned acceptance of their 'restricted' lifestyles and the limited opportunities available to them. Yet children like Mike were also acutely conscious of the opportunities available to their friends and peers.

'I like to go ice-skating and that more often but my mum can't afford it like all my other friends 'cos she ain't got as much money'
Mike 12 years (Ridge 2002: 87)

In Ireland a study by O'Connor, (2002) exploring young people's use of space and time found that children's lives were increasingly scheduled through a range of organized activities. However, research with low-income children found that these leisure opportunities were too costly and the majority of the children were not participating in them and were more likely to spend their free time 'hanging around' in local towns and shopping centres (Daly and Leonard, 2002). The financial and structural barriers to shared leisure consumption means that children who are poor also risk becoming too visible in their societies, and thereby subject to adult scrutiny and censure. Unable to tap into the same degree of fee-paying social activities and managed time as other children in their societies, their social and public presence is perversely often heightened by the relative absence of other children.

In the UK Matthews (2001) found that for many low-income children 'the street' was a key site of leisure activity because there was nowhere else to go, compounded by a lack of space at home and insufficient resources to enjoy the leisure centres and fast food venues available to others. Low-income rural children are particularly visible because they are unable to access affordable transport and leisure opportunities outside of their immediate environments (Davis and Ridge, 1997; Matthews and Limb, 2000). While other children conduct much of their leisure and play outside of their villages and small towns in organised activities, low-income children are effectively contained and visible within their villages (Davis and Ridge, 1997). For young people living in rural areas of Croatia 'poverty is boredom' and a lack of money and transport means that they feel they can't socialise with other young people. For young people in the city being poor was experienced as a loss of future goals and resulted in 'mindless sitting around with friends' (Raboteg- Šarić, 2004:554). Elsewhere, the Italian report reveals that in regions in economic difficulty a growing band of foreign children have become more visible on the streets due both to their identifiable 'difference' and the progressive disappearance of Italian children from the streets. Visible children are in danger of transgressing adult's public spaces and may be more vulnerable to aggressive and restrictive responses by adults (Valentine, 1996).

Virtual realities

The third key area of children's spending identified in cross-country reports was spending on media and the development of real and virtual identities, such as magazines, videos, CDs, PC games and mobile phones. The burgeoning market in mobile phones and the growth in access to PCs and the Internet signals the emergence of new cultural forms in childhood. These are characterised by alternative landscapes of imagination, and accelerated opportunities for the development of virtual identities, which evolve and are produced and reproduced in 'real' and 'virtual' space. Valentine and Holloway (2002) in an exploration of ICT, children's identities and social networks, found that children's 'on-line' identities were not fixed and separate but rather incorporated into their 'real' lives and vice versa. Their research reveals the central place that virtual technologies have come to play in children's lives and the way that children use cyberspace to conduct, develop and maintain their friendships and social networks. Mobile phones and the Internet provide new modes of connection to other children, freed of the temporal spatial considerations of conducting relationships in 'real' time and location. They also spawn new ways to escape from adult control and spatial surveillance (Childress, 2004).

Given the growing significance of cyberculture in children's lives and relationships the perils of being excluded from these new forms of childhood organization, and the everyday interactions and negotiations that give them form and meaning, are apparent. For low-income children cyberspace represents not a new opportunity but potentially a new danger, a new form of difference and exclusion. In all the cross-country reports there is evidence that children's use of ICT and the internet is growing. It is also evident that social class, parental educational qualifications and other indicators of social disadvantage mediate access in many of the countries including Italy, Austria Ireland, the UK, and Estonia. 'On-line worlds reproduce class and gender divisions, and the economic and temporal realities of children's everyday lives impact upon the nature and the extent of their on-line activities (Mayhew et al., 2004: 437). In Israel, new patterns of exclusion are developing as access to virtual space differs between Jewish and Arab children, with over half of young Jewish people (ages 12 – 17) reporting surfing the internet at least once a week from their homes compared with an estimated quarter of Arab youths (Ben-Arieh et al., 2004). In Estonia, where there is a relatively high level of ICT and internet use, computer games and mobile phones are very popular amongst children. There are even '*network parties*' where children get together and bring their own computers. Mobile phone ownership is also growing fast and children identified mobile phone fashions as an important area of competition between children. Without the latest phone Estonian children reported feeling at risk of bullying from other children. Increasingly few children regarded a mobile phone as a luxury but rather as an everyday companion, a social necessity. In Estonia, as in other countries, children living in families without mobile phones were also likely to be without a computer at home. As children's social lives are increasingly developed, explored and negotiated in the world of virtual time and space, new sites of social exclusion are emerging through unequal patterns of access and the unsustainable consumption demands of fashion and high tech accessories.

Children's agency

Listening to low-income children's accounts of their lives and the issues that concern them reveals the sustained challenges that childhood poverty presents for children. It is apparent that the impact of poverty is permeating every area of children's life-worlds, suffusing their everyday lives with economic and material disadvantages, and threatening their social and emotional well-being. Poverty is an intense and for many children an enduring backdrop to their lives. However, easily overlooked is that these are 'ordinary' children, busy in the everyday social world of childhood, determined to stay connected to the social milieu, and striving to be accepted and included in the cultural exchanges of their peers. They are not passive victims of their poverty or their environments, and their strategies of social and economic survival are many and diverse.

Children are also thoughtful, responsive and sensitive actors within their homes and families, where making ends meet and sustaining family life on a restricted income are a daily challenge. As Brannen et al (2000) point out children are well able to empathise with their parent's needs and perspectives, and low-income children play an active and important role in their families (Ridge, 2002). Many of the children in Ridge's study had taken part-time employment to gain access to their own income source. Income from employment was used to secure fashion goods and purchase leisure activities so that children could join in with their social groups as much as possible. This gave them some measure of control of their situation while also being instrumental in improving the financial well-being of their families. By catering in some part for their own needs they helped to free up income within the household. Some children were also contributing money directly to help relieve the financial strain within families. Thus access to work was a key strategy employed by children to generate some measure of autonomy. However, children also revealed a different set of strategies within their families that were potentially more problematic. Studies in the UK, which have explored the dynamics of low-income family life, have found that parents, especially mothers, try very hard to protect their children from the worse effects of poverty (Kempson, et al., 1994; Middleton et al., 1997; Goode et al., 1998). But Ridge's study shows that children may also try to protect their parents from the realities of the social and emotional costs of poverty on their lives. Managing on a low-income frequently requires trade-offs between different needs and demands and children are fully aware that their parents cannot afford to provide for all their school and social needs. Therefore they engage in a series of strategies which can range from overt forms of self-restraint and the moderation of wishes and demands to more co-vert self-denial of needs and wants, and the lowering of expectations and aspirations. These strategies were also evident in Daly and Leonard's (2002) study of low-income children in Ireland, which found that in general children tried to live within their means and consciously refrained from making too many monetary demands upon their families.

Listening to children's accounts of their lives is to become aware of their agency and resourcefulness. However, children's discourse of poverty is also often suffused with despair and uncertainty, and the fear of being excluded, isolated or seen as somehow different and 'other' is very real. Children are engaged in an intense social endeavor to be accepted and included but their agency and resourcefulness is bounded and circumscribed by their material and social realities. Lowering aspirations, moderating needs and containing and controlling desires are rational and strategic responses to the realities of many children's lives. But they are not in essence responses that will enhance children's lives or benefit them in the short or long term.

Final thoughts

Children are cogent thoughtful rapporteurs on their own lives. Where it has been possible to include children's accounts from the cross-country reports they reveal a remarkably similar set of concerns. They indicate the importance to children of social settings, social relationships and the mediums thorough which children form and express their identities. However, while children show a generally similar set of concerns their childhood experiences are mediated by a disparate range of factors including age, gender, class, ethnicity and culture. To understand the social, cultural and symbolic context in which children experience poverty and give their experiences meaning, a subjective analysis, which incorporates, and values childhood diversity is essential.

It is apparent from children's accounts that they are not passive victims of poverty but equally it is important to recognise the manifold constraints on their lives and the challenges these present to their capacity for self realisation. Low-income children are reflexive social agents, who engage with their lives and their circumstances, constructing and reconstructing their lives in dynamic and imaginative ways. They are also thoughtful and competent social agents who are fully aware of social and economic realities of their lives. However, their childhoods are organised around the constraints of poverty, therefore any understanding of childhood poverty, while encompassing the discourse, agency and identity of the child, must also recognise the social, material and cultural boundaries, constructions and institutions that shape the life worlds of children who are poor.

Bibliography

Bradshaw, J. (ed.) (2000): *Poverty: The Outcomes for Children* London. Family Policy Studies Centre.

Brannen, J., Heptinstall, E. and Bhopal, K. (2000): *Connecting Children Care and Family Life in Later Childhood,* London: Routledge Falmer.

Brusdal, R. (2001): *Hva bruker barn og unge penger på? En beskrivelse av ulike forbruksmønstre blant barn og unge i alderen 8 til 24 år* [What do children and young people use money on? A description of different consumption patters among children and young people 8-24 years old] SIFO: Prosjektnotat nr. 1-2001.

Candappa, M. and Egharevba, I. (2002): 'Negotiating boundaries: tensions between home and school life for refugee children'. in R. Edwards (2002) *Children, Home and School: Regulation, Autonomy or Connection?* London: Routlege Falmer. pp 155-171.

Cantillon, S., B. Gannon and B. Nolan (2003): *The Allocation of Resources within Households: Learning from Non-Monetary Indicators.* Dublin: Combat Poverty Agency.

Childress, H. (2004): 'Teenagers, territory and the appropriation of space' in *Childhood* Vol. 11, No. 2 May 2004 pp 195-206.

Christensen, P. and James, A. (2000): Introduction: Researching Children and Childhood: Cultures of Communication in P. Christensen and A. James (2000): *Research with Children: Perspectives and Practices* London: Routledge Falmer pp 1-9.

Daly, M. and M. Leonard (2002): *Against all Odds: Family Life on a Low Income in Ireland.* Dublin: Institute of Public Administration.

Davis, H. and Bourhill, M. (1997) 'Crisis': The Demonization of Children and Young People' in P. Scraton (1997) *'Childhood' in 'Crisis'?* London: UCL Press Ltd. pp 28-57.

Davis, J. and Ridge, T. (1997): *Same Scenery, Different Lifestyle: Rural children on a low Income,* London: The Children's Society.

Esping-Andersen, G. (2002): 'A child-centred social investment strategy' in G. Esping-Andersen, D. Gallie, A. Hemerijck and J. Myles (2002): *Why We Need a New Welfare State*, Oxford and New York: Oxford University Press. pp 26-67.

Goldson, B. (1997): 'Childhood': An Introduction to Historical and Theoretical Analyses in P. Scraton (ed.) *Childhood in Crisis,* London: UCL Press Ltd.

Goldson, B. (2001): 'The demonization of children: from the symbolic to the institutional' in P. Foley, J. Roche and S. Tucker (2001): *Children in society: Contemporary theory, policy and practice,* Buckingham: OUP. pp 34-41.

Goode, J., Callender, C. and Lister, R. (1998): *Purse or Wallet. Gender Inequalities and Income Distribution Within Families on Benefits,* London: Policy Studies Institute.

Grover, S. (2004): Why wont they listen to us? On giving power and voice to children participating in social research *Childhood* Volume 11 Number 1 February 2004, pp 81-93.

Gunter, B. and A. Furnham (1998): *Children as Consumers.* London: Routledge.

Hengst, H. (2001): 'Rethinking the Liquidation of Childhood' in M. Du Bois-Reymond, H. Sünker and H. H. Krüger (2001) *Childhood in Europe: Approaches, Trends and Findings.* New York: Peter Lang. pp 13-34.

James, A. (1993): *Childhood Identities: Self and Social Relationships in the Experience of the Child* Edinburgh: Edinburgh University Press.

Kutsar, D. (2000): *Training Against Social Exclusion*. Project VET Against Social Exclusion. Tartu: Report of Estonia for European Training Foundation in Turin.

Kutsar, D. and Trumm, A. (eds) (1999): *Poverty Reduction in Estonia*. Tartu: TU Pres (UNDP)

Lee, N. (2001): *Childhood and Society: Growing up in an age of uncertainty,* Buckingham: OUP

Lister, R. (2003): 'Investing in the Citizen-workers of the Future: Transformations in Citizenship and the State under New Labour' in *Social Policy and Administration*. October 2003, Vol. 37 No. 5 pp 427-443.

Matthews, H. (2001): *Children and Community Regeneration: Creating Better Neighbourhoods*. London: Save the Children.

Matthews, H. and M. Limb (2000): *Exploring the 'Fourth Environment': Young People's Use of Place and Views on Their Environment*. ESRC: Children 5-16 Research Briefing. Swindon: Economic and Social Research Council.

Middleton, S., K. Ashworth and R. Walker (1994): *Family Fortunes*. London: Child Poverty Action Group.

Miles, S. (1996): Use and Consumption in the Construction of Identities. Paper at British Youth Research: The New Agenda 26-28 January 1996. Glasgow.

Miles, S. (2000): *Youth Lifestyles in a Changing World,* Buckingham: Open University Press

Mizen, P., C. Pole and A. Bolton (eds) (2001): 'Why be a school age worker?' in P. Mizen, C. Pole and A. Bolton (eds): *Hidden Hands: International Perspectives on Children's Work and Labour*. London: Routledge Falmer.

O'Connor, P., C. Kane and A. Haynes (2002): 'Young people's ideas about Time and Space', *Irish Journal of Sociology* 11: 43-61.

Oppenheim, C. and Harker, L. (1996): *Poverty the Facts,* London: Child Poverty Action Group.

Prout, A. (2000): Children's Participation: Control and Self-realisation in British Late Modernity *Children and Society* **14** pp 304-315.

Qvortrup, J. (1990): 'A voice for children in statistical and social accounting: A plea for children's right to be heard', in A, James and A, Prout (eds) *Constructing and Reconstructing Childhood: Contemporary Issues in the Sociological Study of Childhood,* New York: Falmer Press pp 78-98.

Qvortrup, J., Bardy, M., Sigritta G. and Wintersberger H. (eds) (1994): *Childhood Matters Social Theory, Practice and Politics,* Aldershot: Avebury.

Qvortrup, J. (1997): A Voice for Children in Statistical Accounting: A Plea for Children's Right to be Heard in James, A. and Prout, A. (eds) *Constructing and Reconstructing Childhood,* London: Falmer Press pp 85-106.

Ridge, T. (2002): *Childhood Poverty and Social Exclusion: From a Child's Perspective*. Bristol: Policy Press.

Ridge, T. and Millar, J. (2000): Excluding Children: Autonomy, Friendship and the Experience of the Care System *Social Policy & Administration* **34** (2) pp 160-175.

Roker, D. (1998): *Worth More Than This. Young People Growing up in Family Poverty*. London: The Children's Society.

Ruxton, S. (1996): *Children in Europe,* London: NCH Action for Children.

Sandbæk, M. (ed), (2004): *Children's level of living. How much does family income matter?* NOVA-report series 11, 2004.

Saporiti, A. (2001): 'A Methodology for Making Children Count' in M. Du Bois-Reymond, H. Sünker and H.-H. Krüger (2001): *Childhood in Europe: Approaches, Trends and Findings.* New York: Peter Lang. pp 243-264.

Scraton, P. (1997): 'Whose 'Childhood'? What 'Crisis'? in P. Scraton (1997) *'Childhood' in 'Crisis'?* London: UCL Press Ltd. pp 163-188.

Shropshire, J. and S. Middleton (1999): *Small Expectations. Learning to be Poor?* York: Joseph Rowntree Foundation.

Steinberg, S. and Kincheloe, J.L. (eds) (1997): *Kinderculture, The corporate construction of childhood,* Boulder Colorado: Westview Press.

Valentine, G. (1996): 'Children should be seen and not heard! The Production and Transgression of Adults Public Space' in *Urban Geography* No. 17 pp 205-20.

Valentine, G. and S. Holloway (2001): 'On-line dangers? Geographies of parents' fears for children's safety in cyberspace', *Professional Geographer*, 53, 1: 71-83.

Whyte, J. (1995): *Changing Times: A Comparative Study of Children – Belfast, London, Dublin.* Aldershot: Avebury.

Willis, P., S. Jones, J. Cannan and G. Hurd (1990): *Common Culture. Symbolic Work at Play in the Everyday Cultures of the Young.* Milton Keynes: Open University Press.

COST A19 Country Reports

Jensen, A.-M., Ben-Arieh, A., Conti, C., Kutsar, D., Nic Ghiolla Phádraig, M., and Warming Nielsen, H. (eds) (2004) *Children's Welfare in Ageing Europe.* Volume I and Volume II, Trondheim: Norwegian Centre for Child Research.

Beham, M., Wintersberger, H., Wörister, K. and Zartler, U. (2004) 'Childhood in Austria: Cash and Care, Time and Space, Children's Needs, and Public Policies' in Jensen et al.(eds) 2004, Vol. I., pp. 19-79.

Kutsar, D., Harro, M., Tiit, E.-M., and Matrov, D (2004) 'Children's Welfare in Estonia from Different Perspective' in Jensen et al.(eds) 2004, Vol. I., pp. 81-141.

Alanen, L., Sauli, H. and Strandell, H. (2004) 'Children and Childhood in a Welfare State: The case of Finland' in Jensen et al.(eds) 2004, Vol. I., pp. 143-209.

Devine, D., Nic Ghiolla Phádraig, M. and Deegan, J (2004) 'Time for Children – Time for Change? Children's Rights and Welfare in Ireland during a Period of Economic Growth' in Jensen et al.(eds) 2004, Vol. I., pp. 211-274.

Conti, C. and Sgritta, G. (2004) 'Childhood in Italy – A Family Affair' in Jensen et al.(eds) 2004, Vol. I., pp. 275-334.

Jensen, A.-M., Kjørholt, A., Qvortrup, J. and Sandbæk, M. with Johansen, V. and Lauritzen, T. (2004) 'Childhood and Generation in Norway – Money, Time and Space' in Jensen et al.(eds) 2004, Vol. I., pp. 335-402.

Mayhew, E., Uprichard, E., Ridge, T., Bradshaw, J., and Beresford, B. (2004)

'Children and Childhood in the United Kingdom' in Jensen et al.(eds) 2004, Vol. I. pp. 403-457.

Raycheva, L., Hristova, K., Radomirova, D. and Ginev, R. (2004) 'Bulgaria: Children in Transition' in Jensen et al.(eds) 2004, Vol. II. pp. 469-526.

Raboteg- Šariä, Z. (2004) 'Children's Welfare in the Context of Social and Economic Changes in Croatia' in Jensen et al.(eds) 2004, Vol. II. pp. 527-590.

Kouloumou, T. (2004) 'Chidren's Welfare and Everyday Life in Cyprus: A Family with Intergenerational Implications' in Jensen et al.(eds) 2004, Vol. II. pp. 591-647.

Kampmann, J. & Warming Nielsen, H. (2004) 'Socialized Childhood: Children's Childhoods in Denmark' in Jensen et al.(eds) 2004, Vol. II. pp. 649-702.

Jurczyk, K. Olk, T. and Zeiher, H. (2004) 'German Children's Welfare Between Economy and Ideology in Jensen et al.(eds) 2004, Vol. II. pp. 703-770.

Ben-Arieh, A. Boyer, Y. and Gajst, I. (2004) 'Children's Welfare in Israel: Growing Up in a Multi-Cultural Society' in Jensen et al.(eds) 2004, Vol. II. pp. 771-811.

Jensen, A.-M. and Qvortrup, J. (2004) 'Summary – A Childhood Mosaic: What Did We Learn?' in Jensen et al.(eds) 2004, Vol. II. pp. 813-832.

Notes

1 See report references at the end of the chapter
2 Using a 50% poverty line and basic deprivation measure.
3 Both below the 60% poverty line and experiencing 'basic deprivation'

Children's right to a decent standard of living

Mona Sandbæk

Introduction

As a part of the EU's ambitions for a more integrated social policy, a group of leading experts were invited to present their perspectives on new challenges for the welfare state. In his contribution to this discussion, Esping-Andersen (2002) elaborates extensively on what he calls a »child-centred social investment strategy.« The basic arguments are that in order to stay competitive in the future knowledge society, Europe needs to improve its investment in children considerably. Not only do they have to handle high demands in order to succeed in a competitive working life, but children will also have to provide for numerous pensioners. Today several EU countries have low fertility and the fact that many children grow up in poverty can be considered as a bad investment. In order to safeguard our common future, it is important to enhance children's life chances.

The social investment strategy provides valuable reasons to combat child poverty. However, whether to treat children as an investment for the future or as citizens of the present can be described as a key tension in policy reforms. The argument for investing in children provides little rationale for attending to the needs of people who may not have an educational future, like older or disabled people, or children with learning disabilities (Williams 2004). The social investment strategy therefore needs to be supplemented with perspectives emphasizing that children do not only have a value as »human becomings«, but also as »human beings«, to apply a well-known expression formulated by Qvortrup (1985). While childhood is a transition phase for each human being, it is also a permanent category in every society. The children who at any given time constitute this category, negotiate, produce and reproduce, in other words, they are actors, not only through numerous tasks in the various arenas, but also as co-producers of their own development (Qvortrup 2002). Children have a life of their own at school, in their leisure time and among their friends. Another reason to invest in children is therefore attached to their rights as citizens here and now. The UN Convention on the Rights on the Child, article 27, states that children have the right to an adequate standard of living. Parents, or other adults in their stead, have the primary responsibility to provide for the child, but the state is also expected to assist them.

This chapter explores what characterises the situation of children in low-income families and what elements a strategy based upon children's right to a decent standard of living could encompass. A policy directed towards children themselves can be value based and grounded, for example, in Article 27 of the UN Convention on the Rights of the Child but it should also draw upon the findings of empirical research. First, I will present results from poverty research about risk as well as protective factors, before elaborating more extensively upon a Norwegian example in order to explore more in detail the situation of children in low-income families. Finally I will discuss what kind of strategies could be derived from this kind of data.

Findings from poverty research

International poverty research has in recent years been dominated by three areas of interest. First, how many are poor in different countries? Second, for how long are they poor? And third, how poor are they? In other words, researchers have looked at the scope, duration, and degree of the problem in different countries (Vleminckx and Smeeding 2001, Bradbury, Jenkins and Micklewright 2001). The interest in children and poverty can be highlighted as a fourth key topic that has attracted increasing attention among European poverty researchers, and similar questions have been addressed in order to highlight children's situation. Research has focused upon the proportion of poor children in each of the EU countries and examined what the long-term consequences for children of growing up in poverty seem to be. While children and their own experiences used to be invisible and unexplored within the social sciences, we can now find complex datasets about children and childhood, with children not only as the unit of analysis, but also as informants (Alanen 2003, Jensen et al 2004). This development can also be traced in poverty research.

There is reason to conclude that being a poor child means being at statistical risk. Quantitative as well as qualitative studies show that children who live in low-income families are more exposed to risk factors than their peers from better-off families. Garbarino (1998) uses the concept of social toxicity to refer to the multiple threats to child development, like environments filled with violence, racism, unstable care arrangements, economic deprivation and community insecurity.

Based upon a comprehensive research review, Evans (2004) states that poor children in America are exposed to more family turmoil and violence, experience less social support and have less responsive and more authoritarian parents. He claims that the search for explanations of the processes by which poverty affects children has focused almost exclusively on psychosocial characteristics within the family, and ignored the physical settings that low-income children and families inhabit. This happens in spite the fact that low-income neighbourhoods are more dangerous, offer poorer municipal services and suffer greater physical deterioration. To the list of disadvantages that poor children are more likely to experience, Seecombe (2002) adds violence, hunger, poor health, stress and abuse, having difficulties at school and possibly dropping out, and becoming teen parents. She claims that the discussion about resilience should not focus solely on resilience as an individual disposition, family trait, or community phenomenon. Attention should also be paid to structural deficiencies and to the social policies that families need in order to function better in adverse situations.

Poor children in Europe are also more exposed to risk factors. Bradshaw (2001, 2002) found that poverty in Britain and other European countries is associated with increased illness and mortality, child abuse, teen pregnancy, low-standard housing, poor school achievement and youth suicide. Studies from the Nordic countries also indicate some of these correlations. Based upon a follow-up study of long-term effects of unemployment on children, Christoffersen (1994) found that violence, separation from parents and parents' addiction problems were significantly more common in the risk group than in the control group.

Such statistical information provides an overview of distinctive features of a childhood in poverty. It allows us to compare the vulnerability of different groups within the population and to assess the ways in which poverty expands or contracts (Seecombe 2000). However, this kind of information does not tell us how the individual child is experiencing his or her everyday life (Lister and Beresford 2000, Ruxton and Bennet 2002). Recently we have seen a growing number of studies addressing children's own experiences of growing up in families with unemployment and low-income (Näsman and Gerber 1996, Roker and Coleman 2000, Ridge 2002, van der Hoek 2005). The children's age and situation vary, but the studies still have some findings in common that are worth mentioning. They show that many children in low-income families are materially and socially deprived, in the sense that they cannot access items and activities that are common among their better-off peers. The children show insight into the consequences of living on a low-income, and worry more than their peers about the present situation as well as about the future. Children and young people try to help their parents out in various ways, by paying household bills, taking care of their own expenses for clothes and leisure activities or asking for money as seldom as possible (Roker and Coleman 2000).

The fact that children who live in low-income families are more exposed to risk than their peers who live in better-off families does not imply that all children who grow up in poverty have sorrowful childhoods or grow up to have miserable lives as adults. Van der Hoek (2005) found that not every child in low-income families was social or materially deprived or emotionally burdened. This was partly due to the fact that the parents' situation varied, and that some of them were able to protect their children by inventing effective solutions or finding inexpensive alternatives. For the individual child the risk associated with poverty is mediated by numerous factors. To understand better how risk mechanisms work, one often distinguishes between distal and proximal risk factors. Distal risk factors do not directly impinge on the child, but act through mediators, such as social class while proximal risk factors, such as parenting, affect the child directly. Proximal risk factors may be mediated through parenting priorities and style (Luthar 1993). In this context I will draw attention to two aspects that have often been mentioned as protective factors for children who grow up in poverty, namely the quality of the relationships between family members and the distribution of resources within the family.

Protective factors

There can be considerable differences in how a family's economic resources are shared. Recent research indicates that the sources of household income make a difference for the priority given to children (Corak 2005). Some studies have found that women and children are frequently allocated least resources (Pahl 1989, Ringen and Halpin 1997). Others have concluded that children are prioritized, and that quite often parents themselves go without necessary items and/or abstain from desirable activities, while their children do not (Middleton, Ashworth and Braithwaite 1997, Adelman, Middleton and Ashworth 1999). However, these studies also point to the fact that the smaller a family's resources are, the more difficult it is for the parents to give their children what they need. They conclude that parents seem able to protect their children from deprivation to some extent when poverty is present, but not when poverty is severe.

Another factor which mediates the effects of poverty is family climate. Family conflicts were early identified as risk factors while a good child-parent relationship was regarded as protective (Rutter 1971). Within resilience research positive interaction between care givers and children have been identified as a main contribution to positive development. Werner and Smiths' (1982, 1992) longitudinal studies from Kauai showed that when children mainly received positive responses from their environment, it enhanced resilience, even when confronted with chronic poverty, disorganised environments and parents with mental problems. However, the more problems the children experienced, the more protective circumstances or influences were needed in order to balance the risk.

Elder's (1999 [1974]) classic study *Children of the Great Depression* is of major interest in this respect. Elder explored the long-term consequences of the Great Depression, which altered the economic situation of many families dramatically. He emphasizes that there is no simple effect of socioeconomic loss. His work shows that in a life-course perspective, the consequences for children's adjustment depends upon several factors, like the child's age and gender, whether the family is originally middle- or working-class, and family »climate«. Changes in family life, not the deprivation of material resources, appeared to be most damaging to the welfare of children, and marital compatibility seemed to be of major importance.

Looking at areas that mediate poverty may provide valuable insight regarding what kind of policies a welfare society should develop in order to strengthen the families' and children's own efforts. But such an approach may also have serious disadvantages. Drawing the attention to the family's way of handling economic strain may construct poverty as a private matter and contribute to familialisation of children and child-hood. In her chapter in this volume, Ridge indicates that attention is drawn away from social policy measures and directed towards the families' internal lives, portraying child poverty as a family failing. Good parents are expected to succeed in protecting their children from the negative consequences of poor circumstances, while those who are not able to protect their offspring may be perceived as bad parents. Such a twist would be rather unfortunate and must be avoided. However, the way to avoid it is not by ignoring empirical evidence showing that quite a high proportion of children growing up in poverty do fare well. Ignoring these facts does not do justice either to the tremendous efforts taken upon themselves by many poor parents, or to the experiences of children who have overcome a childhood in poverty.

There are many ways to define poverty, and the poverty line can be draw at various levels. There is still a general agreement that the core characteristic of being poor, is having fewer material resources than people in your contemporary society (Pedersen 2002). This fact in itself deserves attention and should lead to a discussion about what kind of policy can create more equal life conditions for poor families and their children. The measures to be taken must not depend solely upon demonstrating negative outcomes associated with a childhood in poverty, but should also mirror the kind of childhood children are entitled to, and what kind of support parents need in order to bring up their children in acceptable circumstances.

Children in low-income families – A Norwegian Example

The child poverty rate in Norway is low. A comparison of 25 countries in Europe, Russia and the US ranked Norway among the five countries with the lowest child poverty (Bradbury and Jäntti 2001). Other studies have drawn slightly different conclusions, but Norway is consistently among the countries with the least extensive child poverty (Bradshaw 2001, Corak 2005). A report from Statistics Norway (Epland 2001) indicated that around 3 per cent of Norwegian children lived in poverty, defined as 50 per cent of the median income. Considering that child poverty is a phenomenon of relatively low frequency, one may question how a Norwegian example can contribute to the discussion of poverty. At least three important contributions may be identified. First, exploring poverty in a welfare state may shed light on the extent and characteristics of residual poverty in a state based upon universal measures. Second, since child poverty is not an acute problem, Norwegian data may make it easier to address more salient questions. Third, empirical research shows that the problems faced by poor families in different countries are comparable and concern the effects of long-term low income and lack of access to the labour market, consumer goods, health services etc. Even though the extent of poverty may vary, there are no major differences in the types of problems that people living on low income have to deal with.

The study »Children's level of living – the impact of family economy for children's lives« (Sandbæk and Sture 2003, Sandbæk 2004) was designed to examine whether there were any connections between the family's economic situation and certain aspects of children's daily life, such as performance and adjustment at school, participation in leisure activities and friendships. The aim was also to extract information about adequate measures, based on the children's and parents' own experiences.

Samples and methodology

The survey contains two representative samples of informants from all parts of Norway.[1] *The low-income sample* consists of children in families with equalised incomes below 60 per cent of the median income, while the smaller *control sample* is made up of children in families in all income groups. The design makes it possible to explore whether there are any differences in living conditions between children in the low-income sample, and children in the control sample, as experienced by children and parents themselves.

The data was collected by Computer Assisted Interviewing, where the interviewer reads questions from a computer screen and registers answers directly on the computer.

The main focus was on children's own experiences and children were the unit of analysis as well as the main informants. However, parents are best informed about certain aspects of children's living conditions, and in order to produce as comprehensive a picture as possible, they were also included as informants. 779 10-12-years-olds answered questions related to their everyday lives, while 1937 parents answered questions about the family's standard of living and also on behalf of children aged 6-9.[2]

The overall response rate for the survey was 54. 4 per cent: 52. 9 per cent in the low-income sample and 63. 8 per cent in the control sample. The high proportion of non-responses was to be expected, given that the target populations frequently chose not to participate in surveys. Yet, the low response rate calls for particular caution when interpreting the results. There is reason to believe that the proportion of non-participation in such surveys is particularly high among those families who suffer most difficulties.

Despite the low response rate, the families in the low-income sample presented characteristics that concord with similar studies. While the majority of the control sample consisted of two-working-parent families with Norwegian or western background, this was the case for one-third of the low-income sample. In the low-income sample there was an over-representation of lone parents (21 per cent compared to 14 per cent), families with ethnic minority backgrounds (21 per cent compared to 3 per cent) and workless families. The workless families overlapped to a large degree with the other two categories (Skevik 2004 A). In this article the data will be used to highlight two major findings, namely that parents in the low-income sample reported expected differences compared to the control sample, while the differences between the children in the two samples seemed to be less obvious.

The parents reported expected differences

According to the parents' information, there were distinct and consistent differences between the two samples regarding their material living standard as well as the parents' health situation. Low-income families were more likely to report an unstable housing situation and fewer families owned their own house (55 per cent compared to 85 per cent), they were more likely to experience housing deprivation, and fewer children had their own room (69 per cent compared to 91 per cent). Almost all families owned a phone, TV and CD-player, but the low-income families more often lacked other key consumer goods like washing machines, video/DVDs, cars, PCs or dish washers. Still, a car or PC was owned by nearly 80 per cent of the low-income sample compared to over 90 per cent in the control sample (Skevik 2004 B). Regarding social activities, low-income families were more likely to report that they refrained from activities such as going on holidays, going to the cinema and eating out. For example, 17 per cent of the low-income respondents did not go on annual holidays, compared to 4 per cent of the control sample (Skevik 2004 C).

Parents in the low-income sample also reported more somatic and mental health problems than those in the control sample. A larger proportion perceived their general health conditions to be bad (22 per cent in the low-income compared to 13 per cent in the control group), they suffered more from psychological stress (35 per cent compared to 25 per cent) and reduced quality of life (26 per cent compared to 14 per cent). They did not, however, report more lasting chronic illness (32 per cent compared to 31 per cent). This may be related to the fact that in order to diagnose such problems, one needs to see a doctor, which low-income families do more rarely (Elstad 2004 A).

Although they reported clear and significant differences on almost all variables, quite a low proportion of the families reported that they had problems making ends meet: only 12 per cent said that they had insufficient money to cover their needs, and 5 per cent that they had to use their savings in order to do so (Skevik 2004 B). Preliminary analysis of the qualitative interviews with the parents may shed light on why relatively few parents said they found it hard to make ends meet.[3] The interviews showed how they lowered their lifestyle and consumption expectations according to the resources available, instead of pursuing the living standard they wished they had. (Thorød 2006). There is reason to believe that when they consider their means to be sufficient, this reflects whether or not they are able to keep to their tight budget, and not whether the budget covers their real needs.

Fewer differences reported by the children

When analysing the children's answers regarding their life at school and in leisure activities, with friends and family, the differences were less obvious and consistent. Most of the children – about 8 out of 10, in the low-income sample as well as the control sample – enjoyed school, and more or less the same proportions experienced their relationships with teachers and with other pupils as good. Children in the low-income sample were, however, more exposed to bullying than children in the control sample (36 per cent versus 26 per cent)[4]. Regarding their school performance, nine out of ten children felt that they performed as well as or better than the other pupils. The proportion of children who considered their performance to be below average was higher among children in the low-income sample (13 per cent compared to 6 per cent, p< 0,05), and a higher proportion of children had received special education, compared to children in general – 22 per cent compared to 14 per cent (Stefansen 2004 A).

A large majority of children in the low-income sample (three quarters) as well as in the control sample (nine out of ten) participated in organised leisure activities. However, girls with ethnic minority backgrounds were particularly likely to report little or no participation in organised activities. Between 70 and 80 per cent of the children in both samples, reported that they had stable friendships, but children in low-income families did not invite friends home or visit friends in their homes as often as the other children. 28 per cent reported that this happened rarely, compared to 15 percent. This was particularly true for children with minority backgrounds, but the differences remained significant when controlled for ethnic background.

The majority of children in both samples owned material objects that are usual among Norwegian children, like bikes, cross country skis/ snowboards and CD-players. The percentage who owned three of what can be defined as essential objects were lower among the low-income sample (55 per cent compared to 79). Again, this was particularly true for children with a non-western background. This also applied to the children's own economic resources: While most of the children in the low-income sample had access to money, the proportion who had no money of their own was larger among the low-income children than among other children (Stefansen 2004 B).

The vast majority of children in both samples reported their overall health situation to be very good (Elstad 2004 B). They also described their relationship with their parents in rather positive terms, and there were no differences among case and control on the sum scores measuring relationships with their parents. However, perceived self-confidence, measured by Harter (1982), was lower among children in the low-income sample (86. 07 compared to 88.90, $F = 8.88$, $p < 0.003$). They also scored higher on external locus of control (88.10 compared to 85.45, $F = 13.25$, $p < 0.000$), measured by Nowicki and Strickland (1973). These tendencies increased in non-working households and families where parents reported that they did not make ends meet or could not pay unexpected expenses of 10 000 NCr.

Parents protect their children

The differences between the parents' and children's responses were not only reflected in their answers about their objective situation, but also in their subjective perception of their economic situation. While 17 per cent of the parents in the low-income sample reported that they had insufficient money to cover their needs, or had to use their savings in order to make ends meet, only 6 per cent of the children in the low-income sample confirmed that their families were badly off (Stefansen 2004 C). Further, there was a significant correlation between parents who reported that their economic situation was difficult and their children reporting the same, but the proportion of children who said their situation was difficult was much lower. 38 per cent of the children whose parents said their situation was difficult reported that the family's economic situation was good.

These results seem to indicate that the parents perceive their economic situation to be more difficult than their children. There may be several reasons why these results emerge. Children's economic situation may not be identical to that of their parents. They may receive money from relatives, or the other parent in cases of divorce. They may also have income from their own work. Another explanation may be that some of the areas where parents report differences in living standards matter little to children.

Whether or not the family has a dishwasher or the furniture needs renewing, does not necessarily affect the children's quality of life. However, this argument should not be taken too far. Children in low-income families brought their friends home more rarely, and this could be related to the state of their homes.

A more likely explanation may be that parents do manage to protect their children in terms of how the resources are distributed within the family. Our results indicate that parents cut down on their own consumption in order to let their children have a normal life. As far as they can, parents function as buffers, reducing the cost of maintenance and repairs rather than their children's activities. However, this strategy also has its limits. Like Middelthon et al (1997), we found that parents who find themselves in the most difficult economic circumstances, more often than the other parents, reported that lack of money did have consequences for their children in terms of their access to leisure activities or to the necessary equipment (Stefansen 2004 C).

The finding that parents seem to perceive themselves to be poorer than their children does not change the fact that they have the family budget at their disposal. They are in a position to decide how the money should be used and to a large degree define what children need. In spite of parents' efforts to meet the needs of their children, and their feeling that this is their responsibility, the asymmetry of power relations and the division of economic resources between childhood and adulthood, and between children and adults, remain relevant questions (Mayall and Zeiher 2003). There is a challenge to safeguard parents' concern and willingness to provide for their children, and at the same time look upon the division of resources between childhood and adulthood as a structural and generational question.

No consequences of being a poor child?

While most of the low-income children were doing as well as their friends with better- off parents, it is still important to emphasize that in most aspects of children's lives examined in this study, there were differences to the disadvantage of the children living in low-income families. The incongruity touched upon important aspects of children's lives, like their perception of coping at school, bringing their friends home, participating in leisure activities and going on vacation. However, these problems cannot be generalized to all children living in families with 60 per cent of the median income, which is not surprising. A sample of families with less than 60 per cent of the median income in a society will be rather heterogeneous. The families will have low income for a wide variety of reasons. For some low income will be a temporary situation, while for others it will be more permanent. A sample of families on long-term social assistance, for example, is likely to differ in a number of ways from a sample of families with less than 60 per cent of the median income. A reasonable assumption is that people with long-term social assistance will be more deprived. Still, also in our study we find the kind of severe problems in accordance with qualitative studies of groups at particular risk referred to earlier. Their situation needs particular attention.

Further, the lack of statistically significant differences in some of the areas examined does not mean there are no differences in real life. Our results do not say anything about the quality of the children's possessions. A bike can be anything from an expensive status symbol to a wreck, inherited from a sibling or second-hand. Vacations can also cover a wide range, from expensive trips abroad to public summer camps, just to mention these two examples. Lack of statistically significant findings should not make one jump to conclusions that there are no differences between the daily lives of children growing up in poor families and their more affluent friends.

There is also reason to examine further what it means to fare well. When relatively few children say that they are experiencing negative consequences of economic strain, this may also be due to a reluctance to describe themselves as poor. In a society like Norway's, poverty is perceived as an individual problem and is still associated with stigma. There is reason to believe that even young children are aware of this and try to avoid describing themselves as poor. Methodological questions may also influence the children's answers. While these interviews were structured, qualitative interviews give more room for children to talk about their everyday life and reveal possibilities as well as restrictions, without using concepts like »can't afford« which may easily be associated with poverty.

Our results showed that self-confidence was lower among the poor children and that they were more inclined to have an external locus of control. These findings underline that even though the parents try to protect their children, they are affected by the economic constraints of the family. Ridge (2002) raises questions of whether children are learning to be poor, by reducing their expectations to what they can have as well as to what activities they can participate in. This can have long-term consequences for their autonomy and aspirations.

A rights-based approach to combat child poverty

A strong defence for universal welfare arrangements

When many children, even in the low-income sample seem to do well, this is likely to be attributed not only to the individual family's effort to protect them, but also to the welfare level in Norway, which makes it possible for parents to exercise this kind of protection. Esping-Andersen (2002) has claimed that the Nordic countries, with their low child poverty rates, represent an exception from the welfare polarisation that is taking place elsewhere in Europe between income- and work-poor households on one hand

and resourceful families on the other hand. He points to two major explanations. One is the relatively generous universal benefits, as well as social transfers. Another reason is the fact that almost all mothers work, including lone mothers. This is made possible because the necessary infrastructure is provided, like day care facilities, parental leaves and allowances. Esping-Andersen (op.cit) argues that strategies to minimize child poverty can be reduced to the earning capacity of households with children and the level of social transfers to which they are entitled. When the Nordic countries secure minimal child poverty, it is by combining these two strategies of generous transfers and support for working mothers. Esping-Andersen and Sarasa (2002) claim that this approach can reduce child poverty at a fairly reasonable cost, and that the investments will pay off not least by enhancing the welfare of future retirees. In their opinion a generational clash can be avoided through policies that take such cohort dynamics into consideration.

In many respects our results support the arguments advocated by the authors referred to above. However, while these policies are recommended in a European context, there seems to be a need to defend them in Norway. Having realised fairly recently that child poverty exists also in the Norwegian welfare state, there seems to be a trend to seek new efforts to target the relatively few families who are falling outside the security net, traced for example in the Government's Plan of Action to Combat Poverty (St.meld.nr. 6 (2002-2003). Targeted measures are more stigmatising than universal, with the potential danger of leading families into welfare traps. It is crucial to avoid a readiness to reach the very poorest being exercised on behalf of the working poor, who are able to make a decent living and secure an acceptable standard for their children, under the existing arrangements.

Defending universal measures and transfers, does not, however, imply that there is no need for specific, targeted efforts. Actually, as shown by Corak (2005), general family and labour market policies have limited capacity to lower child poverty rates below a certain per cent. Also, in our study of low-income families, workless households, whether lone- or two-parent, reported particularly difficult living circumstances in most of the areas examined. Efforts to facilitate people's participation in the labour force are therefore significant. However, our expectations of such measures must be realistic. Some people will have a long way to go before they can join the labour force, and some never will (Dahl and Lødemel 2003). There must be arrangements to secure that those not working are included and not further marginalised. There may also be reason to warn against cutting down on benefits in order to motivate people to work. There is no evidence so far that this is necessary as long as there are systematic efforts to activate the unemployed (Esping-Andersen 2002). Williams (2004) argues that the ethics of paid work is not a broad enough principle to meet the aspirations which people have concerning their use of time and the quality of their relationships. In her opinion we need political principles about care which are equivalent to that about paid work, in order to link the two together in an adequate way.

A child-based perspective on existing welfare arrangements

Our results seem to support the hypothesis that helping parents means helping their children, and we argue strongly in favour of a welfare policy that enables parents to take care of their offspring. A policy that enables parents to care for their children can be seen as putting into practice children's right to adequate provision in keeping with Article 27 of the UN Convention on the Rights of the Child. However, these strategies should be supplemented with measures directed towards the children themselves. After decades of analysing social policy through the lenses of previously neglected groups, the political debate still revolves around the rights and duties of adults, while children still occur as objects rather than as subjects of social policy (Skevik 2003). One way to attend to children's own rights is to undertake an audit of welfare arrangements with particular regard to their consequences for children. For example, new restrictions in Norwegian unemployment benefits imply that the holder no longer has the right to holiday pay, and may also have to attend training courses during summer. These regulations will make it more difficult for unemployed parents to take their children on vacation and may affect children negatively in unintended ways. For children growing up in families who are in need of means-tested measures, the legal framework and service approaches to social assistance and child welfare protection are also important. Serious shortcomings have been highlighted in these institutions' ability to see, as well as in their measures to meet, children's economic and social needs (Andenæs 2004). Children's position vis-a-vis these institutions can be strengthened by revising the legislation from the perspective of children, then training professionals in order to sensitise them to children's rights and needs in situations of economic hardship. The institutions must further be provided with measures to address the children's situation in a proper way.

Educational institutions and leisure activities

The right to high quality day care, school and after school activities has broad support. These institutions provide children with learning opportunities which are significant in securing children's future life chances (Esping-Andersen and Sarasa 2002, Seecombe 2002, Duncan et al 1998). Esping-Andersen and Sarasa (2002) suggest that parents should be compensated as a measure for supporting their children in completing their education. Qvortrup (2002) has proposed that children themselves should receive economic compensation for their schoolwork. This proposal also raises the question of distributive justice between generations, and the extent to which children get a fair share of resources in society in exchange for the efforts they make. The theoretical debate about compensation for children's school work raises far-reaching questions of principle, while in practical policies such facilities are not available for all children and they are far from free. Prices are quite high, even in the Nordic countries, favourising children from well-off families. The costs connected with schools are still numerous, such as occasional or regular contributions to various arrangements, ordinary supplies like school bags, pencils, gym gear and not least school trips, which can be expensive and require special outfits. Such costs should be eliminated, and free school meals should be included. Leisure time activities can be regarded as part of children's education and culture. Children should also be entitled to at least one free leisure activity, including equipment and transportation. Ridge (2002) has pointed to transportation as a considerable problem for many children in low-income families.

The measures proposed in this chapter should be expanded with further exploration of parents' and children's own suggestions as to how they would like to be supported. In her interviews with children in low-income families, Van der Hoek (2005) found that children managed best when they were using active coping strategies, trying to change the circumstances or appraise the poverty situation. Passive coping strategies, such as avoiding inviting other children to their homes and not expressing many of their wishes, seemed to have negative outcomes. Such findings are interesting, but it is important not to standardise children's way of being, and not to expect them all to be active and outgoing. Children are also agents when they are passive and choose not to act. It is therefore necessary to have a broad range of approaches at our disposal.

Concluding remarks

Researchers have argued to let children's perceptions of their needs inform definitions of child poverty as well as measures that should be given priority (Ridge 2002, Corak 2005, van der Hoek 2005). Ridge (2002) claims that this may facilitate children's social inclusion and integration with their peers, while van der Hoek (2005) underlines that child-specific policies can open up chances for children in poor families by not letting the family's economy restrict their access to school and leisure activities. In this chapter I have also argued the case of policies being directed towards children themselves, based upon their own rights as citizens. My main argument for a rights-based approach is that children have independent claims on society. Society should no longer accept that children grow up in poverty. However, a rights-based approach puts the role of the state on the agenda. The measures discussed in this chapter, seem to presuppose an active state. This may appear contradictory to the trend in many European countries towards including civil society more explicitly in public policy, as seen, for example, in the Council of Europe's revised strategy for Social Cohesion (2004). The strategy talks about a welfare society, rather than a welfare state. There is no doubt that civil society and non-governmental organisations can contribute to providing some of the measures discussed here. Even if one accepts such a division of labour, there is in my opinion still the welfare state within the welfare society that must ensure people's basic rights through a legislative framework. The interventions that have been put forward in this article can hardly be provided as rights without the active role of the state.

Although I advocate a rights-based approach to fight child poverty, I also find it necessary to draw attention to some pitfalls that a rights-based approach may entail. One of them is to overestimate children and put too much responsibility on their shoulders. Brannen and O'Brien (1995) have argued that the language of rights presupposes an autonomous, unsupported individual, and this image does not conform to the experience of many women and children who prefer to emphasise their connectedness to others rather than their autonomy and separateness. They argue for a concept of children as agents that includes their right to protection, dependency and care.

Another pitfall is to underestimate children and approach them with an idealized perception of what childhood should be like. Boyden (1997 [1990]) has described the Western view of childhood as a happy and protected phase in their lives. Research on child poverty reveals children who worry, have restricted access to possessions and activities and take on extended responsibilities at home. Such results challenge the views of childhood as a »worry-free zone« and address some important normative issues. It is by no means obvious that every kind of restriction on children's consumption or activities should be regarded as negative. In my opinion, children's claims upon society should therefore not be based on a view of them as unconnected individuals, or as beings referred to an idealised world of happiness and protection.

A rights-based approach in order to secure children's needs should also not be practised in a way that creates contradictions between parents and children. On the contrary, there is reason to build on parents' efforts and willingness to take care of and give priority to children. At the same time it is also necessary to recognise that these expectations are putting poor parents under considerable pressure. Many pay a high price for protecting their children, in terms of worries and health problems. It is likely to be perceived as a positive contribution if the state shares the responsibility for safeguarding the rights to a decent standard of living of the youngest generation, while at the same time recognising the efforts made by most parents to bring up their children.

References

Adelman, L., Middleton, S. and Ashworth, K. (1999): *Intra-household distribution of poverty and social exclusion: Evidence from the 1999 PSE survey of Britain*: CRISP – Centre for Research in Social Policy, Working paper no. 23.

Alanen, L. (2003): *Theorizing children's welfare. Working Paper*. Cypros: Cost Action A19 Children's Welfare.

Andenæs, A. (2004): Hvorfor ser vi ikke fattigdommen? [Why do we not see the poverty?] *Nordisk Sosialt Arbeid. 24*, 1: 19-33.

Boyden, J. (1997): Childhood and the Policy Makers: A Comparative Perspective on the Globalization of Childhood. In A. James and A. Prout (2nd edition). *Constructing and Reconstructing Childhood. Contemporary Issues in the Sociological Study of Childhood*. Londont: The Falmer Press: 190-229.

Bradbury, B., Jenkins, S. and Micklewright, J. (2001): Beyond the Snapshot: A dynamic view of child poverty. I B. Bradbury, S. Jenkins and J. Micklewright (red), *The dynamics of child poverty in industrialized countries*. Cambridge: Cambridge University Press.

Bradbury, B. and Jäntti, M. (2001): Child poverty across twenty-five countries. In Bradbury, B., Jenkins, S. and Micklewright, J. (2001): Beyond the Snapshot: A dynamic view of child poverty. In B. Bradbury, S. Jenkins and J. Micklewright (eds): *The dynamics of child poverty in industrialized countries*. Cambridge: Cambridge University Press.

Bradshaw, J. (eds) (2001): *Poverty: The outcomes for children*. London: Family Policy Studies Centre/National Children's Bureau.

Bradshaw, J. (2002): Child Poverty and Child Outcomes. *Children & Society, 16*, 2: 131-140.

Brannen, J. and O'Brien, M. (1995): Childhood and the sociological gaze: Paradigms and Paradoxes. *Sociology, 29*, 4:729:737.

Christoffersen, M. N. (1994): A follow-up study of long-term effects of unemployment on children: Loss of self-esteem and self-destructive behaviour among adolescents. *Childhood, 2, 4*: 212-230.

Corak, M. (2005): *Principles and practicalities for measuring child poverty in the rich countries*. UNICEF Innocenti Research Centre: Working Paper No 2005-01.

Council of Europe (2004): *A new strategy for Social Cohesion*. Strasbourg; European Committee for Social Cohesion (CDCS).

Dahl, E. and Lødemel, I. (2003): Tiltaksplan mot fattigdom – en vurdering. [Plan of Action to combat poverty – an evaluation] *Tidsskrift for Velferdsforskning, 6*(2), 125-130.

Duncan, G. J., Brooks-Gunn, J., Yeung, W. J. and Smith, J. R. (1998): How much does childhood poverty affect the life chances of children? *American Sociological Review, 63* (June), 406-423.

Elder, G. H. (1999): *Children of the Great Depression. Social change and life experience*. Boulder, Colorado: Westview (first printed in 1974).

Elstad, J. I. (2004 A): Foreldrenes helse og livskvalitet. [Health and quality of life among the parents]. In M. Sandbaek (eds). Barns levekar. Hva betyr familiens inntekt? [Children's level of living. The impact of family income]. Oslo: NOVA rapport 11/04: 79-88.

Elstad, J. I. (2004 B): Barn i lavinntektsfamilier: helse og livskvalitet [Children in lov-income families:health and quality of life]. In M. Sandbaek (eds). Barns levekar. Hva betyr familiens inntekt? [Children's level of living. The impact of family income]. Oslo: NOVA rapport 11/04: 139-156.

Epland, J. (2001): *Barn i husholdninger med lav inntekt Omfang, utvikling, årsaker.* Oslo: Statistisk Sentralbyrå, Rapport 01:09.

Esping-Andersen, G. (2002): A Child-Centred Social Investment Strategy (26-67). I Esping-Andersen, Gøsta m.fl. (red). *Why We Need a New Welfare State.* Oxford: Oxford University Press.

Esping-Andersen, G. and Sarasa, S. (2002): The generational conflict reconsidered. *Journal of European Social Policy, Vol 12* (1): 5-21.

Evans, G. W. (2004): The Environment of Childhood Poverty. *American Psychologist, 59*(2), 77-92.

Flåte, S., Lagerstrøm, B.O. and Wedde, E. (2004): *Barns levekår i lavinntektsfamilier. Dokumentasjonsrapport [Children's leve of living in low-income families. Report of documentation].* Oslo: Statistisk Sentralbyrå. Notater.

Garbarino, J. (1998): The stress of being a poor child in America. *Child and Adolescent Psychiatric Clinics of North America, 7,* 105-119.

Harter, S. (1982): The percieved competence scale for children. *Child development* 53: 87-97.

Jensen A-M, Kjørholt, A-T, Qvortrup, J. and Sandbæk, M. with Johansen, V. and Lauritzen, T. (2004): *Country report from Norway.* Trondheim: NOSEB; NTNU.

Lister, R. and Beresford, P. (2000): Where are »the poor« in the future of poverty research? I J. Bradshaw and R. Sinsbury (Red.), *Researching Poverty.* Avebury: Aldershot.

Luthar, S.S. (1993): Annotation: Methodological and Conceptual Issues in Research on Childhood Resilience. *Journal of Child Psychology and Psychiatry, 34* (4), 441-453.

Mayall, B. and Zeiher, H. (2003): Introduction. In B. Mayall and H. Zeiher (eds). *Childhood in generational perspective.* London: Institute of Education: 1-24.

Middleton S., K. Ashworth and Braithwaite, I. (1997): *Small Fortunes. Spending on children, childhood poverty and parental sacrifice.* York: Joseph Rowntree Foundation.

Näsman, E and von Gerber, C. (1996): *Mamma pappa utan jobb [Mum and Dad without job].* Stockholm: Rädda Barnen.

Nowicki, S. and Strickland, B.R. (1973): The Locus of Control Scale for Children. *Journal of Consulting and Clinical Psychology 40* (1): 148-54.

Pahl, J. (1989): *Money and Marriage.* London: MacMillian.

Pedersen, A.W. (2002): *Om fattigdomsbegrepet og dets implikasjoner for praktisk politikk [The concept of poverty and its implications for practical policymaking].* Oslo; NOVA Skriftserie 1/02.

Qvortrup, J. (1985): Placing children in the Divison of Labour. I Close, P. and Collins, R. (red). *Family and Economy in Modern Society.* London: Macmillian.

Qvotrup, J. (2002): *Children and Childhood in social structure.* Presentation in Cost Action A19: Trondheim.

Ridge, T. (2002): *Childhood poverty and social exclusion from a child's perspective,* Bristol: The Policy Press.

Ringen, S. and Halpin, B. (1997): Children, Standard of Living and Distributions in the Family. *Journal of Social Policy, 26* (1): 21-41.

Roker, D. and Coleman, J. (2000): 'The invisible poor': Young people growing up in family poverty'. In Bradshaw, J. and Sainsbury, R. (eds). *Experiencing Poverty,* Aldershot: Ashgate.

Rutter, M. (1971): Parent-child separation: Psychological effects on the children. *Journal of Child Psychology and Psychiatry, 12*: 233-260.

Ruxton, S. and Bennett, F. (2002): *Including children? Developing a coherent approach to child poverty and social exclusion across Europe.* Brüssel: Euronet.

Sandbæk, M. and Knudsen Sture, C. (2003): *Barns levekår. Teoretiske perspektiver på familieøkonomiens betydning for barns hverdag. [Children's level of living. Theoretical perspectives on the impact of family economy on children's everyday life].* Oslo: NOVA-Skriftserie 9/03.

Sandbæk, Mona (eds) (2004): Barns levekår. Hva betyr familiens inntekt? [Children's level of living. The implications of family economy]. Oslo: NOVA report 11/04.

Seecombe, K. (2000): Families in Poverty in the 1990s: Trends, Causes, Consequences, and Lessons Learned. *Journal of Marriage and the Family. 62.* November 2000: 1094-1113.

Seecombe, K. (2002): »Beating the Odds« Versus »Changing the Odds«: Poverty, Resilience, and Family Policy. *Journal of Marriage and the Family. 64.* May 2002: 384-394.

Skevik, A. (2003): Children of the Welfare State: Individuals with Entitlements, or Hidden in the Family? *Journal of Social Policy, 32*(3), 423-440.

Skevik, A. (2004 A): Hva kjennetegner familiene med lave inntekter i Norge? [What characterises low-income families in Norway?] In M. Sandbaek (eds). *Barns levekar. Hva betyr familiens inntekt. [Children's level of living. The impact of family economy].* Oslo: NOVA rapport 11/04:32-42.

Skevik, A. (2004 B): Lavinntekt og levekarsproblemer – to sider av samme sak? [Low income and poor levels of living – two sides of the same coin?] In M. Sandbaek (eds). *Barns levekar. Hva betyr familiens inntekt. [Children's level of living. The impact of family economy].* Oslo: NOVA rapport 11/04:43-64.

Skevik, A. (2004 C): Lavinntektsfamilienes familieliv og sosiale nettverk. [Family life and social networks among low-income families]. In M. Sandbaek (eds). *Barns levekar. Hva betyr familiens inntekt. [Children's level of living. The impact of family economy].* Oslo: NOVA rapport 11/04:65-78.

Stefansen, K. (2004 A): Barns skolehverdag: Prestasjoner, sosiale relasjoner og trivsel [Achievements, social relations and well being]. In M. Sandbaek (eds). *Barns levekar. Hva betyr familiens inntekt [Children's level of living. The impact of family economy].* Oslo: NOVA rapport 11/04: 89-108.

Stefansen, K. (2004 B): Fritid og sosial deltakelse [Leisure and social participation]. In M. Sandbaek (eds). *Barns levekar. Hva betyr familiens inntekt [Children's level of living. The impact of family economy].* Oslo: NOVA rapport 11/04: 109-126.

Stefansen, K. (2004 C): Barns opplevelse av familieokonomien og egne okonomiske ressurser [Family economy and children's own economic resources]. In M. Sandbaek (eds). *Barns levekar. Hva betyr familiens inntekt? [Children's level of living. Implications of family economy].* Oslo: NOVA rapport 11/04: 127-138.

St. meld. nr. 6 (2002-2003): *Tiltaksplan mot fattigdom [Plan of Action for Combating Poverty].* Oslo: Sosialdepartement.

Thorød, A-B. (2006): En normal barndom? Foreldrestrategier for å skjerme barn fra konsekvenser av å leve med lav inntekt. [A normal childhood? Parents' strategies to protect their children from the consequences of low income]. NOVA rapport 2/06 – in press.

Van der Hoek, T. (2005): *Through children's eyes. An initial study of children's personal experiences and coping strategies growing up poor in an affluent Netherlands.* UNICEF Innocenti Research Centre.

198

Vleminckx, K. and Smeeding, T.M. (2001): *Child Well-being, Child Poverty and Child Policy in Modern Nations. What do we know?* Bristol: Policy Press.

Werner, E. E. and Smith, R. S. (1982): *Vulnerable but invincible. A longitudinal study of resilient children and youth.* New York: McGraw-Hill.

Werner, E. E. and Smith, R. S. (1992): *Overcoming the Odds. High Risk Children from Birth to Adulthood.* Ithaca: Cornell University Press.

Williams, F. (2004): Rethinking Families. London: Calouste Gulbenkian Foundation.

Notes

1   The study was conducted by NOVA, in cooperation with Norwegian Women's Public Health Association (N.K.S.). Statistics Norway was responsible for drawing the sample and interviewing. The sample was drawn from household income records. Information on the number of people in the household was added from Statistics Norway's Family Statistics for 2002. The concept of income used to draw the low-income sample was total household income after taxes and benefits. This includes income from work, income from assets and interest, and social transfers (child, housing and cash-for-care benefit, social assistance). The modified OECD scale was used to calculate equalized incomes. For further details see Flåte, Lagerstrøm and Wedde 2004.

2   The children answered questions about <u>school, leisure activities, health, family relations and their own financial means</u>, and also filled in Harter's (1982) »The perceived competence scale for children«, Nowicki and Strickland (1973) »Locus of Control Scale« as well as questions about bullying. The questionnaires to the parents covered issues like <u>demography</u> (family type and size, education, age and employment conditions), <u>the family's standard of living</u> (housing conditions, consumer goods etc), <u>social networks and health</u>. The parents also filled in questions about the relationship between parent and child and satisfaction with their relationship as a couple.

3   As part of the study, qualitative interviews were conducted with 26 children and 26 parents, drawn from parents in the low-income sample, who reported that they could not make ends meet.

4   The question did not include information about whether this happened on a regular basis. The figures can therefore not be compared to other figures reporting the frequency of bullying.

Working Children and the »Descholarisation« of Childhood

Máire Nic Ghiolla Phádraig

This paper sets out to review the studies of the combination of full-time schooling with part-time economic activity by children and young people in the affluent industrialised countries. Far from being a thing of the past, levels of participation have increased in recent years. This observation has prompted responses regarding the developmental implications both positive and negative. Explanations have ranged from the structural – such as continued hidden poverty, and the demands of the labour market – to the pressures of consumerism. Indeed, working children and young people are reduced to victims by such explanations. It is argued that the increase can only be understood as part of a complex interplay of schooling, continued poverty, labour market, cultural and family factors which give rise to a new 'generational division of labour'. Furthermore, the phenomenon may also be viewed as a way in which children and young people exercise agency to negotiate the boundaries between childhood and adulthood.

The 'modern concept of childhood' defines children's place as in family, care and school settings. The extension of universal schooling was identified as one of the major elements in the social construction of modern childhood.

> »Scholars…seem to agree that scholarisation was the event which most dramatically changed childhood.«(Qvortrup 2001:102).

Moves to extend schooling to all sections of the young population went in tandem with campaigns to eliminate child labour in the early industrializing nations, which now constitute the affluent North. Indeed, legislative changes restricting child labour in the nineteenth century and making schooling compulsory were underpinned by bourgeois ideology, promoting the family as the protector of children. Trade unions, in turn, used bourgeois ideology in pursuit of improved wages for men. »These elements gradually came together to create an arena of »legitimate« child activity. Children's main activity was to gain a »useful education«. (Lavalette 2002: 157). However, this did not rule out work that could be combined with school. This flexibility to retain children as workers, albeit on a part-time basis, resonated with bourgeois ideology stressing hard work and respect for money. Jobs such as newspaper delivery were defined as 'children's jobs' and regarded as harmless ways of useful occupation and earning pocket money. In this way, children's work was trivialised and became invisible (James, et al.: 115; Ridge: 50-51; McKechnie and Hobbs 2001: 12).

Child labour has become a renewed focus of international concern in connection with its prevalence and the harshness of its impact on the lives of children in the South. International organizations such as UNICEF, the ILO (International Programme on the Elimination of Child Labour) and Global March have mounted intensive campaigns to raise awareness of the issues and work to eliminate abusive aspects. The World Bank has also examined the problem. (HCO Working Paper) Child labour in the South is clearly linked to family poverty. An interesting common feature, of such global campaigns regarding child labour, is that the focus has shifted to the extent to which it curtails or prevents children's participation in education. (»School is the right place to work« being the slogan of Global March in 2003)

The phenomenon of children and young people of school age working remained largely unrecognised and unproblematised in the North, however. It is regarded as a historic phenomenon, not part of the modern concept of childhood. ILO studies of child labour only feature one EU country – Portugal – where levels of participation by 6-16 year olds are very low in both economic (4%) and domestic (7.7%) activity (www.ilo.org/public/english/standards/ipec/simpoc/portugal/report/english). There was some evidence of dislike of school or failure to progress as reasons prompting work, but most liked the activity and were engaged in family enterprises. By contrast, the ILO report from the Philippines indicates a much higher level of work participation (16.2%) and a more serious impact on educational levels (e.g. 6% of 5-9 year olds worked and of these almost 10% did not attend school). (www.ilo.org/public/english/standards/ipec/simpoc/philippines/report/english.

The direction of these findings links plausibly with the 'historical-poverty' model of child labour as associated with periods of economic disadvantage. Patterns of universal schooling in the North are interpreted as indicating that child labour is a thing of the past there.

Yet a number of studies from affluent countries point to an increasing level of participation by children and teenagers in economic activity (Alanen et al.; Kampmann and Warming Nielsen; Lavalette; James, Jenks and Prout; Leonard; Whyte; Morgan; Hutson and Cheung; McKechnie et al.; Dustmann; Larson and Verma; Basu and Tzannatos; McKechnie and Hobbes; Ridge; Siddiqu and Patrinos; McCoy and Smyth, 2004: 18: Unicef.org; Unicefusa.org; Short; Hansen et al.; Ingenhorst; White). McCoy and Smyth report that by the fourth year of second level schooling over 70% of Irish students had paid jobs, but that the numbers were slightly lower for the 6th year Leaving

Certificate examination candidates (2004:18). Furthermore, this has become a feature of a majority (From 2 in 3 to 4 in 5) of the teenaged school-going population in a number of countries (US, UK, Denmark, Finland, Germany and Ireland – Alanen et al.; Frederiksen; Lavalette; Ingenhorst; Hansen; Larson and Verma; McKechnie and Hobbs, 1999; Morgan; Leonard, 2004).

> »In looking at child employment in developed countries it becomes apparent that economic development, the reduction of poverty and a compulsory education system have not removed children from employment«. (McKechnie and Hobbs, 1999:97)

As a result, some commentators refer to part-time work during the school term as a 'normal' part of adolescence. Most research concentrates on term-time work, as holiday jobs are not seen as problematic in relation to academic work. Studies vary also, as to whether babysitting, or work for payment within the family should be counted. A smaller, but significant proportion of the pre-teen population are also engaged in paid employment, although this seems to vary cross-culturally (e.g. White found in her study of 12 year olds, that 1 in 3 in London, but 3 in 4 in Belfast and in Dublin had engaged in some form of gainful activity, but a study in the US by Hofferth and Sandberg reported only 4% of 9-12 year olds as 'engaging in market work':300). The range of jobs undertaken by these young people is very extensive and is well beyond the traditional 'children's jobs'. There would appear to be some tendency for children to first work in informal ways, often for family and neighbours and later to access work in more formal employment contexts. For the majority, their motivation differs from that of their peers in the South. Money is the main but not sole reason they offer for working, but instead of a contribution to the family kitty, or towards the expenses connected with schooling, the income helps fund expenditure on extra clothes, music, mobile phones, drugs, alcohol and holidays. (e.g. McCoy and Smyth, 2004:38). This is not to underestimate the importance of the direct or indirect ways that those from disadvantaged backgrounds contribute to their family's income. Leonard reports that 24% of Belfast working children hand up some of their earnings at home (2002:200). The most detailed of the studies indicate that for children from reasonably affluent backgrounds also, having paid employment helps to reduce the demands on their parents for pocket-money and 'extras'. While the combination of light work with schooling is regarded as offering positive outcomes, a significant proportion consistently work in excess of what is compatible with a good participation in school and a sufficient leisure opportunity. In some instances, students may leave school early, without qualifications, in order to work fulltime. Again, the activity is frequently in the informal sector and exposes the young people to possibly hazardous and exploitative conditions of labour.

Negative Developmental Aspects – Does Work Impede Schooling?

McKechnie and Hobbs (2001:10) argue that 3 perspectives have sought to interpret the phenomenon of children's part-time work and to relate it to children's educational task:

1. The view that part-time work gives good experience and preparation for adult roles.
2. »Benign« view of policy-makers who believe that legislation has taken the harm out of it.
3. Zero-sum model – education is the central task for children. Time in employment is at the expense of education

They argued elsewhere that a 'balance model' is required to weigh costs and benefits, which will vary from place to place and that this should be established empirically. (1998:40-41)

We find that when educational outcomes of part-time work are studied that results can be found to support all three models! Some researchers conclude that »a little part-time work« does no harm to grades or attendance or continuing participation in education. This finding is more typical of US than UK research (Larson and Verma, 1999:711; Basu and Tzannatos, 2002:160; Mizen, 1999:426). However, UK research mainly points to a negative linear relationship with grades earned. (e.g. McKechnie and Hobbs, 2001:16-17)

Aries' arguments that childhood is socially constructed and that 'scholarisation' was the main process, which brought about the modern concept of childhood, were further extended in Postman's analysis in »The Disappearance of Childhood« (1983). The main thrust of his argument is that childhood is being 'socially deconstructed' through the media making education and literacy irrelevant as a key to knowledge of the 'secrets' that were formerly reserved for the world of adults. Postman does not discuss young peoples' work, or the extent to which children may reduce their commitment to schooling because of work involvement. Instead of Postman's 'disappearance of childhood', Hengst (2004) prefers to use the term liquidation of childhood, to convey an image of blurring of boundaries between child and adult status. This seems particularly apt for the combination of work and scholarly roles for children and young people. Insofar as this can be established, we may talk about a process of the 'descholarisation of childhood.' But is this, in fact, what is happening? To establish this we need to ask

a) Is there a trend for those engaged in part-time work to drop out of school?

b) Does part-time work have a negative impact on academic performance and if so, is this a linear relationship or can a 'safe' level of participation in paid employment be identified?

a) Part-time work and early departure from or dropping out of school.

The results vary from one study to another. McKechnie and Hobbs report findings from Davies 1972 study that part-time work was associated with a negative attitude to the school leaving age (2001:16). Middleton and Loumidis study of 11-16 years old pupils in 1995 found that part-time workers have lower career aspirations than non-workers but contrast this with a recent study by Leonard of 15 year olds in Belfast, which found that participation in boring work by part-timers encouraged them to stay on at school (2001:34). Hutson and Cheung's Welsh sample of 16-19 year olds found that the majority intended to go on to further education, with some citing their Saturday job experience as having acted as a spur to them to stay on in education and move into more interesting and better paid areas of work (1992:51). The latter two samples were from a later period and their participants were older than the first two, which may account for the different patterns found. A Canadian study, which formed part of the McKechnie and Hobbs report, found that »in economically sound regions« children are more likely to drop out of school if they engage in part-time work (1998:16). McCoy and Smyth also report the trend for part-time workers in Ireland to drop out of school (2004:78).

b) The impact of part-time work on academic performance.

The zero-sum view of part-time work by school-goers points to the reduction of time available for study and homework as the source of negative impact on academic results. This is countered by the argument that time can be 'lost' in other, less productive/beneficial ways, and that provided relatively short hours are worked, that this should not affect grades.

There is a striking similarity in results from different studies of children's views on whether working impacts on their schooling. At least one quarter in the Belfast study (Leonard, 2001:288) report being tired at school, rising to approximately one third in a number of British studies (McKechnie et al., 1996:199-200; McKechnie and Hobbs, 1998: 51) but almost half (46%) in Morgan's study (2000:24). Ingenhorst refers to some children as working a 60 hour week, when the school day and homework are added to paid working hours (2001:143).

The immediate impact of working hours is likely to be on homework with large percentages of young people, in a number of studies, indicating that this is a problem for them. (Ridge, 2002:46) The proportions in this category again fell in the range from one in four (Short) to one in three (McKechnie et al. 1996:199-200; McKechnie and Hobbs, 1998:51) to almost one in two (45% – Morgan, 2000:24). However, Hutson and Cheung, in a study of older teenagers, did not find any difference in time spent on homework by part-time workers and nonworking peers (1992:60). Warren refutes the zero-sum depiction of working time and study time and found that one hour 'lost' to work means a loss of only about 20 minutes (2002:384) as

> »Students who work a lot do, in fact, do a little less homework and spend a little less time in extracurricular activities. However, they spend a lot less time with friends, with family and/or watching television« (Ibid:389).

Only if the social and practical benefits of working, are equivalent to those foregone in order to take a job, can we share Warren's enthusiasm for his findings.

The linking of academic grades to working or nonworking during the school year is examined in a few studies, with varying results. Lavalette argues that the evidence is inconclusive (1994:32). Dustmann (1996:96) found that nonworking pupils averaged 25% better results in O levels/CSE than did working pupils. But Hutson and Cheung quote a study by Courtney which found that those who had obtained the best results in O levels were more likely to be working in fifth form (45-52%) and that the proportions working fell progressively for those with lower results. They argue that

> »there has been a change from the traditional association of Saturday jobs with working-class origins and educational failure to viewing part-time employment as enabling students to stay on« (1992:47).

Indeed they claim that employers deliberately recruit 'smart youth' to attract similar customers. This is a contrast to Davies' study in 1972 which found very poor educational outcomes for those working part-time, (McKechnie and Hobbs, 2001:16) and may indicate that the differences found in his study were mainly a reflection of class origins rather than the direct impact of work as, at that stage, few middle class youths worked. McKechnie and Hobbs' own studies also found negative associations with educational tests with the exception of those working less than 5 hours who had better attendance, better rates of staying on at school and better exam results than did those who never worked. (Ibid:17). Among Irish students at Junior Certificate level, only those who worked more than 15 hours a week had lower average grades than non-workers. But the average grades of part-time workers at Leaving Certificate level are lower, regardless of the number of hours worked. (McCoy and Smyth, 2004:78-9).

It is interesting that researchers in the US who find that a little work can be harmlessly combined with high school refer to 'no more than 20 hours' – i.e. a half-time position (Mizen, 1999:426; Frone quoted in McKechnie and Hobbs 2001:19). By comparison, 5-10 hours is the upper limit, which emerges in the case of research in the UK and 12-15 hours in the case of research in Ireland (Morgan, 2000; McCoy and Smyth, 2004:78). It may be that homework demands or examination pressures may be tailored in the US to the 'normalcy' of work by adolescents, whereas perhaps this is not the case in the UK and Ireland. In Ireland, teachers are largely negative in their attitudes to part-time work and the packed curriculum they must cover and the pressure for results, makes this view inevitable. (Morgan, 2000:25)

Results from the US mainly support the view that working can be beneficial if hours fall below a threshold of 10 hours and only yield mainly negative outcomes, if in excess of 20 hours. Mizen et al. synthesise these findings:

> »there now appears to be a consensus that moderate levels of work (i.e. 10 hours per week, or less), in relatively benign jobs, can be beneficial for children, promoting self-reliance and disengagement from the family, as well as encouraging the development of effective, committed and well-adjusted students and workers. For the academically 'less able' paid work is also seen as a source of practical knowledge…In contrast, levels of working greater than 20 hours per week, especially involving low quality work, have been correlated with a range of adolescent problems ranging from poor grade point averages, truancy and premature disengagement from school through to increased levels of substance abuse, delinquency and occupational cynicism«. (1999:426)

The authors point out that the developmental perspective on children's work ignores children's agency (Ibid:426). However, Marsh's findings are much less favourable to the combination of part-time work and full-time school.

> »The negative effects of working were predominantly a linear function of the number of hours worked and were reasonably consistent across ethnicity, sex, ability levels and levels of SES … saving for college was a notable exception… it favourably affected 16 of 22 outcomes and had particularly beneficial effects on actual attendance at college, educational aspirations, academic self-concept, and time spent on homework« (1991:185).

Marsh contrasts these findings with his earlier study, which found that participation in non-academic extracurricular activities (such as sports) favourably affected academic outcomes, despite the time 'lost' in their pursuit. His conclusion was that participation in these, school-based, activities, enhanced commitment to the school, whereas

»In the present context, working apparently detracts from investment in, or commitment to, the school, which is why working has so many negative affects. My interpretation of the present findings suggests that investment in, commitment to and identification with school and the workplace are typically antagonistic« (Ibid:186).

Warren also supports this view by his findings that the link between lower grades and work intensity is mediated by a relatively higher commitment to work by comparison with commitment to school. (2002:389) McCoy and Smyth, however, found that other out of school activities were also negatively associated with lower grades – apart from sport (2004:79). Perhaps this is because pupils often work to fund various social activities.

The context of the employment may also play a role in positive or negative outcomes, but is rarely a focal point of studies of school-goers' gainful work. Hansen and Jarvis (2000) found that adolescents who were employed in family businesses or school-based work programmes fared better overall than did those employed by private enterprises.

Lack of Recognition for Children within the Education System

While school and educational activity is constructed as the main focus of children's lives, it is clear that many children and young people find little that is positive in the experience. Furthermore, the degree of negative reactions to schooling may increase with age. The main aspects of the educational experience which children may find alienating are its contents, its authority structures and the gap between the rhetoric of the value of education and the reality of the low status of pupils and students.

a) Content

An over concentration on academic preparation for Third Level may seem irrelevant to those whose interests and plans lie elsewhere. Failure at school-work may prompt searching for alternative sources of a feeling of self-worth, which paid work may supply. In particular, education with an academic focus, may alienate children from the working class, or those who have low achievement levels. This may prompt them to look for satisfaction and status from paid employment (McKechnie et al., 1996:202; McKechnie and Hobbs, 1998: 30). However, Marsh's analysis suggests that while part-time work contributes positively to self-concept in the early years of high-school, that in later years the association is negative (Marsh, 1991:186). The argument advanced by

Qvortrup (1985), that school is actually work by children, as without it they would be less effective workers in the future, is not always shared by children. Mayall's study of 13 year olds finds them unconvinced on the scholarisation thesis

> »Whilst school activity can be described as work, it is much less hard than parents' work, and takes up less time« (2002:68)

b) Authority

School tends to be experienced as increasingly rigid and restrictive as pupils grow older and young people frequently see greater autonomy and flexibility in work situations, by comparison. Authority structures, which fail to incorporate increasingly competent children and youth, are also alienating. It is striking that this response is reported as early as primary school, for many children (Christenson and James, 2001:79; Devine, 2003:117-124). Ironically, both studies also refer to teachers themselves reporting feeling lack of control due to curricular and regulations pressures.

c) Rhetoric

Although adults preach »deferred gratification« as the rationale of education to children, this rhetoric is not matched in the lifestyles of adults around them, providing yet another instance for children, of 'don't do as I do, do as I say'. Consumerism, readiness to incur debt and failure to continue their own education, may instead be the example set by significant adults.

Hidden Poverty – Children's Work and the Reproduction of Class

Aries claimed that the concept of »childhood« originated with the upper and middle classes and only later reached the lower classes. This can be roughly linked to the introduction of compulsory schooling. A frequent comment by researchers is that while in the early twentieth century, only working class children worked, now all do and it is no longer stigmatised (McKechnie and Hobbs, 2001:21; Lavalette, 1994:219). When we look at the evidence regarding current patterns of work by children and youth, we find subtle class differences, which help explain »how working class kids get working class jobs« (Willis). Jones' work has been very helpful in pointing to diverging pathways by class background (1991). Summarising the US research, Hansen concludes that there are two pathways

a)   Lower socio-economic kids have high intensity employment in high-school, moving directly to fulltime adult employment.

b)   Middle class kids have lower intensity employment, which serves as a complement to the academic pathway to higher education. (Hansen, 2001:131-133)

Although Warren does not utilise class as a variable, his description of this process complements that of Hansen:

> »One function of the educational system is to sort young people into various post-high school trajectories: college, work, family and others.
>   …At some point during their educational careers, students form some ideas about what awaits them after high school. This understanding has important implications for students' decisions about how to spend their time, which courses to take, how hard to work in school, and so on. Students who see paid employment (and not college) as the activity that will occupy them after graduation quite understandably turn to intensive paid employment while still enrolled in school« (2002:390).

Although academic results can be crucial for future progress to higher education and hence to higher qualifications and employment opportunities, most commentators would not make a judgement on the advisability of combining part-time work with full-time schooling based solely on this dimension. For other students, who do not aspire to third level education, part-time work is often a predictor of good employment outcomes after leaving school.

> »Students who have paid work experience before they leave school appear to make a smoother transition into the labour market. They are less likely to experience unemployment and, when employed, they receive moderately higher pay and are more likely to enter white-collar occupations« (McCoy and Smyth, 2004:79).

McCoy and Smyth refer to the combination of part-time work with full-time schooling as offering a 'safety-net' to the less academic (Ibid: 89). Given that about one third of Irish students with part-time jobs plan to work in the same or a similar job after leaving school, this would seem a good way of testing the employment scene. (Ibid: 38). The view that part-time work can promote development of skills with social interaction, responsibility, experience of handling money, time management, etc. as well as harmlessly engaging energy and time, is quite widespread among parents and helps to encourage children's participation in part-time work (Hutson and Cheung, 1992:60; Justegard, 2002:203; Morgan, 2000:24-25). Parents were often helpful in accessing work opportunities (Justegard, 2002:203) viewing this as a broader socialising experience as well as offering an income to their children.

Currently, children from disadvantaged backgrounds are less likely to be engaged in paid work, because they have less contacts who are employed and less openings in their localities, due to higher levels of unemployment (Morrow, 1994; McKechnie and Hobbs, 2001:21; Dustmann, 1996:88; Middleton and Loumidis, 2001:28). Nevertheless, most children and young people in poverty aspire to getting a part-time job (Ridge, 2002:49). There may also be internal competition in disadvantaged families regarding which members can be released for employment participation. Older children in the household may be pressed into service, as unpaid childminders and housekeepers, for parents who cannot afford commercial services. (Dodson and Dickert, 2004) But in times and places of labour shortage, a greater percentage of disadvantaged children and youth take up part-time work while at school (Morgan, 2001:18; McCoy and Smyth, 2004:32). When such children hold jobs, they typically earn lower pay and work longer hours than middle class children (Morgan, 2001:18-19; McKechnie and Hobbs, 2012:21; Middleton and Loumidis, 2001:29-30; McCoy and Smyth, 2004:32).

Legislation regarding children's work and compulsory schooling has led to a complacency that it has been cleansed of its more harmful aspects and is 'harmless' – whereas its largely informal sector location can be hazardous for child workers. (James, Jenks and Prout, 1998:112-114) The 'socialisation/developmental' view of children predominates in professional and public discourse and it becomes natural to view children's work as a preparation for adult roles (Mizen, 1999)

Children's niche in the labour market

It has been argued by Jens Qvortrup that children's waged or domestic work, in affluent societies, »is somehow residual and anachronistic« (2001:93) as the modern capitalist economy has entered a new phase in which manual work has lost importance to abstract or symbolic activities – from producing use values to producing exchange values and from simple to extended production« (ibid:96). Children's time in school expanded to reflect this. While the 'knowledge-based economy' is undoubtedly dominant, nevertheless, as Braverman argued in 1974, and I would still argue today, the expansion of service sector employment includes not just highly skilled jobs requiring an educated workforce, but also many unskilled and semi-skilled jobs – precisely the range which are identified as employing children and adolescents, along with other marginalized groups in society. Many such jobs are in enterprises catering to new tastes/needs such as fast-food outlets, rather than simply anachronistic articulations with receding modes of production.

»Overall, students are most likely to be employed in service jobs, particularly in petrol stations/shops, pubs/off-licences and the hotel/restaurant/fast food sector« (McCoy and Smyth, 2004:49).

Mizen et al. argue that to talk about »children's jobs« is to ignore the similarity of children's jobs to those of other marginalized workers (1999:428). The concept of 'children's jobs' (keep them occupied and provide a little more pocket-money) leads to a too ready dismissal of poverty as the real reason for working, in the case of children from disadvantaged backgrounds. This happens despite the evidence of increased levels of child poverty (ibid:429).

The Labour Market context of children's employment is identified as significant by Lavalette (1994:3) and also by Mizen et al:

> »…given that children work in the same sectors as young workers, the hotel and catering, wholesale and retail sectors… there is strong justification for believing that school age children have been caught up in employer's greater use of part-time youth and student labour more generally…
>
> This is because children represent a useful source of additional flexible labour, particularly in those undercapitalised and intensely competitive areas of the service sector where they tend to work … Like older students working in the service sector…children are a flexible and relatively quiescent group of workers, willing to work irregular hours at short notice, and unlikely to anticipate high wages. What is more, given the constraints of schooling and the absence of direct pressures to maintain a regular wage, working children are also uninterested in full-time work or in acquiring long-term or secure employment« (1999:428).

Case-study: Recent labour market changes in Ireland and school-goers' employment

As an example of the impact of labour market changes and the combination of part-time work and full-time schooling, we find a very striking example in Ireland which has experienced an economic boom from the mid-1990s with a small dip since 2001. The main growth in GDP can be attributed to the establishment of plants in the Computer and Pharmaceutical industries by US-based Trans National Corporations (O'Hearn, 2002; 2003; Allen, 2000). But the main expansion in employment occurred in the service sector and low pay and part-time jobs also increased (O'Hearn, 2003; Kirby, 2002:52; Allen, 2003:68 and O'Reardon, 2001:138). The preliminary phase of the boom was sustained by the incorporation of the 'Reserve Army' of women workers, (Census and QNHS, 2001) and from the late 1990s there was an influx of immigrant workers to fill various labour shortages (Census, 2002:24; Department of Enterprise, Trade and Employment) but it is striking how the number of second-level students working in part-time jobs also expanded over this period. In 1994 25% of Junior Cycle students and 31% of Senior Cycle students held part-time jobs but just seven years later, in 2001 these rates had risen to 70% Junior and 73% Senior Cycle students (McCoy and Smyth, 2002; 2004:15)

Far from being an 'anachronistic residue', children's work can be situated in the contemporary phase of capitalism as regards labour market segmentation and the extent to which goods and services have been commoditised. There is evidence also, that work which children might previously have carried out »to help« in their own homes, or for neighbours, now sometimes receives payment.

Consumerism

Within globalised capitalism, consumerism and the role of the media in advertising products, play a role in developing a need for greater income. The commoditization of leisure (from the days of skipping ropes in the streets to bowling alleys) has created new pressures for children to find money or to risk social exclusion (Mizen et al. 1999:433, 435; Mizen et al. 2001: 53-4; Ridge, 2003:57). At its most extreme, these pressures may manifest themselves in the bullying of those whose clothes are deemed 'uncool' (Ridge, 2003: 67; Daly and Leonard, 2002: 132-138). Consumerism is frequently linked with the »Disappearance of Childhood« in relation to the marketing of products, formerly reserved for adults/adolescents, to children – make up, sexualised clothes, pop videos, etc.

Children's first encounter with capitalism is through their construction as consumers. Their development of a sense of identity is linked to awareness of possessions.

> »Economic independence begins with the receipt of a personal income from pocket money, or from a part-time job, which allows the child to enter the market place, with the power to buy, to barter and to give« (Jones, 1992:27).

To the extent that goods and services have been commoditised, empowerment of children and young people increasingly comes from access to money. The sums at the disposal of the »average« child have increased accordingly – Danes quotes expenditure data from the US population of 7-18 year olds as having risen from $36 million in 1979 to $56 million in 1990, although the youth population itself had declined by 4 million over this period (Danes, 1991:Chap. 4: 1)

> »The colonisation of children's leisure time by commercial organisations, together with the commercialisation of civic responsibility by local authorities, means that

the socially inclusive provision of the past has been replaced by the more (socially) exclusive standards of the market« (Mizen et al., 2001:53)

While parents make big efforts to provide pocket money, even in disadvantaged circumstances (Ridge, 2002:39-42; Daly and Leonard, 2002:148-150; Hutson and Cheung, 1992: 53-57), it is striking how frequently the reasons offered by young people for their part-time work, prioritise not just »money« but »independent money« which they could spend without reference to their parents' views (Hutson and Cheung, 1992:59; Justegard, 2002:205; McKechnie and Hobbs, 1998:52; Ridge, 2002:47-48; Mizen et al. 2001:44-45). Ingenhorst expresses this process very well:

> »Children's autonomous income is the material aspect of their separation from parents and the basis upon which the moulding of their own cultural world takes place. Commercialised as this culture is, it is also part of the symbolic politics of youth, through which they can express their autonomy and independence and initiate a break or departure from the modes of conduct of previous generations« (2001:142).

Mizen points out that, for the powerless, among whom he numbers children, leisure is a hugely important vehicle for agency:

> »It is precisely because they are so powerless, that their school and family lives are so constraining and that they exercise so little influence over their lives, that leisure is invested with such significance« (2001:432).

We have already looked at constraining aspects of schooling and will now do so for family. Have family and educational contexts changed (or failed to adapt to the times) in a way that promotes the phenomenon of part-time work?

Changes in the Family

Reformist movements in the industrialised countries during the nineteenth and early twentieth century, brought about a social construction of the family as comprised of male breadwinner, schooled child and fulltime homemaker wife. (Humphries, 2003; Lavalette, 1994). This achieved such normative status, that any other arrangement (work by child, or wife) was regarded as stigmatised. This model held good up to the middle of the twentieth century, when labour shortages brought a peace-time call-up for the reserve army of female labour, who were now also in a position to control their fertility. The growth of consumerism gave wage-earning mothers a higher status than housewives and so the new role model for children gave paid labour a higher status than domestic or unpaid labour. The family as a site for 'intensive care' of preschool children, gave way to day-care arrangements, with crèches repackaged as 'early education'. Day-care has, in many ways, brought down the age of childhood into infancy at a time when compulsory schooling ages have risen. (Nic Ghiolla Phádraig, 1994:93-4) The outcome for children has been a lengthening of their childhood at both ends, at a time when personal autonomy and individualised incomes have been emphasised.

Patterns of domestic labour have also changed in a way that devolves more responsibility onto the child and thereby reduces their »social age«. For example, the extensive use of »self-care«or the 'latch key kids', from middle childhood onwards. Zeiher has pointed out that the combination of mothers in paid work, and the restructuring of domestic labour due to developments in technology, service markets and lifestyles

> »could lead to a dissolution of the domestic community, each member of the family attending primarily to their own interests and needs« (Zeiher, 2001:53).

Other changes affecting children have taken place within the household. Consumption patterns have changed, with 2-3 family meals a day being replaced by newer, independent sources of food such as takeaways, individual freezer to microwave meals, 'grazing' from the fridge, or eating when in the vicinity of food outlets, etc. Dane's data indicate that not only do children have more to spend, but also, they often buy for their own subsistence. (Dane, 1991:2) Other studies also refer to children using earnings to buy school meals, etc (no more uncool packed lunches). (Justegard, 2002) We can see other aspects of the 'individuation' of consumption patterns, not just meals but also media usage, outings, holidays – formerly all were 'in common', but now there is more and earlier individuation of such activities, e.g. separate TVs in bedrooms rather than a single, communal set.

A major change in family life since the mid-twentieth century has been the extent of relationship breakdown, divorce, second unions, cohabitation, births outside marriage and lone parenting. Any given child could potentially experience some or all of these situations while they are growing up. Any change in the legal and domestic situation of parents has implications for both economic resources and domestic labour within whatever household the children now find themselves. The linkage of relationship breakdown/separation to diminished economic resources has been well documented and this may even affect higher socio-economic groups. It is not difficult to project 'covert poverty' as part of the reason for work by children from a more diverse class background than formerly.

Changing patterns of family life are not the only way in which the family circumstances may increase the likelihood of young people dividing their time between work and school. Some older forms of economic activity continue such as family owned small businesses (especially farming), which may still draw on the (largely unpaid) labour of school-going children (McCoy and Smyth, 2004:87; Song, 2001)

Generational Division of Labour

The concept of generation, in Alanen's sense of

> »a historically positioned age group whose members undergo a similar socialisation process, which brings about a shared frame of experience and action and makes them into an 'actual' generation« (2003:31),

is of value in drawing together the separate strands of the discussion so far. This has the advantage of locating children and young people in their consumerist, family, historical and labour market situations simultaneously. Wintersberger (2005) offers a detailed analysis of the transformation of the generational division of labour over time. The present account seeks to sketch the phases in a more abbreviated manner.

We can divide children's participation in economically valued employment as follows:

1. Pre-Capitalism and early Capitalism/Industrial Revolution – During this period childhood has not yet been constructed in its modern sense. The boundaries between household members are not rigidly distinctive as regards economic activity in which children are included, as are all other household members, to varying degrees.

2. Mature Capitalism – from mid-19th Century onwards until about 1970 –
    During this period we find clearly distinctive generational and sexual divisions of labour. Nuclear families, within a Fordist model of stable employment and stable conjugal relationships, consisting of men as wage-earners and producers, but women restricted in their economic activity and domesticated as homemakers/ unpaid housekeepers and caregivers (Lee, 2001:72-3). The value of this reproductive labour is ignored and they are categorised as 'Consumers', whose economic dependence is partly underwritten by the Welfare State. School was developed as a new special institution for children, which removed them from the family domain and from economically rewarded activities. Children are excluded from gainful employment. Compulsory schooling provides a response to the demands of this phase of capitalism for a more educated work-force. School is presented as a service to children in a developmentalist perspective, but its importance to capitalism and the expanded white collar sector of employment is a key factor

in its universal, compulsory nature. Children are not rewarded for their efforts in school and are constructed as beneficiaries and consumers (Qvortrup, 2001). The economic costs of children, to families, escalate, they are constructed as dependants and this has a depressing impact on fertility levels (Qvortrup, 1987). The Welfare State underpins the new order and the elderly are reconstructed as pensioners.

3. Late Capitalism/Globalization Commoditisation – late 20th Century on
   There is a 'blurring' or 'liquidation' of boundaries, first sexual with the new feminist movement and then generational. Labour shortages are created by the combination of the commoditisation of goods and services (formerly supplied by the unpaid labour of mainly women), the greater level of production of consumer goods, the development of technology and also demographic declines. These labour shortages are initially solved, by the 'Reserve Army of Women' being reincorporated in economically rewarded activity. Consumerism and the importance of being able to purchase a wide range of domestic appliances and goods help to motivate women to participate in the labour force. This, in turn, leads to further changes in the family and the greater trend of economic independence of women makes lone parenting more feasible, although frequently, where wages are low, the outcome may be poverty. In dual-earner families also, the role models presented by parents, is of the greater importance of economically gainful activities over unpaid activities. Although the new industries are typically more technologically sophisticated, the greatest expansion of jobs occurs in the less skilled services and production. A new 'Reserve Army' is needed and children and young people are reincorporated in a part-time, marginal capacity. Because their employment is mainly in the informal sector, they have none of the protections of health and safety regulations, or wage and holiday entitlements of adult workers. Consumerism, which helped to stimulate women's participation in the labour force, also plays a role in the recruitment of young people. With a majority of young people combining part-time work with second-level schooling, two paths emerge for them. In the first, school takes priority and work is curtailed, particularly in examination years, to give precedence to study. In the second, the satisfactions of work, both intrinsic and extrinsic are given priority over schooling. The less academically inclined find this of value later in accessing employment. In the face of continuing decline in the birth-rate, older members of the labour force are deconstructed as prospective pensioners, in response to the pressure on pension funds. Instead, they are directed to remain economically active for additional years, before qualifying for State benefits, or to make private provision for pensions.

The discourse of developmentalism masks the impact of global capitalism on the increased economic activity of children and young people in the affluent countries. The dominant culture of the current period evaluates everything in terms of economic returns and promotes a work-ethic linked exclusively to economic activity.

Can we argue that 'descholarisation' is taking place?

It is also important to note that part-time work promotes early school-leaving in some cases and dilutes grades in others. But it is difficult to unravel the extent to which lower school achievement precedes or follows involvement in part-time work.

Part-time work is a hugely important part of a positive self-concept for many children and young people. It affords them recognition that they are growing up and ready to take on more adult-like roles, without taking on the full responsibility of adulthood (Hengst's preferred term of 'liquidation of childhood' rather than its 'disappearance' may be more appropriate here (2004)). Parents also mainly support the view that part-time work can be a positive, developmental experience. It may be argued that part-time work has replaced progress through school as a marker of transition to adulthood. In Finland, where the combination of paid work and school work is 'becoming something of a cultural norm' (Alanen, et al. 2004:196) it is concluded that

> »The meaning and value for children of participating in working life cannot be reduced to simply earning money…(but also to) the opportunities that participation in working life gives to children's integration and status in society. Children's claims on access to and place-making in working-life are structured by adult 'ownership' of working life space: participation is experienced as rewarding as such, although the type of work children can obtain, the working conditions and the pay they receive are far from satisfactory« (ibid:197).

> »Recognition in the adult world« was an important part of the reasons young people in Germany gave for part-time work (Ingenhorst, 2001:141). Leonard's sample of 15 year olds in Belfast (2001:273) gave reasons, which included »the ability to be able to renegotiate age and its link with childhood identity…they were able to move between the status of child and adult.«

For some, at least, the status and recognition of competence at work, helps to compensate for a poor school experience. Findings of children being bored at school are not uncommon even at primary level (Christensen and James, 2001:79). Lack of control over what one does and how one does it, in school, is another common finding (Devine, 2003). By contrast many young part-time workers believe that they have more control at work. McKechnie et al. (1996:202) and others would question this belief as having no basis in reality, except for a tiny minority. Yet, having 'chosen' to work would seem to sustain this illusion at least for a time, although experience may bring new consciousness. (McKechnie and Hobbs, 1998:31; Morgan, 2000:27) For example, lack of control and not being treated on a par with adult workers, were raised as important issues by young people in a couple of qualitative studies. (Leonard, 2004:55; Frederiksen, 1999) But it would appear that, for many, the experience of control through work largely refers to access to independent money and the purchasing power it brings. This may indirectly bring status as »The role of consumption has steadily grown as the marker of integration into and membership in society.« (Alanen et al., 2004:197)

The labour market demands for a more educated workforce, which supported a lengthening of years of schooling, have become more nuanced. There is a shortage of service sector personnel, on the one hand, and also a targeting of children and young people as consumers – both of the services partly supplied by their peers, but also of consumer goods for the youth market. This incorporation, of children and young people in the labour-force, has taken place without any reference to the special health and safety risks, pay and conditions issues which arise in relation to them. (Leonard, 2002:198; 2004) The economic forces of a maturing industrial capitalist economy, which banned child labour and contributed to the social construction of childhood as a period of schooling, devoid of economic activity, have come full circle. The impact of the construction of children as economic dependants, on fertility levels (Qvortrup, 1985; Caldwell, 1982) and consequently on the supply of labour, coincides with an increased acceptance of consumerism and a search for the cash to pursue it. This first drew women/mothers back into the labour force and promoted an ideological shift, which valued economic over domestic labour for them. The next phase has been the search for a new reserve army of labour, drawing to some extent on immigrants, but also on young people. There are limits to the need for an 'educated' work-force, many unskilled/semiskilled tasks remain to be carried out. The combination of an independent cash flow and their treatment, when at work, as of adult status, is a big attraction to young people, whose growing social competence is largely ignored in the school system. (Devine, 2003; Lynch 1989) For this group, at least, the secular trend of scholarisation of childhood has ceased and we are now witnessing a process of descholarisation, in which the progressive lengthening of schooling and childhood has gone into reverse.

References

Alanen, L. (2003): »Childhoods: the generational ordering of social relations«, in Mayall, B. and H. Zeiher (eds) *Childhood in Generational Perspective*, London: Institute of Education Bedford Way Papers: 27-45.

Alanen, L., Sauli, H., Strandell, H. (2004): »Children and Childhood in a Welfare State: the case of Finland« in Jensen, A-M., Ben-Arieh, A., Conti, C., Kutsar, D., Nic Ghiolla Phádraig, M. and Hanne Warming Nielsen (eds) *Children's Welfare in Ageing Europe*, Vol. 1, Trondheim: Norwegian Centre for Child Research.

Allen, K., (2000): *The Celtic Tiger*, Manchester University Press.

Allen, K. (2003): »Neither Boston nor Berlin: class polarisation and neo-liberalism in the Irish Republic« in Coulter and Coleman (eds): 56-73.

Aries, P. (1962): *Centuries of Childhood*, London:Cape.

Basu, K. and Z. Tzannatos, (2003): »Child Labor and Development: An Introduction«, *The World Bank Economic Review*, Vol. 17, No. 2,: 145-146.

Braverman, H. (1974): *Labor and Monopoly Capital: the degradation of work in the twentieth century*, New York and London: Monthly Review Press.

Caldwell, J.C. (1982): *Theory of Fertility Decline*, London: Academic Press.

Census of Population, Ireland, various years.

Census of Population, Ireland, 2002: Preliminary Demographic Results, Dublin: Stationery Office. http://www.cso.ie/census/documents/pdr_2002pdf

Christensen, P. and A. James, »What are schools for? The temporal experience of children's learning in Northern England.« In Alanen, L. and Mayall, B. (eds) (2001): *Conceptualizing Child-Adult Relations.* London: Routledge Falmer: 70-85.

Coulter, C. and S. Coleman, (eds) (2003): *The End of Irish History?: Critical Reflections on the Celtic Tiger*, Manchester: Manchester University Press.

Danes, S.M. »Children and Money – Income and Expenditures«, Chap. 4 of Hostler, S.L. *Family-Centered Care: An Approach to Implementation*, http://www.cyfc.umn.edu/adolescents/resources/IB1001.html

Department of Enterprise, Trade and Employment, Ireland http://www.entemp.ie/labour/workpermits/statistics.htm

Devine, D. (2003): *Children, Power and Schooling – How Childhood is Structured in the Primary School*, Stoke on Trent: Trentham Books.

Dodson, L. and J. Dickert, (2004): »Girls' Family Labor in Low-Income Households: A Decade of Qualitative Research«, *Journal of Marriage and Family*, Vol. 66 (May 2004):318-332.

Dustmann, C., J. Middlewright, N. Rajah, and S. Smith, (1996): »Educational Policy and the Growth of Part-Time Work by Full-Time Pupils«, XXX Vol. 17, No. 1:79-103.

Frederiksen, L. (1999): »Child and Youth Employment in Denmark – comments on children's work from their own perspective«, *Childhood*, Vol 6 (1):101-112.

Fyfe, A., Roselaers, F., Tzannatos, Z. and F. Rosati, (2003): »Understanding Children's Work: An Interagency Data and Research Cooperation Project«, *The World Bank Economic Review*, Vol. 17, No. 2:311-314.

MÁIRE NIC GHIOLLA PHÁDRAIG

Hansen, D. D. and P. A. Jarvis, (2000): »Adolescent employment and psychosocial outcomes: a comparison of two employment contexts« *Youth and Society,* Vol. 13, No. 4:417-436.

Hansen, D.M., J.T. Mortimer and H. Kruger, (2001): »Adolescent part-time employment in the United States and Germany: diverse outcomes, contexts and pathways« in Mizen, Pole and Bolton (eds).

Hengst, H. (2004): »Allocation, dislocation and relocation of children's experiences and senses of places« Paper presented to COST Action 19 meeting, Norrkoping, 19.6.2004.

Hofferth, S.L. and J.F. Sandberg, (2001): »How American Children Spend their Time«, *Journal of Marriage and the Family,* Vol. 63, No. 2.

Horan, P.M. and P.G. Hargis, (1991): »Children's Work and Schooling in the Late Nineteenth-Century Family Economy«, *American Sociological Review,* Vol. 56, pp 583-596.

Humphries, J. (2003): »Child Labor: Lessons from the Historical Experience of Today's Industrial Economies«, *The World Bank Economic Review,* Vol. 17, No. 2: 175-196.

Hutson, S. and W. Cheung (1992): »Saturday Jobs: Sixth-formers in the Labour Market and the Family« in Marsh, C. and S. Arber (eds) *Families and Households: Divisions and Change,* London: Macmillan.

Ingenhorst, H. (2001): »Child labour in the Federal Republic of Germany« in Mizen et al (eds).

Ireland, Statistical Abstract, various years.

Ireland, Statistical Yearbook, various years.

James, A., C. Jenks and A. Prout (1998): *Theorising Childhood,* Cambridge: Polity Press.

Jones, G. (1992): »Short-term Reciprocity in Parent-Child Economic Exchanges« in Marsh, C. and S. Arber, (eds) *Families and Households: Divisions and Change,* London: Macmillan.

Justegard, H. (2002): »Earning money of your own: paid work among teenagers in Sweden« in Hutchings, M., M. Fulop and A.M. Van den Dries, (eds) *Young People's Understanding of Economic Issues in Europe,* Stoke on Trent: Trentham Books, pp 193-210.

Kampmann, J. and Warming Nielsen, H. (2004): »Socialized childhood: children's childhoods in Denmark« in Jensen, A-M., Ben-Arieh, A., Conti, C., Kutsar, D., Nic Ghiolla Phádraig, M. and Hanne Warming Nielsen (eds) *Children's Welfare in Ageing Europe,* Vol. I1, Trondheim: Norwegian Centre for Child Research.

Kirby, P. (2002): *The Celtic Tiger in Distress: Growth with Inequality in Ireland,* Hamps: Palgrave.

Larson, R.W. and S. Verma (1999): »How Children and Adolescents Spend Time Across the World: Work, Play and Developmental Opportunities«, *Psychological Bulletin,* Vol. 125, No. 6, pp 701-736.

Lavalette, M. (1994): *Child Employment in the Capitalist Labour Market,* Aldershot: Avebury.

Lee, N. (2001): *Childhood and Society: Growing up in an age of uncertainty,* Buckingham: Open University Press.

Leonard, M. (2001): »Children as Workers: A Case Study of Child Employment in Belfast« in Cleary, A., M. Nic Ghiolla Phádraig and S. Quin (eds) *Understanding Children,* Vol. 1: State, Education and Economy, Cork: Oak Tree Press.

Leonard, M. (2002): »Working on Your Doorstep – Child newspaper deliverers in Belfast«, *Childhood,* Vol. 9 (2):190-204.

Leonard, M. (2004): »Children's Views on Children's Right to Work: Reflections from Belfast«, *Childhood,* Vol. 11 (1):45-61.

Lynch, K. (1989): *The Hidden Curriculum:Reproduction in education a reappraisal*, London: Falmer.

Marsh, H. W. (1991): »Employment during High School: Character Building or a Subversion of Academic Goals?«, *Sociology of Education,* Vol. 64, No., pp 172-190.

Mayall, B. (2002): *Towards a Sociology for Childhood:Thinking from Children's Lives*, Oxford University Press.

McCoy, S. and E. Smyth (2002): »At Work in School: Part-time employment and Student Out-comes«, Seminar paper 28.3.2002 at the Economic and Social Research Institute, Dublin.

McCoy, S. and E. Smyth (2004) *At Work in School: Part-Time Employment among Second-level Students*, Dublin: Oak Tree Press and Educational Policy Research Centre, Economic and Social Research Institute.

McKechnie, J. and S. Hobbs, (eds) (1998): *Working Children: Reconsidering the Debates* (Report of the International Working Group on Child Labour). Amsterdam: Defence for Children International.

McKechnie, J. and Hobbs, S. (1999): »Child Labour – The view from the North«, *Childhood,*Vol. 6(1):89-100.

McKechnie, J. Lindsay, S. Hobbs and M. Lavalette. (1996): »Adolescents' Perceptions of the Role of Part-Time Work«, *Adolescence,*Vol. 31, No. 121: 193-204.

McKechnie, J. and S. Hobbs (2001): »Work and Education: are they compatible for children and adolescents?« in Mizen et al (eds).

Middleton, S. and J. Loumidis (2001): »Young people, poverty and part-time work« in Mizen et al (eds).

Mizen, P., A. Bolton and C. Pole (1999): »School Age Workers in Britain: The Paid Employment of Children in Britain«, *Work Employment and Society*, 13,3:423-438.

Mizen, P., C. Pole and A. Bolton (2001): »Why be a school age *worker*?« in Mizen et al (eds).

Mizen,P., C. Pole and A. Bolton (eds) (2001): *Hidden Hands- International Perspectives on Children's Work and Labour*, London: Routledge Falmer.

Morgan, M. (2000): *School and Part-Time Work in Dublin,* Dublin: Dublin Employment Pact.

Morrow,V. (1994): »Responsible Children? Aspects of Children's Work and Employment Outside School in Contemporary UK« in Mayall, B. (1994): *Children's Childhoods Observed,* London: Falmer.

Nic Ghiolla Phádraig, M., (1994): »Daycare – Adult Interests versus Children's Needs?« in Qvortrup, J. et al (eds) *Childhood Matters: Social Theory, Practice and Politics,* Aldershot: Avebury.

O'Hearn, D. (2002): *The Atlantic Economy*, Manchester: Manchester University Press.

O'Hearn, D. (2003):»Macroeconomic policy in the Celtic Tiger: a critical reassessment« in Coulter and Coleman (eds):34-55.

Postman, N. (1983): *The Disappearance of Childhood*, London:WH Allen.

Qvortrup, J. (1985): »Placing Children in the Division of Labour« in P. Close and R. Collins (eds) *Family and Economy in Modern Society*, Basingstoke: Macmillan.

Qvortrup, J. (2001): »School-work, paid work and the changing obligations of childhood« in Mizen et al (eds).

Ridge, T. (2002): *Childhood Poverty and Social Exclusion – From a child's perspective*, Bristol: The Policy Press.

Short, V. »Child Labour in Britain: A quarter of school children working«, World Socialist Web Site, 14.2.1998
http://www.wsws.org/news/1998/feb1998/britain.shtml

Siddiqi, F. and Patrinos, H.A. »Child labor: issues, causes and interventions«,
http://www.worldbank.org/html/extdr/hnp/hddflash/workp/wp_00056.html

Song, M. (2001): »Chinese children's work roles in immigrant adaptation« in Mizen et al (eds).

UNICEF, »Issue Summary: Child Labor«
http://www.unicefusa.org/childlabor/

UNICEF, »Child protection«
http://www.unicef.org/protection/index_childlabour.html

Warren, J. R. (2002): »Reconsidering the relationship between student employment and academic outcomes: A new theory and better data«, *Youth and Society*, Vol. 22, No. 3:366-393.

Willis, P. (1977): *Learning to Labour – How Working Class Kids Get Working Class Jobs*, Farnborough: Saxon House.

Wintersberger, H. (2005): »Work, welfare and generational order: towards a political economy of childhood« in Qvortrup, J. (ed.) *Studies in Modern Childhood: Society, Agency and Culture*, Basingstoke: Palgrave.

Zeiher, H.(2001): »Children as Family Members in West Berlin« in Alanen, L. and B. Mayall (eds) *Conceptualizing Child-Adult Relations*, London and NY: Routledge and Falmer.

Age order and children's agency

Anna-Liisa Närvänen and Elisabet Näsman

Introduction

The aim of this article is to contribute to a discussion on the complex interplay between structure, culture and agency, focusing on children's agency as a part of childhood welfare. In present-day welfare states, children's agency has surfaced as an important aspect of the discourse on a good childhood. Today, processes of individualization in modernity also include children, because welfare state measures target children as individuals, thus offering them, as individuals, rights with regard to level of living standard, distribution of resources and access to services, particularly in the so-called institutional or social democratic welfare state models. »The egalitarian provision of social right involves an individuation of the population in order to achieve adequate administrative and bureaucratic conditions for social justice« (Turner 1986:121). The state reaches out to the individual child, hence penetrating the privacy boundaries of the family. This also takes the form of institutionalization of children's time and activities. Starting with the decision about compulsory schooling, the childhood school years have successively increased in number, publicly financed institutional day-care facilities are increasing their coverage in the early childhood population and children spend an increasing amount of their non-school time in publicly supported and organized after-school activities. Accordingly, children tend more and more to have their own time-space-activity pattern relative to that of their parents, involving social relations that other family members are not involved in. In this sense, the 'familialization' of children has been reduced as a result of development of the welfare state (Alanen 1992:93). In addition to these processes of individualization and the parallel processes of institutionalisation, there has been increasing emphasis on children's rights, not only in terms of protection and provision, but also in terms of participation, i.e. an emphasis on children's agency. The UN Convention on the Rights of the Child and its ratification constitute a formal expression of this, but there are also tendencies to be found in national legislation, such as the banning of harsh means of fostering children, introduction of children's ombudsmen as well as informal trends towards more democratic ways of raising children. Still another tendency towards individualization is the emphasis placed on the self-realization of individuals – the idea that individuals have a wide scope for making choices in constructing their own life careers and, hence, are also responsible for the possible mistakes they make. »The risk society« and increasing demands for reflexivity are related to the welfare of children in terms of their scope of agency (Beck 1992, Giddens 1991). Accordingly, understanding children's agency in present day Europe is a central element in analyses of the welfare of European childhood. One question here is whether the individualization processes and further changes in the state-family-child relationship have gone so far as to be characterized as a postmodern condition or whether the welfare state and the structures of modernity are still relevant to structuring the scope of children's agency. Addressing these questions requires further theorizing about age, life course and the relationship structure-culture-agency as well as a discussion about empirical tendencies. How is children's agency to be understood in the field of tension between welfare as institutions contributing to an age order and welfare defined also as agency in terms of participatory rights? Does the postmodern condition weaken the welfare state institutions and, if so, does this mean an opening for a larger scope of action for children? If not, how are we to understand the ongoing changes in the child position?

According to some theoretical accounts, the presumed postmodern society is characterized by discontinuity and fragmentation, because social institutions – such as the welfare state, the family, or the life course institution – together with structures such as social class, ethnicity, gender and age, have weakened or lost their social significance (for a discussion, see Dunn 1998; Närvänen & Näsman, forthcoming). Increasingly, such accounts are being called into question for being tendentious, exaggerated or at best able to describe the conditions of only a small category of wealthy people in contemporary, Western society (cf., Furlong & Cartmel 1997; Dunn 1998; Bury 2000; Hockey & James 2003; Närvänen & Näsman, forthcoming).

When postmodern society is described as an *entirely new epoch*, this exaggerates the discontinuities in social change and overlooks the continuities (cf., Dunn 1998; Närvänen & Näsman, forthcoming). The pluralization of life-worlds and the increasing diversification and individualization are indeed processes described and identified *within modernity*, and are ongoing processes in late-modernity (cf., Berger, Berger & Kellner 1974; Giddens 1991; Dunn 1998, Närvänen & Näsman, forthcoming). Individualization may then be understood in terms of »structured individualisation« (Evans 2002: 262; cf., Anisef & Axelrod 2001; Närvänen & Näsman, forthcoming). This does not imply that agency is determined by structures in any unidirectional way, but that agency is *shaped* by such structures, and should be understood through the notion of interpretive practices. According to an overwhelming body of empirical evidence, structures such as social class, ethnicity, gender and age still shape choices and opportunities (Närvänen & Näsman, forthcoming; cf., Furlong & Cartmel 1997; cf., Anisef & Axelrod 2001; Evans 2002). Moreover, although social institutions such as marriage or the life course change over time, the 'longue durée of institutions' (Giddens 1984: 35) and the meanings of these processes in social practices in contemporary everyday life should be acknowledged. »Institutions always have a history, of which they are the products,« stated Berger and Luckmann (1966: 72). They are typifications of patterns of behaviour as well as actors and imply control. Institutions »cannot be created instantaneously« and they do not dissolve instantaneously (1966: 72). The notion of 'structured individualisation' may be further clarified through understanding the temporal embeddedness of agency, the notion of interpretive practices inherent in agency, and the dialectic relations between structure, culture and agency, as discussed in this paper.

The life course is an institution, and is to be seen as both an ongoing process and a product of social and cultural constructions and reconstructions over time; it is constructed through complex processes, such as the development of a welfare state and state interventions, labour market regulations and social policies aimed at life phases or age categories and bureaucratic organizational structures that are related to and reinforced by age-based regulations. During the 1990s, Sweden, one of the most extensive institutionalized welfare states, faced a very dramatic and far-reaching economic crises with subsequent cuts in the welfare system of services and financial transfers[1]. These cuts especially targeted children and young people. Still, the structure of the welfare state with its broad spectrum of measures did not change. The reductions mostly concerned levels of subsidies and transfers, quality of services and limitation of entitlements, but rarely meant abolishment of types of measures. Furthermore, after the crises, many subsidies have been restored to previous levels. Looking more broadly, the conclusion is that even though the welfare state may generally have weakened as a political ideology or with regard to social security, state interventions, social policies and the organizational structures of the welfare state still reinforce and define the different life phases in relation to each other. Due to the increasing age-related regulation of children's lives in various respects, and to recent changes in the educational system and public child-care, processes of further institutionalization in childhood are easily recognized – processes that reinforce the life course institution (Närvänen & Näsman forthcoming). The notion that the welfare state, the life course institution and the age order embedded in it are dissolving can thus be called into question.

The simultaneous processes of institutionalization and individualization and, thus, the complex interplay between structure, culture and agency, should be acknowledged. Institutions have social significance for agency, and vice versa: »institutions […] are emergent products of what people do as much as they are constitutive of what people do. They don't 'exist' in any sense 'above the action'- Institutions are our collective ideal typifications of continuing processes of institutionalisation« (Jenkins 1996: 128),

»they are consequential and constraining« (1996: 128). What we claim here, in contrast to some theoretical descriptions of postmodern life courses (e.g., Featherstone & Hepworth 1989; 1991), is, in accord with Holstein and Gubrium, that »the idea of the life course is a powerful and widely shared design« (2000: 52). In everyday life, the life course is a typification that »elaborates understanding, guides and justifies action« (2000: 55). This means that age, age order and position in the life course are important to agency in terms of the opportunities and constraints of everyday life.

Age order and doing age

Age constitutes a part of the social ordering, as do ethnicity, social class and gender. We claim that there is an obvious parallel between gender order and age order, i.e. that age order can be conceived of as analogous to the former, and that such a conceptualization may contribute to our understanding of the complex interplay between structure, culture and agency. Age, then, is a basis for power relations, as is gender. Relative power and powerlessness are embedded in the age order, and operate through social control and, for example, processes of both exclusion and inclusion. The life course institution consists of socially and culturally constructed, interrelated, sequentially ordered and age-related life phases (Närvänen and Näsman 2004). The age ordering in the life course is seen in that certain life phases and age categories are ascribed a higher social status than are others (Närvänen & Näsman, forthcoming).

One theoretical problem is that there is no good equivalent to the gender concept that may be applied to age. The concept of age is somewhat problematic, because the common-sense notion is tied to chronological age and biological processes of ageing (cf., Närvänen 2004). However, just as we can distinguish between sex, sex category and gender, we can also distinguish between age, age category and socially constructed/produced age. Paraphrasing West and Zimmerman age, as something socially constructed and produced, can be conceived of »as an accomplishment, an achieved property of situated conduct« which also means that the »attention shifts from matters internal to the individual and focuses on interactional and, ultimately, institutional arenas« (1987: 126). In accordance with West and Fenstermaker's definition of gender (1995: 21), we then define age as »a situated accomplishment of societal members, the local management of conduct in relation to normative conceptions of appropriate attitudes and activities for particular« age categories and life phases.

Age and gender both structure interaction and are produced through it. As »doing gender« refers to »situated doing, carried out in the virtual or real presence of others who are presumed to be oriented to its production« (West and Zimmerman 1987: 126), the same can be said about »doing age«. Age is produced in everyday activities and practices, with reference to others, i.e. some audience, real or imagined, and with

ANNA-LIISA NÄRVÄNEN AND ELISABET NÄSMAN

reference to normative age-related conceptions of what is regarded as appropriate (and accountable) for the age category or the life phase in question. The acting individual and others are making assessments of whether or not the activities accomplished are to be seen as age appropriate, or on the contrary, inappropriate. An individual is, thus, »subject to evaluation in terms of normative conceptions of appropriate attitudes and activities« (ibid.: 139) for the particular age category or life phase. In this way, the interacting subjects are not only 'doing' their own age, but also taking part in 'doing' that of others: normatively addressing, accepting or contesting the age performance of the other. Analogous to the distinction between sex and gender, the age category and the various life phases constitute the institutional level and socially produced age the interactional level.

There is, however, an important difference between categorization by sex and categorization by age. With respect to sex categories, the discourse includes two opposite, binary categories, feminine and masculine. Categorization by age is far more diversified. It would be erroneous to create such a binary categorization such as childhood versus adulthood, as this would be a simplification not grounded in the uses of age categorizations. This is important, because categorization, by definition, is about cognitive processes and social practices: »Without categorization, the complexity of the human social world might not be manageable at all« (Jenkins 2000: 8). Categorizations by age, whether in the sciences, other professional practices or in everyday life, differentiate between several age categories and life phases across the life course, and these categories are not oppositional in any simple manner (Närvänen & Näsman, forthcoming). Age categories are 'positioned categories' (Nikander 2002), i.e. there is an age order inherent in age categorization that positions categories in relation to one another in terms of status differences, constituting an age-based hierarchy, but the hierarchy is not cumulative, that is, social status does not continuously increase from childhood to old age (Närvänen & Näsman, forthcoming). Age categorizations may be based on specific chronological ages in certain contexts, such as the compulsory school age period and the specific age grading at school, or in some situations such as maturity tests, targeting, e.g., 4-year-olds. Age categorizations may also be based on cohorts, such as in some scientific research and public statistics. Other age-related categorizations address a period of life that has not (yet) been institutionalized through such processes as the life phases in the life course, but are nonetheless commonly used and understood, e.g. 'tweenie'.

Because the life course and the life phases are age-related (but not specified in terms of chronological ages), the life phases – childhood, adolescence and so on – are age-based categorizations. The normative conceptions of appropriate activities vary between age categories and life phases, but age-specific norms can be seen as part of the wider normative conceptions referring to the life phase in question. There are hegemonic discourses that encompass assessments and criteria concerning what a child of a specific age is expected to manage. Also, there are, for example, hegemonic discourses on all life phases, encompassing sets of social norms that outline what it is to be a child, an adolescent, an old person, etc.

Consequently, 'doing age' may be differentiated according to the various life phases and social categorizations by age. 'Doing age' is then to be seen as a *comprehensive concept* referring to how age works in social practices and with reference to all kinds of categorizations that are based on age, whether based on chronological age (such as in cohorts), on institutionalized life phases or on other social conceptions and understandings of periods of life. Consequently, because age is a situated doing, an understanding of the situation, and of which categorization counts in that situation, is necessary for an acceptable doing of age. The 'doing' may be of a specific chronological age, or a period such as 'doing being tweenie' or 'doing childhood', depending on the situation. 'Doing age' may thus also be differentiated with respect to the various life phases in terms of 'doing childhood', 'doing adolescence', 'doing youth' and so on. This implies that in research on, for example, 'doing adolescence', the normative conceptions defining an adolescent and the life phase adolescence are to be identified, i.e. we must identify the discourses of adolescence and how and in what situations young persons relate to such conceptions, 'do' their life phase, reproduce or contest such conceptions, and what the consequences of not reproducing them are (cf., Raby 2002, for doing adolescence).

It should also be noted that the notion 'doing age' does not imply that an individual, for example a child, is always 'doing' his or her chronological age, or the life phase he or she may be seen as belonging to, or in which he or she may routinely be categorized. On the contrary, we want to emphasize the point that 'doing age' can be related to the notion of borderwork and borderworking, that is, in some contexts and situations, the individual may be 'doing being younger' or 'doing being older' than his or her chronological age or ascribed life phase (for borderwork, see Phillips 2005). This notion again emphasizes the importance of situationality and contextuality, which may also be understood in the light of Haraways' discussion of situated knowledge, the need to »learn to know faithfully from another's point of view« (1988:583), which emphasizes further that one presupposition for situated knowledge is that »the object of knowledge be pictured as an actor and agent, not as a screen or a ground or a resource« (ibid.:592). Such an approach should not be confused with the idea of studying isolated individuals and individualities, as situated knowledge is about commonalities, but as Haraway put it, »The only way to find a larger vision is to be somewhere in particular« (ibid.:590).

The notion of 'doing age' emphasizes how age is 'done', i.e. portrayed in interaction with others in various situations (interactional level) referring to cultural norms, discourses, etc. and defining age categories and life phases (the institutional level). Of course, it is individuals who are acting by 'doing age' (the individual level). As we see it, 'doing age', together with notions such as age order, age ordering and borderworking, may be useful as analytical tools in understanding social meanings of age and age categorizations, as well as in understanding variability of childhood with respect to such age-based categorizations. Processes such as accomplishment and accountability emphasize above all the reproduction of social order and hence the limitations of the welfare aspect of agency. There is, however, some scope for change through the interpretive practices that guide action.

On the dialectical relations between structure, culture and agency

When West and Zimmerman (1987) and West and Fenstermaker (1995) discuss »doing«, they do not present a clear conceptualization of 'structure' or 'culture', or their relations to agency. It is obvious, however, that their main focus is on relations between culture and agency. In the following two sections we discuss the temporal embeddedness of agency and the dialectic relations between structure, culture and agency, notions that we find as helpful in understanding agency, and, hence, »doing age«.

In sociology, the concept 'structure' is often conceived of in terms of patterns of external (material, 'objective') constraints, imposed on an individual or a collective. In empirical studies, 'structure' is quite often used to denote an array of opportunities (Rubinstein 2001). Thus, an age structure may be understood in terms of how age structures opportunities (and constraints), i.e., which opportunities are related to a certain age category or life phase.

Structural explanations fall short, however, in helping us understand agency. Opportunities can, in fact, not be conceived of as external or 'objective' with respect to agency (ibid.). The outcome of unequal opportunity, for example, is not always unequal attainment and vice versa. What is needed is an understanding of the dialectic between opportunity and culture, culture being defined as »systems of belief – norms and values, attitudes, worldviews, and so on « – that have significance for conduct (ibid. 2001:1). What are perceived as available lines of action (opportunities) is influenced by culture, because »opportunities are both expanded and constituted by the values, perceptions, and other features of actors«, i.e. by cultural resources (Rubinstein 2001: 116). The family institution, for example, affords opportunities, but this cannot be understood without acknowledging how family is constructed by cultural norms, values, etc. Thus, structures such as family are constituted by and constitute culture (Rubinstein 2001: 89). The dialectic between structure, culture and agency is obvious: Opportunities are read by an actor in light of cultural understandings, and culture is read in light of opportunities (ibid.). Age and life course structure opportunities, cultural understandings define various ages and life phases, opportunities are read by an actor through such understandings and cultural understandings of age and life phases are read in light of the array of opportunities related to the age and life phase.

Yet, as Rubinstein convincingly shows, the individual is still conceived of as an empty vessel. Understanding the dialectic between structure (opportunities), culture (discourses, beliefs, norms, etc.) and agency (conduct, engagement in a situation) presupposes understanding the actor's (individual or collective) motives, such as wants, desires, feelings etc., i.e. why and how the actor is acting. Again, such motives are read in light of opportunities and culture and vice versa (ibid.). Agency is then about acting and making choices, reflexively interpreting the present situation and the opportunities and constraints at hand in light of what is already known (beliefs, norms, etc.), i.e. the past, and in light of the future in terms of desires, wants and anticipation of consequences.

The temporal embeddedness of agency

The temporal embeddedness of agency is obvious in the notion above, and discussed thoroughly by Emirbayer and Mische, who define agency as »a temporally embedded process of social engagement, informed by the past [...] but also oriented toward the future [...] and toward the present« (1998: 962). Agency is »intrinsically social and relational«, situational and something that is in the present moment (ibid. 1998: 973). Furthermore, agency is »always *toward* something, by means of which actors enter into relationship with surrounding persons, places, meanings, and events. [...] agency entails actual interactions with its contexts« (ibid. 1998: 973). Accordingly, agency is intentional and refers to doing, which presupposes a subject (actor). Because structures (opportunities) are reflexively interpreted by actors, they can also be maintained, questioned, transformed or sustained through processes such as negotiation, resistance or conformity (cf., Raby 2002). Understanding agency, thus, presupposes understanding an actor's definition of the present situation and interpretations of opportunities, constraints and possible lines of action in that particular situation.

Recognition of interpretive practices in everyday life is crucial for understanding agency and presupposes recognition of temporality, the meaning of the past and the future for the present, which sheds further light on what is meant by socially situated agency (Närvänen 1994; 2003: 1; Volkart 1951; Blumer 1969; Rubinstein 2001).

Situations are defined first and foremost in interaction with others, real or imagined, in a continuous process of interaction and reflection. A definition of a situation is an interpretation of the meaning of the situation (Närvänen 1994; 2003: 1). In reflecting on possible futures, a child, for example, may interpret her/his opportunities on the basis of past experiences (success at school, what is known to be typical or untypical for women or men and for a child with a certain social background, etc.), and present interactions with others (what is mediated by teachers and friends, what the parents may reinforce, verify or neglect) and on the basis of what the child may strive for or expect of the future in terms of, for example, occupational opportunities. The child, according to her/his interpretation of the situation, may choose a line of action based on what seems to be possible and plausible (cf., Närvänen 1994). From another perspective, there may be a broader or a smaller repertoire of opportunities than what the child actually interprets as the range of opportunities. It is the *interpretation*, i.e. *the definition of the situation* that guides the action, not the 'objective' opportunities available (cf., Närvänen 2003: 1).

The temporal embeddedness of agency and the significance of culture may be exemplified further through a discussion of the everyday practices of typification. Typifications refer to everyday knowledge that is quite generalized and simplified, pointing out what is seen as typical for an occurrence or a phenomenon and forms »a part of a stock of knowledge at hand« (Holstein &Gubrium 2000: 52). Typifications are necessary for making the world apprehensible (Berger & Luckmann 1966) and mean bringing the past into the present. The typified everyday knowledge of the life course and various life phases is a cultural understanding of how life time is structured and what is expected at different ages and life phases: »typification elaborates understanding, guides and justifies action«, and »all types serve to organize events and courses of action, to give them meaning« (Holstein & Gubrium 2000: 55). Such a typification is thus everyday knowledge about and means of structuring life, making individual experiences apprehensible and assigning meaning to such experiences »in relation to time«, as in assessing present life in light of past experiences and anticipations of the future (ibid.: 24). The institutionalized life course within society also means that individuals may relate to and construct themselves in relation to »the available life course programs« (Kohli 1986: 272), also discussed by Luckmann in terms of biographical schemes, i.e. that each society contains prescription-like versions of what constitutes typical, possible and/or taken-for-granted lives for specific categories of people differentiated by, for example, ethnicity, gender and social class (Närvänen 1994; Luckmann 1983). Such typifications are not automatically transformed into individual biographies, determining individual lives, but serve as tools in interpreting opportunities and choices, i.e. they are tailored individually into personal biographies. For example, there may be a common-sense understanding of the range of typical educational choices for girls from typical working-class families, but the individual choice is a specific education within this range – or, if opportunities and discourses are interpreted differently, and if there are resources available to do so, the individual choice may be to exceed the cultural and social expectations inherent in the typification.

Typifications form one basis of understanding social position vis-à-vis others in the life course, and as they encompass normative conceptions, they define normality and deviance across the life course and, thus, our interpretation of being »on-time« or

»off-time« in relation to such conceptions: »Notions of a typical life course also serve as an interpretative resource for discerning normality in relation to chronological age« (Holstein & Gubrium 2000: 79). The appropriateness or inappropriateness of conduct is often assessed on the basis of the individual's life course position and age, which may constrain action. In Sweden, for example, a relatively new age-related typification is »Pop grandmother«. Being labelled as such is not flattering, as the social meaning is that the person is behaving off-time, acting and dressing as if she were younger than she is.

There is, then, age-related variation in »the degree of agency allowed« (Rubinstein 2001: 157). An opportunity may be definitely closed to some age categories, due to policies, regulations, laws etc., denying children the right to vote in general elections being one example. Most often, though, rules and norms are not followed blindly, but reflected upon. Restrictions of opportunities are then a matter of conformity or non-conformity, subject to modifications and so on, even though individuals are not totally free to circumvent all of them or to choose whatever they wish, for instance owing to the age order. The ideological dominance of adulthood (Hockey & James 1993) means that adults in middle age(s) have the highest status in the age order and, thereby, the privilege of interpretation in relation to other life phases, allowing them to constrain the agency of the others. The power relations inherent in the age order of the life course institution are still decisive with regard to social status, rights and obligations, opportunities and hindrances.

Opportunities are provided by resources. Resources are, according to Giddens, »media through which power is exercised« (1984: 16), which means »anything that can serve as a source of power in social interaction« (Rubinstein 2001: 129). Material objects, emotional and social commitments, physical strength, or cognitive capacity and knowledge may, depending on the situation, be used as resources in acting, making choices, influencing others and maintaining or enhancing power (Rubinstein 2001). The restriction of children's and old people's opportunity to participate on the labour market, as part of the age order, means not only low status, as mentioned above, but also heavy restriction of their access to financial resources and hence the construction of dependency on the welfare state or family members who then become superordinate. But having power resources does not necessarily mean that an individual will use them. What is perceived as a resource in a given situation is a matter of interpretation. As Lin (2001) argues in relation to social capital, actors must be aware of their resources to be able to utilize them. Adults' ability to control children's awareness is, accordingly, another limitation of children's scope of participation (Näsman 2004, 2005)

Social networks and relations may be power resources. The actor may act indirectly, via others, with respect to a particular situation, when acting directly is not possible. A distinction may be made between whether the actor, a child, is acting *in the situation* as an actor, or acting to mobilize some other person or party, who is to be a spokesman for the child. The latter may be called vicarious agency. Furthermore, the child's action in mobilizing the other is agentic and, consequently, this is *children's* agency. Vicarious agency, however, may also refer to a situation in which another person or party is acting on behalf of children, but a situation not involving or initiated by children. Such a situation does **not** constitute children's agency, even though it may ameliorate children's conditions.

In the next section, we will sketch how this general discussion on agency could take shape when focusing on childhood. We start with a look at the discourse on the life phase of childhood, which frames children's agency, and go on to exemplify children's power resources and their doing age.

The futuristic perspective on childhood as a hegemonic discourse

»The idea of the life-course is a powerful and widely shared design« stated Holstein and Gubrium (2000: 52), which again turns our attention to the significance of culture in relation to agency. Notions of the typical life course and constructions of various life phases may be understood in terms of discourses. The most powerful, hegemonic discourse on life course during the 20th century is no doubt the image of stage-like development, defining various life phases in relation to one another, and it is »the current ideological imperative« (Hockey & James 2003: 57) pursued, i.e. it forms the foundation of 'doing age'. This discourse on childhood, promoted by, for example, educational, psychological and other specialist disciplines such as paediatrics, constructs this life phase as one of stage-like development, where maturity is related to chronological age. It pervades various practises in the form of unquestioned 'facts' that are incorporated into institutions such as the family and the schools (Adam 1995). It is fundamentally based on a future-oriented approach to children and childhood, and serves to construct normality and deviance. Consequently, it may have an impact on children's agency as cultural understandings and interpretive schemes and may colour policy-makers and professionals in their welfare state understandings of children's conditions, parents' and other adults' engagement and the child itself, when 'doing childhood'.

Within this discourse, childhood is the first life phase and old age the last. Children are seen as »becomings« (Qvortrup 1987: 5, 1994a: 4), while old people are »has beens« (Närvänen & Näsman 2003). There are some similarities between old age and childhood. Both are constructed in opposition to that part of the life course that is seen as productive and as contributing to the wealth of a society, i.e. middle age, often simply called adulthood[2]. This forms the basis for the ideological dominance of adulthood (Hockey & James 1993). Children inhabiting childhood and adults in old age are constructed as dependent, but not only in financial terms. They are stereotypically seen as being in need of care and supervision. However, ageing during childhood means progress, while ageing during old age is seen as deterioration. This gives childhood a more positive connotation than old age. The futuristic discourse also means that whatever is done to a child within the family, the schools, etc., in terms of assessments, judgements or protection against risks, may be done and legitimated »with the future adult in mind« (James, Jenks & Prout 2001: 74). The welfare conditions of childhood are expressed as conditions of growing up. Problems to be dealt with by the welfare state are those that cause hindrances, time lags or misdirection in this developmental process. Agency during childhood may then be seen primarily in terms of its relevance to positive development, indicating or promoting progress, not as an end in itself as implicated by a rights perspective (Näsman 2004).

The futuristic understanding of childhood rather legitimizes that people in all other life phases restrict children's scope of action, because the child is by definition immature, uneducated, lacking adult competencies, etc. (Qvortrup 1987: 5, 1994a: 4, Näsman 1995). Due to the ideological dominance of adulthood, childhood and the social category of children may be seen as basically subordinated, and in spite of the individuation and individualization of children, they are still subordinate to and dependant upon their parents, i.e. within the family generation structure, also largely in order to access resources and services distributed by the welfare state. Familialization is still working.

Adult responsibility is part of the discourse in which benevolent adults regulate children as well as children's relationships to adults. Benevolence towards children has become one of the main principles regulating policies based on the UN Convention on the Rights of the Child (UNCRC), i.e. the obligation to let 'the best interest of the child' guide all decision-making relevant to children. On the basis of this concept, children's main source of influence may be via adult consideration, i.e. via vicarious agency. In addition to the general demand for this consideration by professionals in public agencies, in Sweden this has been institutionalized in the form of a special official, the Children's Ombudsman at national and municipal levels. Sometimes these officials channel children's initiatives or consult children on an issue, thereby actively opening the scope of children's agency. However, any interpretation by them of what is in the best interest of the child that does not involve any input from children cannot be considered *children's* agency within the conceptualization discussed in this paper. Hence, welfare that involves children's participation is accomplished only to a limited extent in this way.

The notion of 'the best interest of the child' is complicated. One crucial question is who is to decide what is best and on what grounds (Näsman 2004). Another problem is the time reference. Should we be concerned with the best interest of the child during childhood, here and now, or rather for the future? The hegemonic discourse on childhood may reproduce a view on 'the best interest of the child' that is based on cultural, adult futuristic ideas of the 'good childhood'. As Qvortrup and others have argued, the child's best interest may just as well be a smokescreen behind which there are adult interests of various kinds (Qvortrup 1994b, Näsman 1995).

Children's participation

Looking at the political discourse that emphasizes children's participation and children's rights, there are signs of a change away from the child as an object of adult intervention, care and supervision, even though this discourse seems to be related to the hegemonic discourse. Compared to the Declaration of the Rights of the Child from 1959, the UNCRC emphasizes the child as a subject with individual rights, including agency, through an obligation to take children's views into consideration. This right, however, is restricted by the child's age and maturity. Why both age and maturity? In what situations is age per se of interest irrespective of the child's maturity, and vice versa (Näsman 2004)? Chronological age is devoid of meaning (Närvänen 2004). Accordingly, the age concept here refers to a socially constructed phenomenon, which gains meaning through the hegemonic discourse that ascribes competences, qualities, etc. The reservation, thus, may be interpreted as meaning either that the child should have a voice depending on age and maturity, or that what the child says should be judged and have an impact depending on age or maturity, or both. There is an obvious risk that the reservation concerning children's voice will become part of a circular reasoning in which whatever children say that is not in line with adult views will be judged as coming from individuals too young or immature to be listened to (Näsman 2004). The risk of underestimation of children is built into the ideological dominance of adulthood and the typification of childhood. An outcome of the life phase typification may be that adults presume that children cannot make sense of things and communicate a relevant opinion, and that adults, thus, fail to notice what children actually say. It may also block adults' ability to see children's possible competence, because incompetence relative to adult knowledge and experience is what adults, even researchers, often notice. What adults fail to recognize, for instance, is that children's lack of (adult) understanding may not indicate insufficient rationality, but rather reflect limited experience.

The UNCRC has been ratified by most nations of the world, though implementation of a scope for children's agency varies between and within countries. In Sweden, public authorities must report to the government about progress in implementation. Publicly employed staff are educated and groups are established in local authorities to help make children's voices heard for instance via surveys or interviews, or in dealing with individual cases, via personal contact with the child. Such activities as well as children's opinions should be documented. Research in Sweden shows, however, that for instance in custody cases, documentation of contact with children is rare and documentation of children's opinions ever rarer (Rejmer 2003). When social welfare authorities handle various cases, children are rarely involved or asked about their views (Socialstyrelsen 2003). Professionals have given different reasons for this (Näsman 2005). Some state that they lack training in talking to and understanding children, an explanation based on essentialist views of difference. Others argue that they as professionals know what is best, an explanation based on the notion of the child as incompetent. The explanation stating that parents should know the child's best interest is based on the familialization of children. Still others may refer to links in the current discourse between participation and responsibility, i.e. that citizens who experience participation will take responsibility, responsibility being a virtue that grows out of realizing the right to participate. That children might find themselves in a situation where their responsibility is seen as a problem, and as one of the main reasons for not asking children to participate in some issues, because responsibility would become a heavy burden on the child, who is seen as fragile and not mature enough to bear it.

Within the school system, which is dominated by a futuristic perspective, the view on participation and responsibility is the opposite. Participation is seen as an opportunity that children deserve if they take responsibility (Bergström & Holm 2005). This has two objectives: First, to discipline children to take responsibility during childhood, i.e. their options are dependent on their behaviour. Second, to foster children for their future life as active, participating, responsible citizens. The most important issue in the school context – what is to be learned – is not, however, on the agenda for participation (ibid., see further the Swedish curriculum and Skolverket 2000), i.e. participation is an incentive used to foster children's responsibility and not a right children have as citizens.

The idea of the child's right to have a say in decisions that concern them offers a reactive scope of agency. Thus, agency in the sense of actually making a difference, i.e. that children's agency has an effect on the outcome of decision-making processes, presupposes that they are able to state their opinion and are actively asked about it. The opportunity to initiate such a process concerning a particular issue is one of the most important power resources in a democracy, i.e. having an impact on the agenda. A proactive scope for children may be limited, as adult supremacy encompasses a privilege of interpretation that delimits the kind of issues put on the agenda.

The developmental discourse may result in a situation in which problems defined by children, even several cohorts of children, are seen as negligible if they are not expected to have long-term effects (Qvortrup 1994b, Näsman 1995). The fact that children are seen as human becomings means, furthermore, that their understanding of society has limited value. Thus, their viewpoints on their own life, interests and problems need not be considered. Accordingly, the scope for children's initiatives concerning the political agenda is limited and they are excluded from general elections. Because the limitation of children's agency is only related to chronological age, it constitutes a clear case of age discrimination. When debated, alternatives such as granting children the right to vote after examination of relevant qualifications are not discussed, but instead the idea of granting parents multiple votes (vicarious agency), which would not necessarily increase children's agency if children are not involved in the decision-making process within the family.

There are, however, indications that the reactive scope of agency for children is complemented with a proactive scope. One of the objectives of children's ombudsmen in Sweden is to make contact with children in order to take up their issues of concern on the political agenda. Moreover, some kind of formal representation of minors in decision-making bodies is found in several countries. These organizations represent a scope of action for children as a category. This is sometimes formalized, as in youth councils, or simply constructed by gathering a group of children for discussion or consulting. From the welfare point of view, this raises the question of distributive justice in this kind of participation. Here, children's agency takes the form of an often adult-selected group that is to represent the category of children as a collective. The absence of attempts to organize the child population for an election of representatives indicates that just 'any child' is seen as representative. Such a construction mirrors a stereotypical understanding of children as a homogeneous category with common experiences and interests. Every child, thus, carries the 'child perspective' asked for in the political process. This opens the debate in the context of childhood to the same kind of issues that have been causing a turmoil in gender studies, where differences in class, ethnicity, religion, etc. have challenged the idea of a common interest among women, calling for intersectional analysis (Närvänen & Näsman 2005a; 2005b). There are, however, also examples of how children within an adult-chosen age limit have been given some of the citizenship rights granted to adults, such as in local elections concerning changes in the school or changes in the city plan. In one Swedish municipality, the votes of children (i.e., under the age of majority) led to cancelled plans for a new bridge for motor traffic in the middle of town. Politicians motivated inviting children to participate with the fact that children are the future, and that they would have to live with the bridge in adult life. Thus, a futuristic orientation to childhood may in some cases be part of a policy that gives children a scope of action in present time, i.e. when the issue at stake has long-term implications.

Roger Hart (1997) has developed a ladder for children's participation in construction projects, based on the idea of progression with a combination of different dimensions.

Ladder of participation

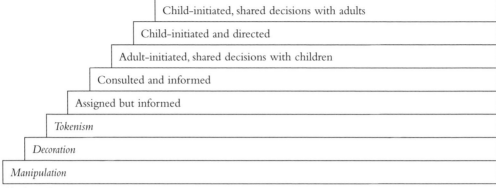

| Child-initiated, shared decisions with adults |
| Child-initiated and directed |
| Adult-initiated, shared decisions with children |
| Consulted and informed |
| Assigned but informed |
| *Tokenism* |
| *Decoration* |
| *Manipulation* |

(ibid.: 41)

The first four steps do not constitute *children's* participation or agency according to our conceptualisation. Hart refers the three first to situations in which children are used by adults in a way that gives the impression of participation without that actually being the case, in which children are manipulated by adults without knowing what they are taking part in, used as decorations, such as the baby on the politician's arm during election campaigns, or invited as tokens to promote adult interests, without having a say or being taken seriously. On the fourth step children are informed, but they do not act.

In the following steps, Hart introduces the dimensions, consulted, taking initiative and making decisions, which gradually increase in autonomy. At the top of Hart's ladder, however, we find making decisions together with adults. The reason may be that the ideal is not some visionary world, where independent children make all decisions on their own, and that participation and democracy are not about total autonomy. Children are, as other citizens, related to and dependent on others and ought to take part in joint decisions in societal matters (Hart 1997).

We may also find discourse on children's agency in informal contexts such as the family. In Sweden, independence is a widely accepted parental goal for fostering children (Dahlberg 1993, Bäck-Wiklund & Bergsten 1997). Two forms of parental orientations offer children a scope of agency. Some parents count on children's ability to take the initiative and do things on their own and allow them a large scope of agency for decision making, though within firm boundaries set up by the parents. The parent's role is to be available to the children when they so wish (ibid.). Other parents, so-called 'modern' project-oriented families, are described as follows:

> »On a general level it seems as if modern family life has opened up towards an emphatic and sensitive discourse among children and parents – parents struggling

to take the position of the child and understand what it means to be a child. This sensitivity may be expressed as respect for the child, children's right to be children, and children's right to their parents' time and involvement. ...parents, through their sensitivity, give the child a voice.« (ibid.: 91, our translation)

In such families, the interaction between parents and children is described in terms of negotiation and references to rationality, i.e. an expectation that the child will establish the competence necessary to take part in the decision-making and then make choices (ibid.). The parents actively try to find ways of checking the impact of the uneven distribution of power resources. As one parent says: »We have made up a speaking order, since some in the family are more dominant than others.« (ibid.: 93, our translation) This parent category, in spite of its 'democratic' ideas of upbringing, does think of children's agency in a futuristic perspective, i.e. these parents treat children in this way so they will become adults who are capable of negotiation and rational decision-making. The futuristic perspective may then be combined with a large scope of action for children, though in combination with careful teaching of what counts as rational thinking (ibid.).

Children's power resources

We can assume that adults as a rule are able to manipulate children's right to be informed, consulted or to participate in decision-making and, that adults accordingly can delimit children's opportunities for participation, formal rights notwithstanding (Näsman 2004). A critical question, concerning children's power resources, then concerns children's ability to understand and make sense of what happens. This may be related to the ideological dominance of adulthood with respect to the construction of people's ideas and the privilege of interpretation. The life course institution mediated by, for instance, the family and the schools provides children with typifications as tools for interpretation, such as an understanding of what is considered normal and deviant in childhood (Holstein and Gubrium 2000). The steps of participation from information and upward may be generally problematic owing to constraints on children's access to power resources such as knowledge and experience. Information can only mean insight into a decision-making process if it is based on critical reflection. The risk of asymmetric access to knowledge is that adults may construct a hidden structure of awareness concerning basic understandings of the relative positions held by the actors involved (including children), of what the situation and the issue at stake mean, and of which arguments count (Näsman 2004, 2005). In the organizational structure of the school, for example, the staff are in a position of having greater power resources relative to children/pupils.

Children, however, may have power resources that are inherent in the relational network of social positions, and may for instance draw on emotional ties between parents and children. When negotiating for pocket money, for example, children describe how they take advantage of their father wanting to be 'a good father', who provides his children with what they need (Näsman & von Gerber 2003). Children may also test the boundaries of agency with regard to parents' emotional ability to sanction agreements. Drawing on emotional ties, a child may feel safe in not following family agreements (ibid.). The status as a good father is also a matter of appearance to an audience outside the family. Children may be aware of this power resource and use it in public by not complying with parental demands for good behaviour. There is also a commitment involved in the parental role, which children may be well aware of. From an early age, Swedish children argue that it is the responsibility of the parents to provide for their children (ibid.).

Material power resources and physical strength are generally lacking in childhood compared to other life phases. Nonetheless, these kinds of resources are of interest in understanding children's agency. The fact that there tends to be a wider gap in material standard among families with children than among children demonstrates that children's material standard is often given priority by parents (Näsman & von Gerber 1996, Jonsson et al. 2001, Hölscher 2003). This may sometimes be a result of children's negotiation and use of emotional power resources, but may also result from parents' taking children's interest into account as part of their parenting practices (vicarious agency). Parents' interpretation of the importance of children's material standards mirrors the way in which material power resources are used by children in interaction with one another. From an early age, children are aware of the social status value of toys, clothes, spare time activities and money as such, and they develop strategies to avoid the risk of status loss (Hölscher 2003; Näsman & von Gerber 2003).

In a country such as Sweden, physical strength is mainly a power resource children may use in interaction with other children. This stresses the importance of growing in a physical sense, as shown in children's way of expressing growing up as getting bigger.

Hockey and James (1993) discuss two more sources of power that a category like children may draw on. First, they consider alternative sources of wealth and social status. Hockey and James do not mention children in this context, but a child may gain a higher social status than even an adult by exploiting other categorizations, for example, a white child in relation to a black adult in a racist country, an upper class child versus a servant in a class society, or a teenage boy versus a police women in a gendered society. Second, Hockey and James (1993) discuss visible membership of a disadvantaged social category. This may seem like a paradox, but refers to the opportunity to act on weakness. If one is defined as having a weak position, there is little to lose by acting out that weakness, for instance in the form of anti-social behaviour.

A marginalized position may also give access to the power associated with the sacred, the set apart or the weak (Hockey & James 1993: 169). A special case is the performance of outsiderhood, such as child stars who symbolize difference. There is also a power source in playing the role of the inferior and from that perspective criticizing and making demands (ibid.).

Children's strategies of 'doing age'

Based on their understanding of their position, the situation they are in, the conditions that apply to that situation and the power resources at their disposal, children, at an early age, develop strategies to reach their goals. Here we will focus on some basic strategies of 'doing age'.

Early in the life course, children become aware of the links between their scope of action and their age position. As Hockey and James (1993) note, »little children, of three and four years old, see themselves as restricted by their lack of age and show an awareness of this implicit patterning of their lives« (1993: 161). The age order is also an order of social status whereby minors and old people share the experience of low status positions: »the passage of calendrical time is experienced as a control system which defines them as members of a marginal social category, separated off as a group apart« (ibid.: 162).

When 'doing age', children may comply with the norms of childhood or negotiate, resist or circumvent them[3]. »Controlled and constrained through adult ordering of time, children none the less discover forms of resistance« (ibid.: 162). Hockey and James (ibid.) and James and Prout (1990: 233) mention a number of examples of children's age-related strategies to increase their scope of action beyond the limitations linked to their 'low' chronological age:

- Maximizing age: claiming an age close to the following year: »almost six«.
- Exactitude: adding parts of the year, months and even days to seem as old as possible.
- Mystification: not answering in years, but for instance by relating to an activity »old enough to…«
- Passing: in Goffman's (1968) terms, i.e. performing in such a way and with such an appearance that the audience accepts them as older than they are. This can be accomplished through their manner of dressing, using make up, talking and using gestures. A place where children normally are excluded, in combination with a place competent performance may add to the probability of success in passing. This passing constitutes borderworking, as discussed above: 'doing being older' than one's chronological age. 'Doing another age or life phase' is also shown in strategies

of marking higher status by doing adolescence or adulthood. A young child may stress that she or he takes care of even younger siblings, and by positioning her-/himself as a care-giver, distance her-/himself from the child position. Thus, she or he is »big« compared with »the little ones« (Hockey & James 1993: 167). For example, a young child who gave money to a parent to buy milk expressed the status increase of crossing the age border that is symbolized by access to money (Näsman & von Gerber 2003).

To these examples could be added:
–   Fraud: a kind of passing, but accomplished by openly stating the proper, but in chronological terms false, age, for instance by simply telling a lie about their age or cheating with an identification card.
–   Hidden crossing of boarders: gaining access to age-inappropriate goods, services and activities without the adults knowing.
–   Conformity: conforming to age-related norms, i.e. 'doing age' in accordance with norms, may extend the scope of action, as parents trust the child to behave well.

Borderwork strategies at the other end of the age ladder involve, for example, trying to reduce the ascribed age in order to make use of the potential gains of being young, incompetent and hence irresponsible. Children may '*infantilize*' themselves, for instance by using baby talk or performing as incompetent and unknowing »to thwart adults' claims that they are »capable« in contexts when children do not want to comply« (Hockey & James 1993: 164). This means that they make use of the typifications linked to the child position, such as being incompetent and needing adult support, thus 'doing being younger'.

Children may react to their subordinate status by stressing their progress within the childhood population for those who are younger and accordingly inferior to them (cf., Moore 2001). The school system is a formalized ladder of status related to chronological age. Children may use the steps of this ladder to mark their own position and to judge other children. Moving to a new class or a new school for older children entails a status shift, which may be demonstrated by talking superimposingly about the former school and the younger/smaller ones whom they themselves belonged to just a year ago (James & Prout 1990: 233; Bergström & Holm 2005). A child may also refer to age-based changes in amount of pocket money and consumption patterns in ways that are degrading to younger children, such as when they go from a weekly to a monthly allowance (Näsman & von Gerber 2003).

Concluding remarks

In this article, we have addressed aspects of children's participation that are related to welfare. We initially discussed dialectical relations between structure, culture and agency, the temporal embeddedness of agency, as well as social situatedness, meanings of culture and interpretive practices, intentionality and the acting subject. In this we agree with Pilcher, that age and the life course institution (still) play an important role »in shaping experiences and relationships and in structuring access to power, resources and citizenship rights« (1995: 146). In conclusion, institutional order does not determine behaviour, but shapes it and limits which patterns of behaviour may be regarded as appropriate in any particular context. Our discussion also shows the strength of not merging structure and culture in this conceptualization. Studies based on this may then sometimes focus on the distribution of opportunities, while others might focus on interpretive processes in understanding and reading opportunities in order to act, and still others might try to capture the complexities of the dialectical relations between structure, culture and agency (cf., Rubinstein 2001).

We have discussed how the life phase discourses on childhood are mediated to children as typifications. The age order of the life course institution structures opportunities and constraints, such that the child position shapes and limits agency in any particular context. But, as discussed, children interpret and reflect upon their opportunities and constraints, through past experiences, by anticipating their future and interpreting their present situation when choosing a line of action. They may have and make use of power resources and negotiate, contest, oppose and overcome the constraints of the age order in the specific situation. In studies of agency among children, it is important to take into account the norms and regulations applied to them by others, and to examine the ways in which children interpret and can influence these norms and regulations in order to stretch the limits they impose.

In terms of children's welfare, the conclusion is that children's agency, on a formal level in the welfare state, is stressed as part of their rights, but we have also exemplified the variation in opportunities offered by professionals and parents, where a futuristic understanding of childhood is still dominant and still puts restrictions on children's scope of participation. We have furthermore argued both in favour of recognizing social change in terms of the scope and conditions for children's agency, and in favour of understanding this as a continuation of the impact of welfare state policies, the institution of parenthood and the structuring of the life course institution, with its embedded age order, as well as other structures of modernity. A welfare perspective is sometimes contrasted to a rights perspective. Here, however, the rights of children are understood as one aspect of children's welfare. Is children's participation good for them? This question, which fits into a more paternalistic welfare perspective, has not been addressed here, as our choice of perspective is that of the new childhood sociology.

References

Adam, B. (1995): *Timewatch: the social analysis of time*. London: Polity.

Alanen, L. (1992): *Modern Childhood? Exploring the 'Child Question' in Sociology*. Jyväskylä: University of Jyväskylä.

Anisef, P. and P. Axelrod (2001): »Baby Boomers in Transition: Life-course Experiences of the 'Class of 73'«, Marshall, V. et al (eds) *Restructuring Work and the Life Course*. Toronto: University of Toronto Press: 473-488.

Beck, U. (1992): *Risk society: towards a new modernity*. London: Sage.

Berger, P., B. Berger and H. Kellner (1974): *The homeless mind: modernization and consciousness*. Middlesex: Penguin Books Ltd.

Berger, P.L. and T. Luckmann (1966): *The social construction of reality: a treatise in the sociology of knowledge*. New York: Doubleday.

Bergström, M. and I. Holm (2005): Den svårfångade delaktigheten i skolan. Ett ungdomsperspektiv på hinder och möjligheter. (Elusive participation in school. A young people's perspective on hindrances and possibilities) Linköping: Linköping university.

Blumer, H. (1969): *Symbolic Interactionism. Perspective and Method*. Berkeley: University of California Press.

Bury, M. (2000): »Health, ageing and the life course, in Health, Medicine and Society«, Williams, S. J., Gabe. J. and M. Calnan (eds) *Key Theories, Future Agendas*. London: Routledge: 87-105.

Bäck-Wiklund, M. & B. Bergsten (1997): *Det moderna föräldraskapet: en studie av familj och kön i förändring*. (The modern parenthood: a study of family and gender in change.) Stockholm: Natur och kultur.

Dahlberg, G. (1993): »Modern barnuppfostran och modernt familjeliv – en komplex och sofistikerad förhandlingsprocess«, *Om moderna familjeliv och familjeseparationer*. (Modern up-bringing and modern family life – a complex and sophisticated process of negotiation. Modern family life and separations.) Stockholm: Swedish Council of Social Research: 87-98.

Ds 2002:32 *Welfare in Sweden: The Balance Sheet for the 1990s*. Stockholm: Edita Norstedt

Dunn, R.G. (1998): *Identity Crises. A Social Critique of Postmodernity*. Minneapolis: University of Minnesota Press.

Emirbayer, M. and A. Mische (1998): »What is Agency?«, *American Journal of Sociology*, Vol. 103, pp 962-1023.

Evans, K. (2002): »Taking control of their lives: Agency in young adult transition in England and the new Germany«, *Journal of Youth Studies*, Vol 5, pp 245-269.

Featherstone, M. and M. Hepworth (1989): »Ageing and Old Age: Reflections on the Postmodern Life Course«, Bytheway, B., T. Keil, P. Allatt and A. Bryman (eds) *Becoming and Being Old*. London: Sage Publications: 143-157.

Featherstone, M. and M. Hepworth (1991): »The Mask of Ageing and the Postmodern Life Course«, Featherstone, M., M. Hepworth and B.S. Turner (eds) *The Body. Social Process and Cultural Theory*. London: Sage Publications: 371-389.

Furlong, A. and F. Cartmel (1997): *Young People and Social Change. Individualization and Risk in Late Modernity*. Buckingham: Open University Press.

Giddens, A. (1984): *The Constitution of Society. Outline of the Theory of Structuration.* Cambridge: Polity Press.

Giddens, A. (1991): *Modernity and Self-Identity. Self and Society in the Late Modern Age.* Cambridge: Polity Press.

Goffman, E. (1968): *Stigma: Notes on the Management of Spoiled Identity.* Harmondsworth, Middlesex: Penguin Books Ltd.

Haraway, D. (1988): »Situated Knowledges: The Science Question in Feminism and the Privilege of Partial Perspective«, *Feminist Studies.* Vol. 14: pp 575-599.

Hart, R. (1997): *Children's participation: – from tokenism to citizenship.* Firenze: UNICEF International Child Development Centre.

Hockey, J. and A. James (1993): *Growing Up and Growing Old. Ageing and Dependancy in the Life Course.* London: Sage.

Hockey, J. and A. James (2003): *Social Identities across the Life Course.* New York: Palgrave.

Holstein, J.A. and J.F. Gubrium (2000): *Constructing the Life Course.* New York: General Hall Inc.

Hölscher, P. (2003): »*Immer must Du hingehen und praktisch betteln*« *Wie Jugendliche Armut erleben.* Frankfurt: Campus Verlag.

James, A., C. Jenks, and A. Prout (2001): *Theorizing Childhood.* Cambridge: Polity Press.

James, A. and A. Prout (eds) (1990): *Constructing and reconstructing childhood: contemporary issues in the sociological study of childhood.* London: Falmer.

Jenkins, R. (1996): *Social Identity.* London: Routledge.

Jenkins, R. (2000): »Categorization: Identity, Social Process and Epistemology«, *Current Sociology.* Vol. 48: pp 7-25.

Jonsson, J.O. and V. Östberg (eds) (2001): *Barns och ungdomars välfärd.* Antologi från Kommittén Välfärdsbokslut. (Children's and young people's welfare. An anthology from the Welfare Commission) SOU 2001:55. Stockholm: Graphium/Norstedt.

Kohli, M. (1986): »Social Organization and Subjective Construction of the Life course«, Sörensen, A.B. et al (eds): *Human Development and the Life Course: Multidisciplinary Perspectives.* New Jersey: Hillsdale: 271-292.

Lin, N. (2001): *Social capital: a theory of social structure and action.* Cambridge: Cambridge University Press.

Luckmann, T. (1983): »Remarks on Personal Identity: Inner, Social and Historical Time« Jacobson-Widding, Anita (ed) *Identity: Personal and Socio-Cultural.* Uppsala: Almqvist & Wiksell: 67-91.

Moore, V. A. (2001): »Doing« Racialized and Gendered Age to Organize Peer Relations. Observing Kids in Summer Camp. *Gender & Society.* Vol. 15, pp 835-858.

Nikander, P. (2002): *Age in action: membership work and stage of life categories in talk.* Helsinki: The Finnish Academy of Science and Letters.

Närvänen, A.-L. (1994): *Temporalitet och social ordning.* (Temporality and Social Order. diss.). Linköping: Linköping university.

Närvänen, A.-L. (2003): *Time, Space and Identities – A Dramaturgical Approach.* Working paper 2003:1, ISAL, Institute for the study of Ageing and Later Life. Linköping: Linköping university.

Närvänen, A.-L. and E. Näsman (2003): *Time and Space in Different Life Phases.* Paper presented at ESA-conference, Murcia, Spain, September 23-26.

Närvänen, A.-L. (2004): »Age, Ageing and Life Course«, Öberg, B.-M., A.-L. Närvänen, E. Näsman, E. Olsson (eds) *Changing Worlds and the Ageing Subject*. Aldershot: Ashgate förlag: pp 65-80.

Närvänen, A.-L. and E. Näsman (2004): »Childhood as Generation or Life-phase?«, *Young* Vol. 12, pp 71-91.

Närvänen, A.-L. and E. Näsman: *Challenging Postmodern Lifecourses?* (forthcoming)

Närvänen, A.-L. and E. Näsman (2005a): *Doing age, doing childhood – performing and contesting the age order.* Paper presented at the conference Childhoods 2005, Oslo, Norway, 29 June-3 July.

Närvänen, A.-L. and E. Näsman (2005b): *Age and intersectionality – the childhood case.* Paper presented at the ESA conference, Torun, Poland, September 2005.

Näsman, E. (1995): »Vuxnas intresse av att se med barns ögon«, Dahlgren, L. and K. Hultqvist (eds) *Seendet och seendets villkor.* (»Adult interests to see with the eyes of children.« To see and the conditions of seeing.) Stockholm: HLS förlag: 279-304.

Näsman, E. and C. von Gerber (1996): *Mamma Pappa utan Jobb.* (Mum, Dad, No Job) Stockholm: Rädda Barnens förlag.

Näsman, E. and C. von Gerber (2003): *Från spargris till kontokort. Barndomens ekonomiska spiraltrappa.* (From piggybank to cash card. The financial ladder of childhood.) Linköping: Linköpings universitet.

Näsman, E. (2004): »Barn, Barndom och barns rätt«, Olsen, L. (ed) *Barns Makt.* (»Children, childhood and children's rights« Children's power.) Uppsala: Justus förlag: 53-76.

Näsman, E. (2005): »Barns perspektiv och perspektiv på barn som informanter.« Vräkning och hemlöshet – drabbar också barn. SOU 2005:88. (»Children's perspectives and perspectives on children as informants.« Eviction and homelessness – also harms children.) Stockholm: Fritzes: 271-308.

Phillips, J. (2005): *Childhood Helping as Generational Borderwork.* Paper presented at the conference Childhoods 2005, Oslo, Norway, 29 June-3 July.

Pilcher, J. (1995): *Age and Generation in Modern Britain.* Oxford: Oxford University Press.

Qvortrup, J. (1987): *The sociology of childhood.* Barndomsprojektet 2/87. Esbjerg: University centre of South Jutland.

Qvortrup, J. (1994a): »Childhood Matters: An Introduction«, Qvortrup, J. et al (eds) *Childhood Matters. Social Theory Practice and Politics.* Aldershot: Avebury: 1-23.

Qvortrup, J. (1994b): *Barn halva priset. Nordisk barndom i samhällsperspektiv.* (Children half price. Nordic childhood in a societal perspective.) Esbjerg: Sydjysk Universitetsforlag.

Raby, R. (2002): »Tangle of discourses: Girls negotiating adolescence«, *Journal of Youth Studies*, Vol. 5, pp 425-448.

Rejmer, A. (2003): *Vårdnadstvister. En rättssociologisk studie av tingsrätts funktion vid handläggning av vårdnadskonflikter med utgångspunkt från barnets bästa.* (Custody disputes: a socio-legal study of the role of district courts in the handling of custody disputes with the child's best interest as a base.) Lund: Sociologiska institutionen.

Rubinstein, D. (2001): *Culture, Structure and Agency. Toward a Truly Multidimensional Society.* Thousand Oaks: Sage Publications.

Skolverket (2000): *Beskrivande data om barnomsorg och skola.* Rapport 192. (Descriptive data on child care and school.) Stockholm: Skolverket.

Socialstyrelsen and Länsstyrelserna (2003): *Barnperspektiv vid handläggning av ekonomiskt bistånd.* (A

ANNA-LIISA NÄRVÄNEN AND ELISABET NÄSMAN

Child perspective on handling of economic aid.) Stockholm: Socialstyrelsen and Länssty-relserna.

SOU 2001:51 *Barns och ungdomars välfärd. Antologi från Kommittén Välfärdsbokslut.* (Children's and young people's welfare. An anthology from the Welfare Commission.) Stockholm:Graphium/Norstedt.

SOU 2000:3 *Välfärd vid vägskäl. Delbetänkande.* (Welfare at a crossroad.) Kommittén Välfärdsbokslut. Stockholm:Nordstedt.

Turner, B.S. (1986): *Citizenship and Capitalism. The debate over Reformism.* London: Allan & Unwin.

West, C. and S. Fenstermaker (1995): »Doing Difference«, *Gender and Society*, Vol. 9, pp 8-37.

West, C. and D. H. Zimmerman (1987): »Doing Gender«, *Gender and Society*, Vol. 1, pp 125-151.

Volkart, E.H. (ed) (1951): *Social Behavior and Personality. Contributions of W.I. Thomas to Theory and Social Research.* New York: Social Science Research Council.

Notes

1 See reports from the Welfare Commission, especially SOU 2001:51, SOU 2000:3, Ds 2002:32.

2 As if old people lose their adulthood (Närvänen & Näsman 2004).

3 The »doing« concept is mostly used for compliance with category norms. We wish to widen this to include other actions performed with reference to the norm, including active resistance.

European Childhood in

Perspective

EUROPEAN CHILDHOOD
– DIVERGING OR CONVERGING?

Jens Qvortrup

The foregoing chapters have presented a host of detailed data about children's material welfare. These data are added to the rich information given in the Action's published country reports. Together the reader is left with a picture of European childhood characterised by diversity and complexity. This picture shall not be contested as such. The wide variety in life conditions from Bulgaria to United Kingdom, from Cyprus to Norway, from Israel to Finland is indeed conspicuous and remarkable. How do we make sense of all the data? Is it true that diversity prevails over convergence? What shall we be looking for?

The renowned British sociologist and social policy expert, Richard M. Titmuss made this observation about comparing social policies in different countries:

> «In so far as these [diversities of different economic, political and social systems, cultural patterns, and ways of life] are reflected in national social policies they represent difficulties for anyone who is expected to discuss programmes and policies with an international audience. None of us know enough of – or can remember – all the facts. We must, therefore, treat the subject, *not by discussing the details* for this or that country, but with the aid of *concepts* and *models*, *principles* and *goals*, and in terms of *categories* of benefits, contributions and users. We have to think of *classes* of benefits, *kinds* of entitlement, *patterns* of utilisation, and *differences* in goals and objectives. This, it is suggested, is the only way in which an attempt can be made to handle comparatively and intelligently the problems of change« (Titmuss, 1967, p. 57, my italics).

Titmuss' observation is to my mind an encouragement to make sense of seemingly striking differences which by closer inspection may nevertheless be comparable. Titmuss is – at the cost of all the details – stepping back in relation to his material; he is abstracting from it while asking for ordering principles.

I shall in the first pages of this chapter likewise step back, i.e. bring distance to the material while putting Europe and European childhood in perspective. By doing this I shall not be sacrificing the concrete data, but rather asking new questions to them. Given a tendency currently to perceive almost everything as diverse and complex it might be sobering simply to position oneself differently to the material.

This brief analysis will suggest that European countries have much in common despite all the nuances and differences, and that reasons for this commonness may be more determining for our everyday life than more close variables. It will be followed by asking questions about generational relations. How do generations compare with each other and are our methods to improve different age groups' welfare highly different or are they basically the same? Finally the chapter shall discuss the extent to which the costs or burdens of financing so-called non-productive groups are equally shared by various 'productive' groups.

Increasing similarities: Europe at a distance

A likely first reaction to a question about childhood in Europe might be that Europe is too diversified to make conclusive statements about this issue (or any other issue). This is true from a number of perspectives. Europe is highly diversified; yet from other perspectives it may well make sense to talk about Europe as a somewhat unified entity. Let me therefore begin with putting Europe in perspective.

It is not at all uncommon to deal with Europe or other such large entities. This is actually what is done in international reports such as Human Development Report and UNICEF's The State of the World's Children, which typically include statistical appendices. These are not only divided into countries, but also give averages for selected clusters of countries, for instance according to levels of development – least developed countries, developing countries and industrialised countries. It is thus possible, as these statistics show, to think in terms of a rich world, a poor world and one in between. It is obvious that such clusters do not eradicate a multitude of differences between countries or within them; it merely – and that is not so little – suggests that in terms of a number of internally correlated indicators of welfare, *clusters of countries or regions set themselves off from each other while exhibiting some degrees of commonness,* as Table 1 demonstrates.

	2004	2004	1993-2004	Adult literacy rate 2000-2004		2004
	GNI per capita in US$	Life expectancy	% of population below 1$ a day	Males	Females	% of population urbanised
Least developed	345	52	41	63	45	27
Developing	1524	65	22	83	70	43
Industrialised	32232	79	–	–	–	77

Table 1 Welfare indicators according in clusters of countries with different levels of development
Source: UNICEF *The State of the World's Children 2006,* Tables 1, 5, 6 and 7

While this table can, rightly, be said to hide considerable differences between – even within – regions and countries, it is also safe to say that the relative similarity in indicator levels within each cluster compared to other clusters allows us to talk – *grosso modo* – about entities that differ from each other in both level and quality of their indicators. It does thus make sense to talk about Europe as a wealthy continent compared with for instance Africa. These statements are not altered by the fact that we may find rich people in poor countries and vice versa. A similar observation can be made about comparisons between contemporary Europe and pre-industrial Europe. To argue against the observation that historical Europe is basically different on this account from Europe to day would be to give precedence to what is exceptional at the cost of what seems to be the rule.

It does, similarly, make sense to talk about a 'Western' *childhood* and 'non-western' *childhood* (see Table 2), although any subdivision into smaller entities tends to threaten the validity of such statements.

	Under 5 mortality rate 2004	Infant mortality rate 2004	Net primary school enrolment/ attendance (%) 1996-2004★	% of under-fives (1996-2004★) suffering from moderate & severe underweight
Least developed	155	98	60	36
Developing	87	59	80	27
Industrialised	6	5	95	–

Table 2 Welfare indicators for children according to clusters of countries with different levels of development
Source: UNICEF *The State of the World's Children 2006,* Tables 1, 2 and 5. ★ Data refer to most recent year

Common parlance in fact uses them; politicians and journalists use them widely too, and in my view research is not only permitted to do so, in fact they must do it from time to time. Any effort to hide behind postulates about complications and nuances, correct as they are as such, only adds to forgetting about the powerful influence of the macro-variables that contribute to making clusters of countries low, medium or highly developed according to certain standards. The fact that we speak about the clusters in these terms proves our acceptance of them: the notion of *'industrialised'* is indeed one way of conceptualising certain countries exhibiting a particular set of indicators which correlate with each other.

Whatever the historical genesis of 'least developed', 'developing' and 'industrialised' countries, it is possible to argue that a certain level of the *forces of production* produces one or another set of interconnected indicators. Other candidates might be mentioned such as *private property and democracy*, which have played together with the development of forces of production and are ingrained parameters of Europe's political-constitutional set up. These three parameters – economically a high level of forces of production, politically an eventually long tradition for democracy and a constitutionally anchored right to private property – are common to European countries. In their wake has followed a number of indicators exhibiting similar values relative to other clusters of countries. I do not intend any attempt to trace them causally, but want rather to make the point that it would be mistaken to disregard forces of production, property rights and democracy as if they did not exist and as if they had no influence. On the contrary, they arguably account for Europe as having historically developed and currently displaying similarities at a high level. They must be borne in mind before one is embarking on the journey to discern differences between Europe's countries. Those who tend to argue in favour of differences of countries as well as of childhoods as preponderant to similarities seem to be overlooking the powerfulness of these parameters; they seem to be dealing with them as *trivia* – as something that is taken for granted. However, they cannot be taken for granted; no item, factor or variable to be analysed are beyond their influence, which in an international context makes Europe and its childhoods converge towards similarity internally while making it appear different from other vantage points.

Increasing differences: Europe from within

As already mentioned the similarity at this level or from this perspective does not contradict the fact that we at the same time, but at another level and from another perspective, envisage Europe and its childhoods more differentiated. Table 3 shows country values of some of the same variables as in Tables 1 and 2.

Even here in such basic indicators the differences are not what catch the eye – apart from values from the former socialist camp, and this latter piece of information demonstrates the point that *countries having similar experiences also show similar patterns*. Otherwise these indicators are surprisingly similar. Some indicators from Tables 1 and 2 – such as primary school enrolment, underweight of children, and adult literacy rates – have not been quoted in Table 3 (no values were shown at all in the UNICEF statistics) either because they were 100 per cent or zero. I want to repeat: the existence of similar data does not mean that we can disregard them as were they of no significance. On the contrary – the fact for instance that all children attend primary schools, the close to eradication of infant mortality, and very high incomes per capita are indeed important, although they appear banal. It is, in other words, *only on the background of this extraordinary similarity that we can proceed to account for differences*. More or less common historical developments, democracy, market economy, welfare state and private property rights and the convergence of level of forces of production account, as suggested above, for these similarities, which are likely to be even more conspicuous as the European Union widens.

	GNI per capita in $	Life expectancy	Under 5 mortality rate	Infant mortality rate	% urbanised population
Norway	52030	80	4	4	80
Denmark	40650	77	5	4	85
Sweden	35770	80	4	3	83
Ireland	34280	78	6	5	60
UK	33940	79	6	5	89
Finland	32790	79	4	3	61
Austria	32300	79	5	5	66
Belgium	31030	79	5	4	97
Germany	30120	79	5	4	88
Italy	26120	80	5	4	67
Cyprus	17580	79	7	6	69
Israel	17380	80	6	5	92
Estonia	7010	72	8	6	70
Croatia	6590	75	8	7	59
Bulgaria	2740	72	15	12	70

Table 3 Selected indicators for COST A19 countries in 2004

Source: UNICEF *The State of the Worlds Children 2006*, Tables 1 and 6

As we now proceed the analysis we will certainly find differences, but their explanation can only to a limited extend be accounted for in terms of economic development, which by and large appear to be so similar that we are permitted to treat them as constants, which is likely to be one reason why they are typically not given proper attention. Their influence is not diminished by that, I want to reiterate.

Methodologically we might continue – while using the same arguments – to descend towards ever lower levels of analyses. In general terms, differentiation discovered at one level seems to turn into a similarity at the level above, while demanding of the analyst to discover new common causes or denominators while descending (or ascending). It is within the cluster of similar countries that we should find our countries of comparison, where we should expect – according to Marc Bloch – »a certain similarity between the facts observed« and at the same time »a certain dissimilarity between the situations in which they have arisen« (Bloch, 1967, p. 45).

The facts in this book to be observed and which must display a certain similarity are about children's material welfare. The 'certain similarity' must be seen in relation to what is found in other very *different clusters* of countries, which does not prevent us from finding that they actually assume different values. *In the first place they show a similarity as to the nature of the problems and secondly as to the nature of solutions offered.* Thus for instance, the problem of child poverty exhibits some – but comparatively speaking not too much – variation within Europe; its nature is though relatively similar and the ways and means of addressing it quite similar as well. Given a certain and relatively high economic standard the solutions to the problem are rather to be sought in terms of ideological, political and administrative measures that are all predicated a high degree of economic development and a moderate economic growth.

Esping-Andersen's categorisation (1990), for example, is thus basically a political-ideological one, which – without making it explicit – actually takes a certain relative similar (and high) economic development for granted. I think this is legitimate, but what I am arguing is that it should not at the end of the day be ignored. In a global context, similarities between European countries prevail, and it is only between clusters of countries at a global level that dissimilarities become very conspicuous.

Generational differences

It was part of COST A19's programme to look at children's welfare in a generational perspective. For many reasons it is not easy to come to definitive conclusions about this issue. Let me nevertheless look at such a comparison and begin with a quick overview of at-risk-of poverty and poverty rates. In the following table data about both the 50 and the 60 cut off lines are given.

	All		0–15	0–17	65 +	66–75
	60%	50%	60%	50%	60%	50%
Denmark	10	4.3	7	2.4	24	3.8
Sweden	9	5.3	7	3.6	16	4.6
Norway	–	6.3	–	3.6	–	5.5
Finland	11	6.4	9	3.4	18	7.0
Austria	12	9.3	13	13.3	24	7.6
Germany	13	8.9	17	10.9	15	9.7
Italy	19	12.9	25	15.7	17	14.6
UK	19	11.4	24	16.2	25	11.4
Ireland	21	15.4	26	15.7	44	31.1
Estonia	18	–	19	–	18	–
Bulgaria	16	–	19	–	15	–

Table 4 At-risk-of poverty rates (60 per cent cut off line) and poverty rates (50 per cent) by age in a number of European countries. 2001 (EU) and around 2000 (OECD). EU-scale. After tax and transfer.

Sources: 60 per cent: EUROSTAT; 50 per cent: Förster and d'Ercole, 2005, p. 73-75.

In this table we do actually find clear differences among countries which all belong to the category developed countries. As always, one is inclined to say, the Nordic countries are in the lead – in particular as far as children are concerned. Austria and Germany come next while the Anglo-Saxon isles are worst off. This is as expected from Esping-Andersen's categorisation (Esping-Andersen, 1990). The pre-socialist countries Estonia and Bulgaria are in fact doing relatively better than Ireland and the UK.[1] If we add information from the Country Reports (CR), we find that Croatia is slightly behind Bulgaria and Estonia with 22 per cent at-risk-poverty (CR, p. 540), whereas it is merely 16 per cent in Cyprus (CR, p. 600). In Israel the poverty rate (50 per cent cut off) is 25 per cent and thus the country doing worst.

Rates among elderly do not fit into the common pattern. At-risk-poverty clusters elderly in countries like Sweden, Finland, Germany, Italy, Estonia and Bulgaria, whereas Denmark goes together with Austria and the UK and Ireland comes last with some distance. In Croatia the percentage is 32. However, if one does not include the very olds (75 years +), we find that the expected pattern is re-established, and furthermore that differences between children and the relatively early retirees are small – apart from in Ireland.[2] The apparent lagging behind of the very olds may be due to pension schemes which for this age group have not been modernised and/or that this age group is less educated than their successors.

Given this picture it is tempting to conclude that differences prevail, and much more detail could be added to confirm this impression. But again, I want to reiterate that the diversity must be seen also in a more global context. There seems to be three levels of explanations: (1) at the global and historical level there is a correlation between children's life conditions and GNI; (2) at the inter-country level within Europe, this correlation keeps explaining the high level (globally speaking), but there is also a strong influence from the political-ideological level manifesting itself *in terms of welfare state interventions or not*; (3) within countries we must seek more particular explanations, which though assume generality given their occurrence in most countries.

Thus regarding the latter point, irrespective of differences in child poverty levels between countries, there seems to be recurrent causes for, or at least statistical associations between a number of factors and child poverty. Typical factors as mentioned in the CR are such as (a) number of children in the household, (b) living with an adult aged 30 years or younger, (c) living in a family that rents an apartment rather than owns a dwelling, (d) ethnicity, (e) number of earners in the household, (f) female headed households, and (g) living in a family whose main breadwinner is a woman.

Public transfers

We shall not here discuss these recurrent causes, (a)-(g), but rather focus on point 2 above concerning welfare state interventions. As suggested, there are variations between countries, but first of all, I would argue, it is characteristic that European countries in general terms exhibit likeness compared with poorer countries (both historically and contemporary) as far as welfare state interventions are concerned.

As a welfare measure *public transfers* are characteristic for welfare states. Failure to provide transfers will result in both lower levels of welfare and more inequality. It is the rule rather than the exception that wealthy nations dispose of such measures. The pure economic level in Europe safeguards a relatively high basic level (but does not guarantee equality), whereas differences between countries arc explicable in terms of ideological attitudes to interventions.

For improving children's material life conditions public intervention is of great importance as it has been shown first by Luxembourg Income Studies (LIS) many years ago and later by other agencies such as OECD and EU. No countries show acceptable poverty rates under pure market conditions.[3] In a quite clear sense the welfare state functions as a kind of residual agent and is helpful to both employers and employees.

Data from Eurostat (see table 5) show familiar patterns, namely that the highest per cent *changes* in child at-risk-poverty (well above two thirds) from pre- to post-levels as far as tax and transfers are concerned appear in countries with lowest post-level child poverty rates (7-9), i.e. the Nordic countries. And vice versa: in countries where the change rate is low or relatively low – as in Italy (16), Ireland (28) and the UK (38) – you also find highest, although quite similar post-poverty rates (24-26). The change is though small in Germany (29) with middle poverty rate (17), and Austria (63 and 13) comes close to the Nordic pattern. Estonia deviates as being in the middle on both accounts.

Not surprisingly are the changes for the elderly very high given the fact that pensions are included in social transfers rather than as a market based salary. Had the latter been the case and thus pensions not included in the transfers, the pre-transfer incomes are typically reduced to around 25 per cent (apart from in Denmark, where it is as high as 55 per cent, and Ireland with 48 per cent).

	0-15 years		16-64 years		65 + years	
	Pre	Post	Pre	Post	Pre	Post
Denmark	27	7	28	8	87	24
Sweden	22	7	37	11	:	16
Norway (2003)	:	8	:	:	:	20
Finland	33	9	31	10	91	18
Austria	35	13	28	9	84	24
Germany	24	17	23	12	88	15
Italy	30	25	34	18	81	17
UK	39	24	24	15	66	25
Ireland	36	26	29	16	77	44
Estonia	33	19	34	18	86	18
Bulgaria	:	19	:	:	:	15
Croatia (2003)	:	16	:	:	:	31
Cyprus (2003)	:	11	:	:	:	52

Table 5 At-risk-poverty rates by age in a number of European countries. 2001. 60 per cent cut off line. EU-scale. Pre- and post- tax and transfer (pensions included in social transfers)
Source: EUROSTAT

There are, as suggested, two forms of resources families can draw upon to alleviate poverty or to enhance affluence: one is market based incomes through employments and the other is net transfers from the public purse. Although either of them exhibit considerable differences it is worth noting that these are by and large the only instruments to be availed of (cf. Titmuss's point above). What determines the mix of the two is not the level of economic development, which is – as shown – more or less converging, apart from pre-socialist countries which are though likely to catch up. It is rather divergent views of market and welfare state and correspondingly divergent political initiatives. Not surprisingly, countries availing themselves effectively of the welfare state model are doing best in reducing poverty or at-risk-poverty. In terms of public support, Table 5 speaks merely of cash-transfers. To get a full picture it is important to include also in-kind support in the analysis and to see how the two forms are represented.

Cash and kind

People benefit from public support through cash transfers as we have seen, but as important may be support in kind such as hospitals, schools, kindergarten etc. Support in kind is beneficial in the sense that the services received would otherwise have had to be paid for fully or partly by ordinary people. On the other hand they differ from cash transfer because those who avail of them have no choice but receiving them or they get nothing; the services are not changeable into cash. In addition they are nevertheless partly received as a consequence of needs: only if you are ill, you will get hospital services – and you don't get your money back if you happen to be healthy. Thus we may talk about an insurance principle, which in welfare states is administered by the public.

These principles make it extremely difficult to calculate distribution of in-kind services. Even if we can calculate the amount and make preliminary distributions according to for instance gender and age, we have no way really to make statements as to the fairness of the distribution. Obviously elderly will not have a just claim for kindergartens, nor will children justly be demanding health services on par with elderly for equally obvious reasons. Even if elderly and children would not make such claims, they might in principle (or others on their behalf) object to making fiscal contributions to items they do not need.

Nevertheless something could in principle be done to come to a better understanding of the modality of in-kind distributions (cf. Thomson, 1996). One would for instance be able to follow the development of expenses to this or that kind of services over time and thus – controlled for demographic factors – make conclusions about which age groups may be more or less favoured during for instance slump or boom periods (see later the Norwegian case).

What determines the balance of cash and kind? There seems to be an ideological preference among conservatives to favour cash support, while left wing politicians will typically more often opt for in-kind services. This is in particular the case, one would surmise, for expenses for children. Eurostat data give (see Table 6) some hints

– although neither very conclusive nor satisfying; one would have preferred to know about expenses to children rather than to families.

	Cash			Kind		
	Total	Elderly	Families	Total	Elderly	Families
Denmark	17.6	9.9	1.5	11.0	1.8	2.3
Norway	14.2	5.1	1.9	10.9	2.2	1.3
Sweden	17.8	8.8	1.6	12.5	2.7	1.3
Finland	16.4	7.3	1.7	8.6	0.9	1.3
Germany	20.1	11.6	2.2	8.7	0.2	0.8
Austria	19.9	10.8	2.4	7.9	0.5	0.5
Italy	18.2	12.6	0.6	6.3	0.1	0.4
Ireland	7.6	2.4	1.9	7.0	0.3	0.2
UK	17.2	10.8	1.5	9.3	0.5	0.3
Estonia	9.2	5.6	1.4	4.8	0.2	0.6

Table 6 Benefits in cash or kind to elderly and to families as percentage of GDP in some European countries 2001
Source: EUROSTAT

It is though clear that benefits are higher in the Nordic countries, but I would have expected also a tendency to transfer more in kind than in cash for families, which is true merely for Denmark. Given Sweden's strong child care policy I am surprised that this is not more clearly shown in the in kind column. On the other hand it is less surprising that Norway has an even more pronounced cash share, given the introduction a few years ago of a cash-for-care legislation providing a choice for parents to receive money in stead of a kindergarten place under certain conditions (see CR, p. 370-71).

If one looks at the other countries the balance is the same – in favour of cash, even if in some countries like Italy it is negligible. Given pensions it is not surprising that elderly are receiving most in cash, but this tendency has become clearer in recent years since it is less costly to keep the elderly in their own homes rather than having them at old peoples' homes.

Generational budgets

Generational budgets like those highly preliminary ones are far from satisfying. In an effort to better come to terms with differences between age groups, the Norwegian COST team requested a study (see Toresen, 2005). Even if no comparable figures from other countries are available, let me quote a few salient features from it in the hope that they will illuminate some of the points mentioned above and perhaps inspire other countries to repeat the exercise.

Expenses from the public (state, county, municipality and/or other political-administrative bodies – we do not make any distinction here) basically consist of (1) expenses for common purposes (which it does not make sense to divide according to target groups) such as for the police, the military, public administration, and the like; (2) expenses which can in principle be subdivided into (a) cash expenses to households, and (b) in kind expenses. Since (1) is considered to be of common interest and advantage these expenses will not be considered here. Thus 2a and 2b will make up 100 per cent.

It has to be said that what is considered to be of common advantage is far from always easy to determine. Thus of relevance for a generational distribution one should in particular note expenses for education at all levels. Are they primarily to the advantage of pupils, students and perhaps even teachers or should they be considered thus important for the national economy as a whole that it would make more sense to be ranged under (1)? (cf. Bundesministerium, 1994, 291). Should housing transfers be targeted parents or children or divided between both?

In the Norwegian report quoted here education is categorised as expenses for the relevant age groups – i.e. primary schooling for pupils attending such schools, universities for students at universities etc., and housing is considered an income for owners or tenants of dwellings or apartments and not children. Such questions are not unimportant. In fact, if one would distribute educational expenses equally over all age groups, children's part of the public budget would be reduced considerably.

Welfare expenses in Norway (i.e. the sum of cash and in-kind expenses) have more than doubled over the last 20 years (1981-2002) and were for 2002 465 billion NOK = 60 billion €. The share of cash for households was slightly higher than that for in-kind – 49 per cent versus 51 per cent.

The following tables show distributions to three age groups: below 16 years, 16-66 years and over 66 years.

	1981	1986	2002	P8102
IN KIND				
Below 16 years	0,286	0,279	0,312	1,188
16-66 years	0,422	0,424	0,386	0,833
67 years and over	0,292	0,297	0,301	1,073
In kind, total	1,000	1,000	1,000	1,000
CASH				
Below 16 years	0,097	0,088	0,080	0,692
16-66 years	0,437	0,453	0,535	1,392
67 years and over	0,466	0,459	0,385	0,692
Total cash for households	1,000	1,000	1,000	1,000
WELARE EXPENSES, TOTAL				
Below 16 years	0,203	0,194	0,202	0,982
16-66 years	0,429	0,437	0,457	1,126
67 years and over	0,368	0,369	0,341	0,865
Welfare expenses, total	1,000	1,000	1,000	1,000

Table 7 Public expenses for welfare in cash and in kind according to age. 2002-prices. 1981-2002. Per cent.
Source: Toresen, 2005, p. 48

Table 7 shows the distribution of in-kind expenses in the upper part of the table; in the middle part we find distributions of cash transfers, while the totals are shown in the lower part. The last column tells about the changes from 1981 to 2002 and we notice a modest increase for all age groups – slightly more for the adult group than for children and the elderly. In each of the years the adult group receives most, second is the elderly and third the children – which to a large extent reflect the differences in the groups' sizes.

More interesting is to note the big difference in what children receive in kind and in cash. Children are the only group where there is a sizeable difference between the two forms of expenses. The reason is of course that much more is paid on children's 'account' in terms of child care and schools, whereas the cash transfers are much smaller, while this obviously carries a big weight among pensioners.

	1981	1986	2002	P8102
IN KIND				
Below 16 years	1,214	1,306	1,470	1,494
16-66 years	0,663	0,653	0,592	0,753
67 years and over	2,274	2,163	2,236	0,961
In kind, total	1,000	1,000	1,000	1,000
CASH				
Below 16 years	0,411	0,410	0,377	0,843
16-66 years	0,687	0,698	0,819	1,370
67 years and over	3,635	3,349	2,860	0,593
Total cash for households	1,000	1,000	1,000	1,000
WELARE EXPENSES, TOTAL				
Below 16 years	0,863	0,908	0,949	1,209
16-66 years	0,674	0,673	0,700	1,077
67 years and over	2,869	2,690	2,534	0,758
Welfare expenses, total	1,000	1,000	1,000	1,000

Table 8 Public expenses for welfare in cash and in kind according to age. Per capita in 2002-prices. 1981-2002. Indexed.
Source: Toresen, 2005, p. 51

Table 8 is perhaps even more instructive, because it is calculated per capita and thus corrected for demographic differences. In average terms it says, for instance, that while in 2002 each child totally (cash + kind) received slightly less than the population as a whole, and an adult merely a little more than two thirds, each old person got two and a half times more. If we look at distributions between cash and in kind, we find that the differences are even larger as to cash transfers in favour of the elderly – again not surprisingly, given the large share of pensions paid to this age group. It is perhaps surprising that the adults are more advantaged than children in cash terms. On the other hand, children are doing better in kind than adults, although even here the elderly are 'receiving' most on a per capita basis.

If we look at the development over 20 years, there are no changes as to the ranking of the groups. By and large, however, children have improved slightly more than the other age groups – in fact the elderly have lost a little and mostly in terms of cash.

Translated into money terms (see Table 9), we are told that each person in Norway receives on average in welfare income – cash plus the value of in kind – a total of almost 13000€. Each child gets almost the average, while each old person receives more than 32000€. In cash alone a child receives 13 per cent of what an elderly gets, whereas the value of in kind for a child is two thirds of what an elderly gets. Adults' receipts are lower than children's in kind, but higher in cash, but always lower than those of the elderly. If we look at the development since 1981, children have overall been favoured most and the elderly least. In particular is an increase for children noted in kind, most likely due to an increase in number of kindergartens.

	2002	P8102
IN KIND		
Under 16 years	9960	115
16-66 years	4010	58
67 years and over	15152	74
In kind, total	**6775**	**77**
CASH		
Under 16 years	2328	91
16-66 years	5059	148
67 years and over	17671	64
Total cash for households	**6178**	**108**
WELARE EXPENSES, TOTAL		
Under 16 years	12288	110
16-66 years	9070	98
67 years and over	32823	69
Welfare expenses, total	**12954**	**91**

Table 9 Public expenses in cash and kind according to age. € pr capita. 2002 prices.
Source: Toresen, 2005, p. 50

There is no way in which one can determine if these distributions are just in generational terms. The elderly are doing best in absolute terms, but one can note a decrease in their receipts, and although children get much less in absolute terms, their receipts have increased. We can therefore note an equalisation between these two groups of dependents.

One thing is a distribution of cash and in kind receipts; another thing is who is paying for them. An answer to this question would require a distribution of taxes, not according to age but rather according to households with or without children.

We do not have such a distribution, but we might approach the problem by at least accounting for distributions of these types of households.

The actors and their resources

Despite all reverence to children's competence and capacity, to which much attention is due currently, the responsibility for their material provision lies with adults. The notion of adults may take a variety of forms. In concrete terms, the primary responsible adults are and most likely always were *children's parents*. When we often talk about the family as the responsible unit, we do in fact mean parents as providers and carers. Children are rather seen as consumers of parental resources. This is particularly true in modern societies, as children are hardly perceived as contributors, neither to the family economy nor at a personal level as procuring old age pensions to their own parents. Parents obviously contribute with their incomes earned. This is the most direct way in which children come to share resources from the market. This is of critical importance for children's welfare. There is a close association between children's material welfare and the incomes of parents, and in the connection it makes much of a difference whether there are two income earners, one or none at all, whether the latter is due to unemployment or single motherhood.

Adults could also mean *all adults* in society and not merely parents. While parents always had an important role for children's upkeep, in pre-modernity this role was typically shared with other adults in the locality. Also adults without children had a place in the generational exchange, which they could not escape without negative sanctions in the long run. This is not so in modern Europe. Adults without home staying children are exempt from direct responsibility for children, who have been reduced to a private matter.

It does not mean that these 'child free' adults are completely free from responsibility. They may be personally liberated from children, but they assume another role, namely as tax-payers who – to their liking or not – are forced to contribute incomes to and thus also expenses from the public purse. Since their role as tax-payers is shared with parents, this notion of adults in praxis become equated with the state, and their responsibility towards children is thus defined by the state both as to how resources are distributed between various groups and as to how it is administered, i.e. by the state itself or by other administrative levels like municipalities.

Thus the state – or in general terms the public purse – is the redistributive agent which channels resources to groups which are either deemed needy, unfairly treated or thought of as a long term profitable object of investment. Children or families with children are definitely a target of redistributive measures; at the same time they have to compete with other groups for the attention of the public.

JENS QVORTRUP

The last group of adults is 'corporate society'. Again, historically, there was no division between productive and reproductive agents. Nowadays, however, companies, firms, and other trading actors have come to be in charge merely of their own business, while reproduction is exclusively a family decision. Yet, even this is not completely true since also corporate society makes supplies either to the state in terms of taxes or to employees in terms of welfare goods. However, the forms of these contributions vary in complicated political and administrative ways from country to country and will not be considered in this chapter. Corporate society hardly contributes to children as such – parents are not paid more than other employees – but in case they may make life easier for parents in terms of so-called family friendly measures. The extent of the latter is hardly accounted for systematically.

Given these different definitions of adults with various expectations and roles vis-à-vis children and their upbringing, it is easy to imagine that tensions arise. Although it is obvious that 'child free' adults and corporate society have an interest in reproduction of adults (which in the first place means production of children), their assumption of responsibility for this task and for its scope depends completely on state imposed fiscal policies and agreements between employers' and employees' organisations, and as we know they vary considerably between countries in Europe. On the other hand: although it is as obvious that parents also are dependant on a flourishing economy including a sufficient supply of labour, they have hardly an easily perceivable stake in corporate society to an extent that they should be prepared – for close to own costs – to produce a new labour force.

Due to the development of society, its productive forces and concomitantly its division of labour – including a separation of productive and reproductive responsibilities – European countries have been brought or brought themselves to an impasse, the most visible climax of which is the so-called pension-bomb. Its immediate premise is a dire lack of labour force – both for financing explosively growing pensions and for providing labour for taking care of the elderly – but at the end of the day it is caused by the fact that children are born in insufficient numbers so as to make up for a labour force which meets the demands of the day.

This situation is demonstrably *common* to all European countries and thus belongs to the similarities mentioned above. It is true, at the same time, that it assumes different forms both quantitatively and qualitatively. It is true as well that more or less half-hearted efforts to come to terms with the problems vary across Europe.

Any outcome of distribution of resources between groups or agents is basically a result of strength relations between contending parties. The classical conflict over resources has historically been carried out between capitalists and workers – employers and employees, if you like. In this conflict over the price of labour power there was hardly much place for persons outside the labour market. The family wage has long time ago lost its currency to be replaced by the welfare state as a kind of welfare guarantee for persons outside the market. Given the premise that children are a private matter the burden of their upkeep is left with parents – to some extent in collaboration with the public. If, on the other hand, the premise would be that children are also a public good (cf. Folbre, 1994) with positive externalities to for instance childless adults and corporate society, how should 'burdens' be distributed?

Distribution of burdens

One of the more astonishing pieces of information in the CR is from Germany. In its CR it is mentioned that among West-German women born in the 1960s close to 30 per cent will remain without children; indeed, academic women of the same age will remain childless to about 42 per cent, and the same tendency is noted for eastern Germany (p. 707). It is astonishing not only because of its magnitude – an increase from 10 per cent in 1950 and 16 per cent in 1970. It is astonishing also for what it indicates in terms of women's (and most likely more pronounced for men's) inclination to have children, i.e. a beginning change of norms regarding parenthood. For various reasons women have always been expected – and expecting themselves – to be mothers, and typically it has been stigmatising not to have children. Although it can be interpreted positively as a sign of a new opportunity to really choose freely whether or not to have children, it is from a reproductive point of view alarming if it is now becoming normatively acceptable, not to say preferable, given the advantages it entails or is assumed to entail, to remain childless. It is one thing to have a combination of structural constraints towards childbearing and a normative preference for it; quite another thing to have the former combined with a norm for childlessness.[4] The difference in terms of reversing low fertility thus becomes not only to remove structural constraints, but also of reversing the norms, which probably is much more difficult and in any case impossible by law or decree.

We are perhaps not there yet. In any case it is reported in the German CR (loc. cit) that the majority of young people under 30 still would like to have two or more children, leaving us however with a discrepancy between subjective wishes for having children and structural conditions for realising them. This is likely to be an uneven battle, predestined to be lost by prospective parents, other things remaining equal.

The German figures are alarming also for what they suggest in terms of shared responsibilities for children's material welfare. More and more childless people will necessarily produce more and more childless households, which historically used to be rather the exception than the rule – due also to shorter longevity. In Sweden, Norway[5] and Denmark the share of households without children were around 2000 73.2, 73.7 and 76.8 per cent. Or to put it differently: merely ¼ of all households in these countries included children. In other words, in these Scandinavian welfare states it is merely one in four of all households which has an everyday obligation to provide and care for children. It is the income earners of these households who must shoulder the lion's share of expenses to children. Children in this statistics (see Table 10) – and in the UK with 64 per cent childless households – are below 18 years, which makes a difference to statistics produces by many other countries, where children living in households are counted without an age limitation. This means that the share of households without responsibilities for children decreases. Thus, for Germany, there were 61.3 per cent households of that type, in Ireland there were 39.2 and in Italy 42.4 per cent households without children (CR, p. 277).

Country and year	Couple households			Single-parent households	One-person households	Total without children[1]	Other households
	Total	With children[1]	No children[1]				
Denmark, 2001	45.7	18.5	27.2	4.2	49.6	76.8	0.6
Germany, 2000	51.1	25.9	25.2	7.7	36.1	61.3	5.2
Ireland, 2002	59.2	41.4	17.7	11.7	21.6	39.3	7.6
Sweden, 2000	45.8	19.1	26.7	5.8	46.5	73.2	1.9
UK, 2001	58.0	23.0	35.0	6.0	29.0	64.0	7.0

Table 10 Per cent distribution of households by type. Selected countries 2000-2002.

[1] Children are under 18 in Denmark, Sweden, and the UK; and of all ages living at home in Germany and Ireland. Source: Martin and Katz, 2003, p. 12.

These are striking differences concerning households with and without children. It cannot be explained merely by differences in definitions of children (whether up to 18 years as in Scandinavia and the UK or without age limitations as in Germany, Ireland and Italy). This is likely to explain much of the difference between Scandinavia and Germany. The difference to Italy must be due to the fact of what in the Italian CR is called the 'postponement syndrome', i.e. the dramatic prolongation of children's stay in their parental homes (see CR p. 284ff) and low divorce rates. Ireland's low level is likely to be explained by the very recent fertility fall and low divorce rates.

In a historical – and contemporary intercultural – comparison there is no doubt that a displacement has taken place in the direction of much fewer households assuming responsibilities for children – a trend which is *common* to all European countries. But as indicated, differences between European countries force us to look for different causes. Among them are (1) the increase in longevity – more or less equal for all countries; (2) the decrease in fertility, which is much more pronounced – compared to Scandinavia – in Germany and in particular in Italy. Based on these two factors alone, one would have expected a smaller share of adults who are encircled in the obligation to provide for children. This is however not the case, partly because, as we saw, (3) different definitions of 'children', and in addition (4) a much lower divorce rate, especially in Ireland and Italy, which contributes to keep down the share of household units, which is of particular importance since it prevents the development of single-households with children that are mostly at risk of poverty.

The question we are seeking to address is to which extent the societal development is producing a household composition that is conducive to providing and caring for children. Although it may, at first glance, appear as if low fertility countries with low divorce rates are doing better – measured on the share of obliged and committed households – we also know that child poverty rates are lower in exactly countries with higher fertility and higher divorce rates! How can this be explained? One thing is obviously a stronger welfare state. There is also another factor which might suggest that we should perhaps not primarily concentrate on obliged households but rather on obliged income earners. In other words, we suggest that the higher share of parental income earners, the less likely it is to find high levels of child poverty.

References

Bloch, M. (1967): »A Contribution towards a Comparative History of European Societies«, in M. Bloch: *Land and Work in Mediaeval Europe*. London: Routledge & Kegan Paul, pp 44–81.

Bundesministerium für Familie und Senioren (1994): *Familie und Familienpolitik im geeinten Deutschland – Zukunft des Humanvermögens*. Fünfter Familienbericht. Bonn.

Esping-Andersen, G. (1990): *The Three Worlds of Welfare Capitalism*. Cambridge: Polity Press.

Folbre, N. (1994): »Children as Public Goods«, in *American Economic Review*, Vol 84, No. 2, pp 86–90.

Johansen, V. (2006): *Children and Distributive Justice between Generations. A Comparison of 16 European Countries*. Dissertation. Norwegian University for Science and Technology: Trondheim. Forthcoming.

Martin, G. and V. Kats (2003): »Families and work in transition in 12 countries, 1980-2001«, in *Monthly Labor Review*, September, pp 3-31.

M. Förster and M. M. d'Ercole (2005): *Income distribution and poverty in OECD countries in the second half of the 1990s*. Paris: OECD Social, Employment and Migration, Working Paper 22.

Thomson, D. (1996): *Selfish Generations? How Welfare States Grow Old*. Cambridge: The White Horse Press.

Titmuss, R.M. (1967): »The Relationship between Income Maintenance and Social Service Benefits – an Overview«, in *International Social Security Review*, Year XX, No. 1, pp 57-66.

Torcsen, J. (2005): *Offentlige velferdsutgifter. Nivå og aldersfordeling 1981-2002* [Public welfare expenses. Level and age distribution 1981-2002]. Preliminary version.

Notes

1   We must of course always be reminded that the figures are relative with reference to any country's poverty line. As we saw in Table 3, GNI per capita is much lower in pre-socialist countries than in Western countries.

2   In Israel the poverty rate for children and the elderly is the same – around 25 per cent (CR, p. 780).

3   One might of course suggest that without availability of welfare provisions market agents were forced to behave more friendly or people inclined to respond differently (see Johansen, 2006)

4   It is not, eventually, uncommon that adults without children air their dismay for what the see as children's encroachment on their spatial, temporal or financial freedom. Thus, we find in for instance the USA new, so-called 'child-free' movements without embarrassment and, as it were, without thoughts of long term negative consequences even for themselves, make statements to the effect that children are none of their business.

5   For Norway, see www.ssb.no.

CONTRIBUTORS TO THIS VOLUME

Leena Alanen, Professor, Department of Early Childhood Education, University of Jyväskylä, Finland

Jonathan Bradshaw, Professor, University of York, United Kingdom

Nancy A. Denton, Professor, Department of Sociology, Associate Director, Center for Social and Demographic Analysis, University at Albany, State University of New York, USA

Don J. Hernandez, Professor, Department of Sociology, Research Associate, Center for Social and Demographic Analysis, University at Albany, State University of New York, USA

Suzanne E. Macartney, Doctoral Candidate, Department of Sociology, Center for Social and Demographic Analysis, University at Albany, State University of New York, USA

Anna-Liisa Närvänen, Associate Professor in Social and Cultural Analysis, Department of Social and Welfare Studies, Linköping University, Sweden

Elisabet Näsman, Professor, Department of Sociology, Uppsala University, Sweden

Máire Nic Ghiolla Phádraig, Statutory Lecturer, Department of Sociology, University College, Dublin 4, Ireland

Thomas Olk, Professor, Department of Education, University of Halle, Germany

Ilona Ostner, Professor of Social Policy, Institute of Sociology, Department of Political Sociology and Social Policy, Georg August University Göttingen, Germany

Jens Qvortrup, Professor, Department of Sociology and Political Science, Norwegian University of Science and Technology (NTNU), Trondheim, Norway

Tess Ridge, Research officer, University of Bath, United Kingdom

Mona Sandbæk, Research director, Norwegian Social Research, Oslo, Norway

Helmut Wintersberger, Lecturer, Department of Political Sciences, University of Vienna; Consultant, Ludwig Boltzmann Institute for Human Rights, Vienna, Austria